Ethics, Values and
Social Work Practice

Ethics, Values and Social Work Practice

Edited by
Linda Bell and Trish Hafford-Letchfield

 Open University Press

Open University Press
McGraw-Hill Education
McGraw-Hill House
Shoppenhangers Road
Maidenhead
Berkshire
England
SL6 2QL

email: enquiries@openup.co.uk
world wide web: www.openup.co.uk

and Two Penn Plaza, New York, NY 10121-2289, USA

First published 2015

A catalogue record of this book is available from the British Library

ISBN-13: 978-0-335-24529-1
ISBN-10: 0-335-24529-3
eISBN: 978-0-335-24530-7

Library of Congress Cataloging-in-Publication Data
CIP data applied for

Typeset by Aptara, Inc.

Praise for this book

Dedication

Linda dedicates this book to David, Tom and Sarah who help keep her feet on the ground and her heart in the right place.

Trish dedicates this book to Ted and Katie who give her so much pride and joy through their own achievements and who make life fun, and to Emily, my new daughter-in-law.

Contents

About the authors   ix

Foreword   xi

Acknowledgements   xiii

Glossary of key terms   xv

**Part 1: Linking ethics and values to professional identity,
inclusive and reflective practice**   **1**

1 Situating ethics and values in social work practice   3
   Trish Hafford-Letchfield and Linda Bell

2 Major trends in applied ethics, including the ethics of social work   12
   Souzy Dracopoulou

3 The contribution of education and learning for ethical practice:
   situating ethics and values within the social work continuum   23
   Trish Hafford-Letchfield and Jean Dillon

4 Ethics, values and social work identity(ies)   37
   Linda Bell

5 Links between reflective practice, ethics and values   47
   Pat Cartney

**Part 2: Themes for social work practice: 'Power',
'Social justice', 'Partnership', 'Diversity and difference'
and 'Relationship-based practice'**   **61**

6 Power   63
   Trish Hafford-Letchfield

7 Partnership working, ethics and social work practice   76
   Colin Whittington and Margaret Whittington

8 Diversity and difference   90
   Tom Wilks

9 Relationship-based practice   101
   Mina Hyare

10 Social justice   112
   Alison Higgs

   Afterword: Reflecting on ethics and values – continuing the journey   122
   Linda Bell and Trish Hafford-Letchfield

   References   125
   Index   141

About the authors

Linda Bell is Associate Professor in the School of Health and Education at Middlesex University. She has researched various aspects of health and social care practice including collaborative working, ethics, gender issues and parenting, and has a PhD in Anthropology. She has published in journals including *Aging and Mental Health, Equal Opportunities International, Journal of Interprofessional Care, Social Work Education, Sociological Review* and *Women's Studies International Forum*. Linda previously worked on policy applications of practice-based research, with links to organizations including the Central Council for Education & Training in Social Work (London and South East region). She has taught social work and other professional students since 1995, with a focus on research methodology and ethics, is interested in ethical aspects of research practice and has presented conference papers in this area. She is an editorial board member for the *International Journal of Social Research Methodology* (Routledge).

Trish Hafford-Letchfield is Associate Professor in Social Work in the School of Health and Education at Middlesex University, where she is Programme Leader for an inter-professional leadership programme. Trish is widely published in leadership, management and organizational development and she has also written extensively on the quality of care of older people and sexuality in social work, which are key areas of research interest. She is on the executive of the National Association of Education and Aging and is co-chair of a national special interest group in sexuality and social work. Trish is series manager of *Managing Skills in Social Work and Social Care* by Jessica Kingsley and her latest book is with Christine Cocker, *Rethinking Anti-Discriminatory and Anti-Oppressive Theories for Social Work Practice* (Palgrave, 2014).

Pat Cartney is an Associate Professor in Social Work, and Learning and Teaching Strategy Leader for the School of Health and Education at Middlesex University. Pat is a qualified and experienced social worker, including generic, hospital social work, and children and families work in the statutory sector. Since 1996, Pat has worked in higher education and her research interests and PhD are focused on social work pedagogy and learning for professional practice, especially the social and emotional as well as the cognitive aspects of learning.

Jean Dillon is an experienced social work academic currently working at the University of Bedfordshire. Her practice experience comes from being a qualified nurse and social worker, and Mental Health Act manager. Jean has taught ethics and values in social work. Her research interests include exploring ethical issues relating to widening participation, life course development and the importance of students' social contexts, individual trajectories, academic potential within admissions policies and practice. Jean is also a member of the editorial board for the peer-reviewed journal, *Widening Participation and Life Long Learning*.

Souzy Dracopoulou was a Senior Lecturer in Healthcare Ethics at Middlsex University. Her background is in Philosophy and she has taught philosophy, health and social care ethics and law for many years to a wide range of care professionals, law to biomedical scientists and business and environmental ethics. She is the editor of the book *Ethics and Values in Healthcare Management* (Routledge, 1998) and has published widely in the area of moral philosophy and applied ethics both in the UK and Greece. Her current research interests are in professional ethics and the ethics of mental health.

Ann Flynn is a development manager in a multi-agency setting, focusing on services for children and their families and is an associate lecturer with the Open University. Ann is a registered social worker and has several postgraduate awards in related areas. She has had 25 years' experience in social work including management and was formerly a nurse.

Alison Higgs is a qualified social worker with many years' specialist experience in hospitals, working with adults and families affected by life-threatening illness. She has taught medical and nurse practitioners about ethics in practice and has an MA in Medical Ethics and Law. Alison is a lecturer in social work at the Open University and in her previous academic role designed an innovative blended learning approach to ethics in health and social care. She co-chairs an Ethics Interest Group and has been a member of NHS Research Ethics Committees for ten years.

Mina Hyare is an experienced social work practitioner, academic and practice learning manager. Her practice experience includes work in the voluntary sector relating to domestic violence and in statutory services with children and families where she specialized in youth justice. Mina has a Master's in Education and Training, a Practice Teaching Award, and Advanced Award in Social Work. She is working on a Professional Doctorate in Social Work and Emotional Well-Being at The Tavistock and Portman Trust, and is interested in relationship-based practice, child protection and social work education.

Colin Whittington is Visiting Professor at the University of Greenwich and consultant, researcher and educator at whittingtonconsultants.co.uk. He held fellowships at Keele University and King's College London where, respectively, he also gained his Master's and PhD. A registered social worker with experience as practitioner, manager and university teacher, he was Principal, R&D for England's social care training organization and headed the London and South East region of the UK's Social Work Education Council. Colin has published widely on theory and practice, including inter-professional/inter-agency collaboration (IPIAC). He is a member of the Editorial Boards of the *British Journal of Social Work* and *Journal of Practice Teaching and Learning*.

Margaret Whittington is a consultant at whittingtonconsultants.co.uk, a member of the local board of Healthwatch and actively involved in the voluntary care sector, where she is a trustee. She holds an MSc in inter-professional studies, is a registered social worker and has extensive experience as a practitioner and social services manager in several service areas in community and hospital settings. She has particular expertise in services for older adults and in partnership working, especially between social care and health. Margaret has a long record of contributing to research and publications, the training of practitioners and service development.

Tom Wilks is a Senior Lecturer in Social Work at London South Bank University. He worked for many years as a social worker and service manager primarily in mental health and drug and alcohol services. His academic interests are in social work ethics, service user involvement in social work education and advocacy. He is author of *Advocacy and Social Work Practice*, published in 2012 by Open University Press.

Foreword

This book is timely given the fast changing pace of social policy. The book brings together ethics and values in social work practice, powerfully applying them to many areas, including reflective practice, partnership working, relationship-based practice and in relation to power, diversity and difference and social justice. My current professional roles involve working with children and their families within a multi-agency setting as well as teaching new social work students as part of their professional training. Both these roles bring me into contact with many aspects of social work practice and as such I value the leadership this book brings in surfacing some of the key aspects of social workers' engagement in the lives of their service users and social work's exchanges across the multi-agency context.

Social work has always had a strong value base and one that is endorsed in professional standards and employing organizations. This is also true of other professionals and so this book gives good guidance for social work's discrete practice, and ethics and values in order to facilitate effective partnership working. Ethics and values also have a central place in reflective practice. Increasingly we are encouraged to exercise double loop learning and a deep reflective process that impacts at the level of values. This book progresses this debate and informs both social work students as well as practitioners in this process.

The book advises how social work operates in an increasingly neoliberal environment where the relationship of social work to the state is constantly being renegotiated. A commentary suggesting social work takes too robust an action versus too relaxed an action plays itself out constantly in the media, often with damaging consequences. Social welfare organizations have been modernized and we look increasingly to how services can be further transformed – to make improvements; to meet financial efficiencies; as well as to offer service users what they want as an outcome to their engagement and feedback; however, all this is not without its dilemmas. Social work is an integral part of that process and as such we are both challenged and challenging within the multi-agency environment. This book provides an excellent focus on ethics and values and helps us maintain principles and a framework through unsettled times.

Ann Flynn
Development manager, Children's Services

Acknowledgements

Special thanks to all the contributors to this book who despite all the traumas and diversions thrown at them managed to finally complete and help us bring it all together. We also thank the team at McGraw-Hill OUP.

Glossary of key terms

For further discussion of these terms relating to ethics, see Chapter 2 (Dracopoulou).

Applied ethics: During the 1970s and early 1980s, a focus on how to treat practical issues started appearing in the philosophical literature; the field of 'applied ethics' emerged as a distinct academic discipline, with relevance to practice in areas such as social work and health.

Care ethics/Ethics of care: Understanding care as involving attentiveness, responsibility, competence and responsiveness accommodates some of what care ethicists think is at the centre of care ethics: care as a 'relationship'. An understanding of care as a virtue is in accordance with how we understand the (virtuous) caring practitioner. 'Ethics of care' is also associated with some feminist approaches to ethics.

Consequentialism (*see also* Utilitarianism): The basic idea or moral principle underlying Consequentialism is that morally right actions are the ones that produce the best possible consequences. Consequentialism is a general theory that does not define what counts as good consequences. The classic consequentialist approach is represented by **Act-Utilitarianism**, and is associated with the philosophers Jeremy Bentham and John Stuart Mill.

Deontology (*see also* Kantian ethics): In a Deontological approach to ethics, morally right and wrong actions are not determined exclusively by reference to their good outcomes but are considered morally to be right or wrong in themselves.

Kantian ethics (*see also* Deontology): Immanuel Kant provides the classic statement of a **deontological** theory based on what he calls 'the categorical imperative', central to which is the notion of 'respect for persons'.

Metaethics: This involves the analysis of concepts, language and methods of reasoning in ethics. For example, it examines the meanings of terms such as 'rights' and 'obligation'.

Normative ethics: The two dominant normative (top-down) theories in the Western philosophical tradition are Consequentialism (Utilitarianism) and Deontology. These provide frameworks, each based on an overriding moral principle, in which ethical problems are often usefully placed.

Non-normative or descriptive ethics: Non-normative ethics represent a move away from abstract theories and principles towards a particularistic and contextualized approach to moral reasoning and justification. Such approaches to ethics can involve taking account of different contexts and the moral practices of different groups, e.g. in **Virtue ethics**, **Care ethics**.

Principlism: Developed by Beauchamp and Childress, and based on four key moral principles: (1) Autonomy or free will, (2) Beneficence, (3) Non-maleficence and (4) Justice.

Utilitarianism (*see also* Consequentialism): Act-Utilitarianism is based on the claim that the morally right action is the one that brings about the most happiness, or least unhappiness (maximizes utility), to all those who are affected or potentially affected by the action. With **Rule-Utilitarianism**, rules, rather than individual actions, are justified morally on utilitarian grounds.

Virtue ethics: With virtue ethics the focus shifts from general theories and principles to the particularities of character or 'virtues'. The morally right action is not the one that is in accordance with certain principles, but what the virtuous person would do in certain circumstances.

Part 1

Linking ethics and values to professional identity, inclusive and reflective practice

1 Situating ethics and values in social work practice

Trish Hafford-Letchfield and Linda Bell

Introduction

Social workers are one of the core groups of professionals with an international identity. As we argue in this book, issues of 'values' and 'ethics' are both highly topical and integral to current social work practice. These issues have become even more central to how social work operates in the context of relatively new systems of regulation of professional conduct, initially established in the UK by the four Care Councils, and continuing with social work's recent inclusion within the Health Care Professionals Council in England. Each of these bodies has developed documents and processes concerning professional ethics and values that clearly cover concepts, principles and behaviour that social workers profess in their everyday work (see Banks, 2010).

This book is written for social work students and professionals and will also be of interest to those in related welfare professions. Building on theories of applied ethics and values, we aim to examine how key areas of social work values and ethics can be meaningfully applied to specific practice contexts. A number of quality texts on social work ethics already exist (see, for example, Clark, 2000; Beckett and Maynard, 2005; Hugman, 2005a; Banks, 2006, 2012); this text focuses in particular on the application of various ethical theories for practice. Our contributors document the importance of understanding ethics and values for inclusive practice within what we term the continuum of social work. This continuum starts at the commencement of social work education through to the postqualification stage of social work practice and beyond. Recognizing the importance of ethics and values in social work practice forms an essential part of social work internationally. This text aims to explore ethics and values in the context of everyday practice, especially in the UK, and to provide useful strategies, understanding and ideas for practice. These are explored through their application to a range of different scenarios involving everyday work with people who use social work services. We identify important theoretical debates linking issues such as reflective practice, social work identity(ies) and social work education to ethics and values, with a central underpinning premise of social justice. We include some international perspectives, particularly on the relevance of social work identity(ies) to ethics and values.

While not completely privileging one specific approach, our contributors certainly emphasize the kinds of approaches to ethics and values that humanize social work practice. The first part of the book (Chapters 1–5) provides some grounding in ethics theories and principles and emphasizes important debates around education, identity and reflection. In Part 2, the themes of Chapters 6–10 drill down into specific professional ideals/principles such as social justice, power, partnership and working with diversity that go beyond extant professional norms.

Exploring ethics in social work practice

The word 'ethics' derives from the Greek word 'ethos', referring to a person's character, nature or disposition, and is used when making distinctions between right and wrong in relation to actions, volitions or the character of responsible beings (Leathard and McLaren, 2007). The terms *ethics*, *morals* and *values* are often used interchangeably; it is nevertheless possible to make a distinction between these concepts – for example, 'ethics' may be considered as the 'active' form of values (explored by Whittington and Whittington in Chapter 7). Clark (2006) makes specific reference to the 'moral character' of social work, a quality that is not just the ability to be competent in one's role as a social worker but also involves demonstrating a virtuous character; by modelling and subscribing to a way of life in tune with choices of specific individuals or communities that we work with. Similarly, Parton (2000) described social work as a practical-moral act rather than a techno-rational action, which requires a morally active practitioner. The idea of being morally active can be traced to Bauman's (1993) notion of a person's moral impulse coming from within, as opposed to acting in response to externally imposed ethical frameworks. As many people involved in social care do not belong to a traditional 'profession' at all, there is always potential for conflict in understanding what we mean by 'ethics' and 'values'. Moves towards standardizing frameworks and levels of training and education, for example, all need to contribute towards a consensus from which a moral analytical framework and a moral language can emerge.

Applied ethics as a branch of philosophy is relevant to social work and covers several areas underpinning various aspects of social work practice. In Chapter 2, Souzy Dracopoulou discusses dominant Western ethical theories, including *consequentialism* and *deontology* as well as *principlism* (see Beauchamp and Childress, 2001), focusing on *ethical principles* of *autonomy, beneficence, non-maleficence* and *justice*. Dracopoulou introduces us to *virtue ethics* and what is termed 'ethics of care'; together with others (Orme, 2002; Gray, 2010) she highlights how these latter, more 'contextualized' ethics approaches can act as a backdrop to critical social work, as they draw on feminism, race theory and other critiques that recognize economic and political domination (see also Rogers and Weller, 2013). These latter approaches will, according to Webb (2010), enable social work to cast itself in self-promotional terms both as an organized profession and directly as front-line practitioners. Dracopoulou explains the strengths and drawbacks of these approaches to applied ethics, and provides examples of how they can be applied in social work.

Values and ethics have increasingly taken a key position in social work policy, practice and education, and are widely debated within social work literature (Clark, 2000; Beckett and Maynard, 2005; Hugman, 2005a; Banks, 2006, 2012). What have been called spheres of values (Powell, 2005; Barnard, 2008; Shardlow, 2009) have been conceptualized, for example, in four areas:

1 'moral philosophy' that forms 'a backdrop to ethical debates in social work';
2 'legislation' providing a 'context for social work practice';
3 'political ideologies', with the comment that these have differentially 'shaped…social work models, methods and practices'; and finally
4 'the historical emergence of social work as a profession and the struggle for a professional identity' (Barnard, 2008: 6).

Clark (2006) suggests that social work is first and foremost an enterprise imbued with moral purpose and values. Typically, practice has been more micro or individually focused where the best ways of analysing and challenging ethical issues are contested. However, he also describes this as a 'fictional representation of the goals of social work practice' (Clark,

2006: 76), reminding us that the potential of practice is profoundly conditioned by social and cultural circumstances often manifest in a broader structure of oppression, discrimination and inequality. This context mitigates any attempt at neutrality and therefore, as Clark asserts, social workers need to be personally committed to values and ways of life that extend well beyond the scope of their contract of employment.

Some of these ideas are tested in issues around 'suitability' for social work and 'fitness for practice' hearings by regulatory bodies, as well as in ways that some organizational cultures have been interrogated to examine how the physical, psychological and emotional environment has contributed to both successes and failures of care (Hafford-Letchfield et al., 2014). Banks (2010) has argued that construction of professional integrity is not just about conduct that meets commonly accepted standards, but involves maintaining and acting upon a deeply held set of values, often in a hostile climate. Some of these ideas have been tested in recent public enquiries and serious case reviews into failures of care whose findings have offered great potential for transferable learning, to ensure a dignified culture of care.

There is arguably increasing emphasis in the literature on the relevance of philosophical theories (such as 'ethics of care') as a significant *moral* basis for social work and/or related occupations, grounded in particular in notions of 'virtue ethics' (noted by Barnard, 2008; Banks and Gallagher, 2009; Gray, 2010; Weinberg, 2010). This has clear implications for processes of construction of social work identities, as discussed in Chapter 4 by Linda Bell. Gray (2010), for example, debates whether a feminist ethics of care, which he perceives as being close to virtue ethics, can be a more useful ethical stance for social workers than existing approaches based on ethical principles: is this approach more able to address complexities involved in the social problems with which social workers grapple? Does it offer more opportunities to deliver good quality outcomes for clients, or mutual respect than ethical principles based on human rights and social justice? Graham (2007a, 2007b) draws our attention to black women's voices around the 'ethics of care', while Orme (2002, 2003) argues that it is unhelpful to dichotomize 'care' and 'justice', proposing that the principle of the 'ethic of care' ('the different voice') has 'led feminist theory to reinterpret the principles and processes of justice in ways that are meaningful for social work and social care practice' (Orme, 2002: 812).

We argue here that students entering social work will have already been asked to demonstrate their motivation and commitment during the process of recruitment and selection; on entering social work education they may have found it very different to more traditional ways of learning, one which involves encountering and reflecting on the 'self' as well as in relation to professional roles they will play in future. In this book, we seek to cover some issues involved in being and becoming a social worker, from entry to the profession and 'learning how to learn' taking an inclusive and a moral stance, to becoming a critically reflective practitioner using the enhancement of relationship-based practice as a mode of being.

Like many other human service professionals, social workers continue to work within specific and clear lines of guidance in the form of codes of practice (GSCC, 2010; BASW, 2012; HCPC, 2012a, 2012b) and international statements of principles (IFSW/IASSW, 2004). These are fundamentally statements of intent that spell out the ethics, duties and behaviour expected from both social workers and their employers. An analysis by Gilbert (2009) of the similarities and differences in the structure and language of the IFSW/IASSW document and the BASW code situated them both firmly within the tradition of Western liberal ethics, whereas the latter code is argued to pursue a stronger commitment to duty.

A range of case studies and situations, particularly from case-law and human rights perspectives, have influenced some of these debates, particularly in the face of globalized economic downturns and the impact of prolonged austerity. For example, Cocker and

Hafford-Letchfield (2014) argue that concepts of anti-discriminatory practice and anti-oppressive practice, part of the social work landscape since the late 1970s, and which are essential and fundamental areas within social work education, practice and research, have now become part of 'status-quo' thinking; they have long since lost their political edge. Substantial structural changes, various cultural shifts, new social movements and contemporary contests from within the critical tradition of social work continue to challenge core assumptions of social work theory and practice to aid development of new thinking. Statements of intent and codes of practice have not always been able to keep up with these challenges. There are also some practical objections to codes of practice, the first of which is scepticism about how external professional regulation can be the best way of generating ethical conduct. Secondly, they imply that a broad set of principles or practice guidance can meaningfully capture the complexity of ethical decision-making. The third problem is that regulation and bureaucracy can arguably lead to defensive practice with an over-reliance on rules, and meeting obligations, rather than taking actions that are seen as morally right (Banks, 2006). Practice wisdom, knowledge and experience of reflective good practice are important ingredients in addressing these issues.

Global development of agendas involving risk and governance has also increased over the past two decades: documented by writers such as Ulrich Beck since the 1980s, Western nations are said to have become engaged with the idea of 'risk' in many spheres of life, including professional practices (Adam et al., 2000; Webb, 2006). Increasing focus on risk has been linked to the rise of neoliberal policies favouring economic growth in Westernized countries (Mudge, 2008). As the provision and delivery of care has become more sophisticated and determined by the impact of a globalized market economy, increasing technology and a greater consumerist orientation to social care, it can be argued that there is an even greater need to retain and defend a more reflective, philosophical approach to how care is produced and provided, going much further than prescribed codes and guidelines (Leathard and McLaren, 2007).

Within the global context, the development of an international statement of values and principles signed by some seventy countries is a step towards establishing a unifying framework for social work worldwide. This statement has been influenced by universal declarations of human rights covering civil, political, economic and social rights and aims to guide social workers' practice as they seek to manage complex, dynamic situations in a broader context (Gilbert, 2009). Such commitment also has its challenges: Stanford (2010) has analysed how the rhetoric of risk is used within neoliberal societies to mobilize fear as an emotive, defensive and strategic medium for advancing values of safety and security. According to this discourse, Stanford argues that while taking risks has become integral to social workers enacting a moral stance, how we view ourselves, either in the context of personal or social relations:

> has become dominated by the legions of polarised identities that cumulate around notions of risk – dangerousness and vulnerability, independence and dependence, responsibility and irresponsibility, trustworthiness and untrustworthiness, culpability and innocence. Within this analysis, overwhelming fear operates as a core constituent for defining the personal experience of risk within contemporary society. (Stanford, 2010: 1066)

In social work, we can appreciate how values link with engagement with professional bodies and their codes of practice. Ethical principles underpin governance, which is the framework that guides and monitors quality and equality, such as in the way services are designed, delivered and evaluated. Social workers are also expected to hold certain personal values. These are not free-floating, but belong to a person, a team, an organization, a profession as well as to the wider society. They are often framed in vision and mission statements, in lists of principles and in ethical guidelines. To think and act ethically requires a set of values and a mindset that values other people (Dawson and Butler, 2003). Some commentators, however, have noted the problematic, conceptually vague and unsatisfactory ways values are discussed in social work, suggesting that their meaning needs greater clarification. As organizations continue to face relentless new pressures to adapt, learn, innovate and constantly improve performance, social workers need to keep up with rapid technological and other opportunities, and threats. These require greater integration across a range of organizational boundaries through increased collaborative or integrated working (Hafford-Letchfield et al., 2014). The latter has been accompanied by increased complexity as organizations consolidate and in many cases combine structures and resources to promote new ways of organizing service delivery, with raised expectations coming from a consumer culture and among a complex array of stakeholder involvement.

Clark (2000) defines social work values under four headings incorporating different levels: (1) worth and uniqueness of every person, (2) entitlement to justice, (3) aspiration to freedom, and (4) essentiality of community. Despite these efforts at definition, it is widely acknowledged that attempts to pin down what we mean by ethics and values in social work are often contradictory, competing and sometimes too abstract for practical application within contingent, uncertain and transient contemporary social environments.

Ethics and values in professional education

Increasingly complex ethical and legal dilemmas in care, many of which involve working within inter-professional contexts, have for several years drawn attention to the quality and quantity of professional education (Whittington and Bell, 2001; Whittington, 2003a; Hean et al., 2006; Narey, 2014). Therefore, inclusion of ethics and values inevitably underpins professional education, training and continuing professional development and should permeate institutional approaches to staff, students and communities within organizational settings focusing on delivering care, such as in the ways people experience culture and workplace rules. These issues have been well aired in serious case reviews and enquiries where strong links have been made between those imperatives arising from poor workforce management, specifically bullying, supervision and workplace stress-related illness, and serious compromises in and failure of care. Managerialist cultures in care organizations were explored in the UK by the Munro Report (2011), which offered a critique of the defensive process of risk management frequently observed in many social care organizations. According to Dawson and Butler (2003), ethical practice includes demonstrating probity and professionalism and appropriate use of professional status and power on a daily basis, including in our relationships with colleagues. Formal and informal codes of ethical practice are there to govern rules about personal conduct and behaviour, confidentiality, consent and accountability and how we collaborate and enable participation from service users, carers and the community. Students of social work, whether at pre- or post-qualifying level, may therefore have to confront and 'unlearn' some personal values and beliefs as well as learning how to act morally and ethically. This means developing an ethical perspective that is good enough to help cope with the role and tasks that go with the job and an ethical approach that is robust enough to cover dilemmas and difficulties occurring at the front line. This means more than not succumbing to judgemental attitudes, it involves developing skills in creativity, physical and emotional integrity and having enough knowledge and expertise to maximize use of formal and informal structures that can represent perspectives of service users, carers and communities.

Some of these issues will be addressed in Chapter 3 by Hafford-Letchfield and Dillon, who discuss how ethics and values are incorporated into social work education and training and which (according to these authors) involves a lifelong learning approach. Gray (2010) has argued the importance of social workers having at least some grounding in moral philosophy, although social work education has tended to steer away from this. Through examining a feminist ethics of care, Gray further posits that that there are limitations in current ethical theory and questions whether the relational ethics of care holds better prospects for delivering quality outcomes for social work clients than existing ethical theories, which seek universal standards of impartiality. These are just some of the debates about how a focus on ethics and values can address complexities of problems within very harsh practice environments, where maintaining certain values becomes ever more difficult. We expect that you will find these ideas woven throughout this book from different authors, and we make no apologies for some of the differences and debates that are subsequently raised within these contributions.

Summary of themes and content of this book

This book is divided into two key parts. Part 1 provides a general introduction to values and ethics from the perspective of the learner social worker, from pre-qualifying to qualified social workers undertaking continuous professional development. In the first five chapters, we provide an overview of ethical theories and links with values, prioritizing those that promote professional roles/identity, inclusive practice and reflective practice. The chapters in Part 2 go on to illustrate concepts such as 'power' and 'social justice', working with 'diversity and difference', 'partnership' and 'relationship-based practice', using scenarios to apply these concepts to different aspects of social work practice. These chapters provide a number of case scenarios and suggestions to help the reader develop an ethical framework and key strategies when working within different practice situations, striving to balance related processes with social work values. Given the interdisciplinary and multi-agency contexts of social work practice, we have written in a way that we hope will benefit other professionals within wider fields of social care, health and education, such as doctors, nurses and allied health professionals or teachers.

Part 1: Linking ethics and values to professional identity, inclusive and reflective practice

In Chapter 2, Souzy Dracopoulou offers a review of the main theoretical approaches in the field of *applied ethics* with an emphasis on their potential application to social work. Social work ethics is a recent attempt to consider ethical problems and dilemmas arising in social work practice in a systematic way and by appealing to philosophical thinking and methodologies. This chapter is an exposition of central theoretical trends and methodologies, but is also critical of mainstream tendencies that rely too readily on direct application of certain ethical theories and principles to concrete moral problems, with the intention to analyse them and, where possible, resolve them. Dracopoulou reviews key approaches, in particular *consequentialism* and *deontology*, and *principlism*. She then suggests other approaches that rely on a more particularistic or contextualized understanding of moral reasoning and justification (e.g. *virtue ethics* and *ethics of care*). In these approaches, context, history, culture, character, virtue, relations as well as notions of interpretation and comparative case analysis are central.

In Chapter 3, Trish Hafford-Letchfield and Jean Dillon consider the importance of values and ethics to those motivated to enter social work. Drawing upon theoretical ideas related to lifelong learning and life course development, this chapter asserts and illustrates the importance of an understanding of ethics and values for inclusive practice during social work education and training, continuing into the arena of continuing professional development after qualifying. The authors look at some debates about recruitment and retention in social work and ethics underpinning emerging workforce development strategies. Concepts related to 'experiences of being' (Dalrymple and Burke, 2006: 5) and 'becoming' are explored to illustrate the centrality of continuity and consistency in attitude, behaviour and practice *vis-à-vis* inclusive practice and social justice. Some initial cases and questions are presented to illustrate the issues raised.

In Chapter 4, Linda Bell explores the relevance of values and ethics to the construction of 'professional' identity(ies) in social work. She reviews recent literature relating to 'professional' identity(ies), taking the position that professional identity(ies) are (re)constructed in practice rather than being completely fixed and unchanging. Bell explores how professional identity(ies) in social work relate to individual practitioners as well as collectivities; she also considers whether there can be a single social work identity, or if there are several. These processes are connected to issues of ethics and values, noting that for some, the *individual practitioner* is where any focus on identity and values should start. Bell suggests how inter-professional practice and working in different organizational/cultural contexts can help to shape social workers' values and, therefore, professional identity(ies). This chapter notes increasing emphasis in literature on the relevance of philosophical theories (such as 'ethics of care') as a significant *moral* basis for social work and/or related occupations, grounded in particular in notions of 'virtue ethics'. This chapter also widens the theoretical focus of the book in its final section to explore some international influences on processes of identity construction.

In Chapter 5, Pat Cartney focuses on links between reflective practice, ethics and values, aiming to draw on issues raised in previous chapters to 'problematize' the nature of professional knowledge and 'know-how' in social work. The complex, multi-layered knowledge held by practitioners is presented and explored. Practice knowledge is conceptualized as incorporating elements of both formal and informal knowledge. Links are made to literature on reflective practice and the relationship between 'internalist' ways of knowing and more 'externalist' ways of justifying our actions, for example, by drawing upon research evidence. Cartney explores the nature of current tensions in social work, suggesting that a more holistic, nuanced understanding of the nature of practice knowledge is required. Such understandings are especially relevant to applied ethics and values, as professional judgements in this arena are often very complex and may require the balancing and prioritizing of different, conflicting interests and rights. Cartney illustrates the issues she raises through a case scenario and related questions, leading us into themes covered in Part 2.

Part 2: Themes for social work practice: 'Power', 'Social Justice', 'Partnership', 'Diversity and difference' and 'Relationship-based practice'

In the second part of the book, we focus on ethical issues arising within different social work practice contexts and associated with specific concepts commonly cited in social work. In Chapter 6, Trish Hafford-Letchfield focuses on the concept of professional power and related ethical issues and dilemmas through closer examination of two familiar scenarios. She theorizes competing discourses of empowerment in social work with particular reference to those within UK government policy and examines key concepts around power and empowerment. Drawing in particular on the explanatory powers of selected critical systems theorists such as Foucault (1980) and those from more radical traditions, she examines how power might be conceptualized within different levels of practice. The concept of power is problematized by explicitly drawing on users' and carers' own accounts from the literature to demonstrate different external and internal influences on root causes of disempowerment. Hafford-Letchfield then illustrates these through case studies on 'safeguarding' and 'vulnerability' in relation to how different service users are supported to make decisions about their own care and support, using more creative approaches (such as those involving narrative) and relationship-based approaches. These, she argues, emphasize the centrality of experience, critical reflection, meaning-making and the importance of flexible and facilitative relationships within social work practice.

In Chapter 7, Colin Whittington and Margaret Whittington focus on the theme of 'partnership'. This chapter has several main components: exploration of aspects of partnership and its place in policy and practice agendas, together with examples of evidence on partnership working; consideration of ethics and values in social work and the location of partnership ideas within them; discussion of practice scenarios, explored through the narrative of a single 'case' relating to an older adult, in which the authors identify particular spheres of partnership and collaboration, raise ethical issues relevant to partnership and suggest responses to them. Whittington and Whittington leave us with some reflective questions about the limitations of partnership, the importance of taking a questioning stance and the role of the social worker in promoting commitment to service user-centred services within this agenda.

In Chapter 8, Tom Wilks applies concepts of 'diversity and difference' to various practice scenarios in social work. There is discussion about how services users' unique social, ethnic, economic and cultural contexts can be recognized and responded to both sensitively and appropriately. That diversity has a central place within social work practice is universally acknowledged in professional codes and underlying principles of practice; however, achieving such worthy goals for social work as a whole is not always straightforward in practice. Wilks considers two different ways that this concern with diversity manifests itself: in broader goals of social work as a professional activity (headline statements of ethical codes of practice, for example) at a macro level; and in specific roles and tasks undertaken by social workers at a micro level. How diversity should be addressed by the profession as a whole (and by organizations providing social work services), a macro level consideration, and how individual social workers should respond when faced with dilemmas concerning diversity, a micro level consideration, are interrelated and are illustrated by examples of practice dilemmas at both these levels. At a macro level, important sources of such dilemmas are how far social work should go in its commitment to supporting diversity and social change. The issue of separate services of specific groups or inclusive services for all can also raise important challenges to social work values. At a micro level, dilemmas can often revolve around what respect for difference means in practice.

In Chapter 9, Mina Hyare builds on some of this discussion, especially in relation to the concept of 'relationship-based practice'. Taking a contemporary conception of relationship-based practice informed by psychodynamic, attachment and systems theory, she asserts that these provide a knowledge base for facilitating and enabling development of highly sophisticated communication skills that can help work within emotionally charged situations and with service users who can be hostile or resistant. Hyare provides some case material to illustrate the application of relationship-based practice, asserting its superiority in developing professional confidence, maturity and thus an ability to utilize discretion, which is important in achieving genuine change.

In Chapter 10, Alison Higgs takes forward the argument that being morally active encompasses not only individual conduct and personal belief but choices about participating in a broader social justice agenda, which, she argues, should be at the heart of the contemporary social work endeavour. Taking up the macro debate, Higgs documents in more detail how neoliberal economic and social policy has influenced social work, asserting that it has the primacy of the market, while operating at an ideological level to affect those who need services. She suggests that furthering understanding about the meaning of social justice in neoliberal contexts is vital, but this must be combined with political action in order to make changes. The political and philosophical nature of social work requires a definition of social justice that goes beyond an abstract 'thinking about' what a fair society would look like. Through case examples, Higgs illustrates how social work is about acting and doing, as well as thinking, and consequently social justice is something that needs to be struggled for as well as conceptualized. She makes a counter-argument against current brutal neoliberal policies being inflicted on populations globally being inevitable and the only possible response to the crisis of world capitalism. Higgs concludes that there is an urgent need to develop a social work ethics that embraces both intellectual understanding and political action in relation to social justice.

In a final afterword, Linda Bell and Trish Hafford-Letchfield draw together key arguments presented in this book. They briefly explore possibilities for social work values and identity(ies), based on social justice and critical reflexivity that can link or transcend different social work contexts, with suggestions for a possible practice-led ethical framework and key strategies to assist students' and practitioners' ethical decision-making when working within different practice situations.

Chapter summary

This chapter has provided a general introduction to how ethics and values are situated within the continuum of social work practices, including a discussion of some broader debates about what it means to social workers to 'act ethically'. The 'ethical' social worker is likely to be guided by a number of issues in their decision-making, including: an awareness and ability to recognize dilemmas and conflicts and how they arise; being aware of their values and having the capacity to reflect on their practice, and to learn from it. These issues will be discussed in the following chapters with the opportunity to consider examples of the types of ethical dilemmas that might arise for social workers in practice.

2 Major trends in applied ethics, including the ethics of social work

Souzy Dracopoulou

Introduction

The field of *applied ethics* has flourished in the last 35 years or so. The interest in *applied ethics*, or in understanding, analysing and addressing ethical issues that arise in various practical contexts, whether in business, the environment or healthcare, has increased constantly during this time. Healthcare ethics (or bioethics or biomedical ethics) is at the forefront of this expansion of applied ethics, as the incredible technological advances in biomedicine, as well as the shift in the importance given to rights and autonomy in the last part of the twentieth century, have challenged our traditional moral views and obligations.

An interest in the ethical issues that arise in the context of social work is a more recent trend in applied ethics, and with the profound changes that are happening in this area in the UK as well as in other countries, this interest is not surprising (e.g. Banks, 2006, 2012; Clark, 2000). The theoretical basis of social work ethics, however, is not different from that of healthcare ethics or indeed of applied ethics in general. Being a branch of moral philosophy, applied ethics (or applied philosophy) is concerned to examine and analyse ethical issues in various practical contexts in a systematic way, and by appealing to philosophical thinking and methodologies. After a brief descriptive and historical account of applied ethics in general and social work ethics in particular, I will offer a critical review of the main theoretical trends and methodologies, with the aim of bringing out the challenges that they each face and how these challenges are addressed by rival approaches. Throughout my discussion, there will be an emphasis on issues arising primarily in social work, but also in healthcare practice.

The nature of, and a critical overview of major trends within, applied ethics

Applied ethics is a field within the discipline of ethics or, synonymously, moral philosophy. More specifically, it is a branch of normative ethics, that area of moral philosophy that is concerned with which moral views are justifiable, and thus morally acceptable. Normative ethics is distinguished from (although, arguably, not unconnected with) metaethics, the area of moral philosophy that attempts to understand the metaphysical, epistemological and conceptual presuppositions of moral thought. It is also distinguished – and in this case logically – from descriptive ethics, the aim of which is simply to describe and causally explain (rather than attempt to justify) existing moral views, a discipline which therefore belongs to the social sciences.

At a general level, normative ethics is concerned to establish a justificatory framework or a theory that provides answers to questions about what kinds of actions are morally right or wrong. For example, as I will discuss later, it advances a theoretical framework within which actions that lead to overall happiness are morally right or obligatory; or an opposed theoretical framework that discounts consequences as non-important and identifies the morally right actions by appealing to the notion of moral duty. In contrast to general normative ethics, applied normative ethics (or applied ethics) brings these justificatory frameworks into context by focusing on the examination of specific controversial issues. It is thus concerned to address particular ethical (or moral – I will be using these two terms interchangeably) problems and dilemmas, such as whether it is morally right or acceptable to coerce a service user who finds it difficult to look after himself to have a home care assistant or to withdraw treatment from a terminally ill patient.

The concerns of applied ethics are not new. Since ancient times, moral philosophers have debated various practical ethical questions, including the issues of suicide, infanticide, unjust wars, telling a lie and the moral status of animals. However, no specific programme or method of practical or applied ethics was developed throughout the history of moral philosophy. Rather, issues were discussed topically, in a relatively unsystematic way, and generally by appealing to intuitions and social norms. General moral theories that were formulated about what is right and what is good appeared hazy about whether and how they may be applied to address moral problems (Beauchamp, 2005). It was not until the 1970s and beginning of the 1980s that a focus on how to treat practical issues and on methodology started appearing in the philosophical literature and the field of applied ethics emerged as a distinct academic discipline. Within moral philosophy of the twentieth century, this turn towards normative ethics, and a systematic understanding and treatment of specific practical problems, can be seen as a rebellious move, as an emphasis on metaethical concerns, and a strong scepticism about any role the moral philosopher may claim in the practical realm dominated the discipline. Unsurprisingly, the impetus towards this move resulted from the interaction of moral philosophy with biomedicine and the pressing moral issues that arose within the latter. However, ethical issues in other practical areas, such as social work, were soon after to be addressed by means of this more systematic methodology.

The frameworks of Consequentialism and Deontology

In the relatively short history of applied ethics as a discipline, specific ethical problems and dilemmas (predominantly in healthcare) were first addressed by appealing to one or other of the two main normative ethical theories – Consequentialism or Deontology. These two dominant theories in the Western philosophical tradition still today provide frameworks in which ethical problems are (often usefully) placed. The basic idea of Consequentialism is that the morally right actions are the ones that produce the best possible consequences. For example, when considering whether to treat with antibiotics pneumonia that has developed in a terribly suffering terminally ill patient, the possible consequences of the treatment on those affected or potentially affected (the patient, the relatives, the hospital staff, society as a whole) will determine the morally right way to act. The morally right act is the one that produces the best, or least bad, consequences. Consequentialism is a general theory that does not define what count as good consequences. However, according to utilitarianism, the most prominent consequentialist theory, good consequences (referred to as utility) is defined in terms of happiness. The classic formulation of Utilitarianism, a theory associated with the nineteenth-century British philosophers Jeremy Bentham and John Stuart Mill, is based on the claim that the morally right action is the one that brings about the most happiness, or least unhappiness (maximizes utility), to all those who are affected or poten- tially affected by the action. In the example above, it might be that the least unhappiness will be experienced if antibiotics are not prescribed, the pneumonia is not treated, and the patient's suffering ends earlier than originally anticipated. The unhappiness might be less for the patient, the relatives, the staff, indeed even for society as a whole if this particular case contributes to an unspoken acceptance that the life of a severely suffering terminally ill individual should not be prolonged unnecessarily.

As described above, Utilitarianism in fact conforms to what in contemporary qualifica- tions of the theory has been branded as Act Utilitarianism, to be distinguished from Rule Utilitarianism, where rules, rather than individual actions, are justified morally on utilitar- ian grounds. A morally right action for Rule Utilitarianism is then the one that conforms to a rule that has a utilitarian justification. The rightness of the action is not determined by its consequences alone. For example, as conceptualized by the Rule Utilitarian, telling the truth to a service user is morally right, even if in certain circumstances this may lead to more unhappiness than happiness (think of the situation where deceiving a patient about their condition may help their recovery), because the action falls under the 'rule of truth telling', which has a utilitarian moral justification: the adoption of the general observance of truth telling encourages trust, which is of fundamental importance in the confines of the professional–service user relationship.

Utilitarianism (and Consequentialism more generally) provides a deductivist frame- work that can be used to determine which, from a possible number of alternatives, is the morally right course of action to take. It is deductivist in the sense that it is based on a single fundamental principle (maximization of utility) that is meant to provide justifica- tion for all moral judgements, given relevant factual information (e.g. about the possible consequences of an action). It is accordingly applied top-down – actions that bring about the most happiness or least unhappiness to all those affected or potentially affected are morally right (premise 1); action X (e.g. withholding treatment by antibiotics) is likely to bring about the least unhappiness (premise 2); therefore action X is the morally right action (conclusion). Another deductivist framework in which moral dilemmas were placed during the early life of applied ethics as a discipline, and which is still widely appealed to, is provided by Deontology.

The deontological approach can be perhaps characterized best by its contrast to the con- sequentialist one: morally right and wrong actions are not determined by reference to their outcomes, at least not exclusively; on the contrary, they are intrinsically right or wrong, right or wrong in themselves. Just as the classic formulation of Utilitarianism is found most prominently in the works of Bentham and Mill, the eighteenth-century German philosopher Immanuel Kant provides the classic statement of a deontological theory.

There is a basic moral principle from which all our moral duties derive, according to Kant, which he calls 'the categorical imperative'. Kant offers a number of different formula- tions of the categorical imperative, but in the context of a discussion of the application of moral theory to practice, the formulation that is most relevant, and which is almost invari- ably used in argumentation in this area, is the one that could be expressed by saying that no person should be treated merely as a means (object to other people's ends) but always also as an end in themselves (beings with their own wishes, desires and choices). What is central to this formulation is the notion of 'respect for persons'. For Kant, all persons, by virtue of being rational agents, capable of rational thought and self-determined action, are entitled to respect, and should therefore never be treated simply as a means, for their usefulness to others. Such treatment would be incompatible with respecting them.

Of course, on many occasions we all treat others as a means to achieving our ends. For example, a social worker uses her clients as a means to having a job and a salary. A student uses his lecturers as a means to acquiring knowledge and skills. Kant would find nothing morally wrong in all these human interactions. The Kantian claim is rather that we should never treat others *merely* as a means: to the extent that other people exercise their free choices and desires when they interact with us, and there is no coercion involved, using them as a means to achieve our ends is perfectly morally justified.

From the basic moral principle of the categorical imperative a number of duties to ourselves and to others derive, some of them 'perfect', which allow for no exceptions, others 'imperfect', which can be overridden by perfect ones. The notion of 'respect for persons' imposes duties on us towards ourselves, for example the duty not to get drunk or inebriated or to commit suicide – all of these actions involve treating ourselves as a means to pleasure or avoiding distress. But it is the duties to others that are of most importance in the context of the present discussion. Perfect duties to others are the duties not to kill, not to lie and to keep promises, while the duty to act in the best interests of other people and to promote their well-being – the duty of beneficence – as well as the duty to refrain from harming others – the duty of non-maleficence – are both imperfect duties. It would follow from this distinction of duties that, for example, a social worker would not ever be able to lie (perfect duty) to a service user on a particular occasion in order to prevent great harm (imperfect duty) to a family member or to the community; a researcher would never be able to use placebos in placebo-controlled trials; an individual would never be able to break a promise, even of trivial nature, in order to prevent a huge embarrassment or distress.

Both Utilitarianism and Deontology have a certain appeal, as they each capture some important aspects of our moral life. We often think in terms of maximizing happiness and minimizing unhappiness when contemplating about which is the morally right way to act. Indeed, utilitarian thinking is prominent in policy-making, as aggregate benefits and human welfare become the focus. At other times we think in terms of having certain duties, and corresponding rights, independently of any consequences, as for example when we are repulsed by the abuse or killing of a child, and not because of the distress that this will bring to so many people.

However, both theories also fail to take into account fundamental aspects of our moral lives, and hence face serious objections. One of the many problems with Act Utilitarianism in its application to practise is its intrinsic disregard for the individual and individual rights. Under Act Utilitarianism, an individual may be tortured or unjustly punished, and this may be morally permissible, if the greatest balance of happiness over unhappiness (greatest utility) is brought about by this action, such as if a large-scale disaster, say a terrorist attack, is prevented. Rule Utilitarianism fares better with respect to individual rights, as a consideration of the rights of an individual might be a requirement incorporated into a rule. However, Rule Utilitarianism faces another, more general problem – that it may be unsustainable as a theory distinguishable from Act Utilitarianism. In certain circumstances, breaking the rule may bring about greater utility than keeping it. Consider the example of lying to a seriously ill patient, whose recovery would be affected if they knew the truth about their condition, in an environment where the rule is to always tell the truth. In a situation like this, Rule Utilitarianism collapses into Act Utilitarianism. As Rule Utilitarianism may be confronted with this challenge at any time, the objection is that it cannot exist as a theory independent of Act Utilitarianism.

In its insistence that individuals should never be treated merely as a means, Deontology is very well placed to account for individual rights. However, there are other aspects of this theory that cannot be easily reconciled with our ordinary moral experience. One such aspect is the exceptionless character of its perfect duties. Surely in certain circumstances it is not morally wrong to lie or to break a promise, such as when, for example, this is the only way to avoid extreme distress to another person. Yet, according to the deontologist the above situation presents a conflict between a perfect duty (not to lie or break a promise) and an imperfect duty (to avoid doing harm), and under no circumstances is it morally acceptable for the latter to override the former.

Objections such as the above (and only a taste of these has been given here) weaken aspects of the two major ethical theories, and unavoidably their appeal in the area of moral reasoning and decision-making in practical contexts. But their historical appeal in applied ethics has been also, and most significantly, tarnished by two further challenges. The first one has to do with the abstractness and remoteness of these theories, and their consequent inability to decide very complex and diverse ethical issues in a very complex world of particularities – of intricate relationships, cultural beliefs and institutional commitments and responsibilities. Their deductivist style, where a single, overarching value (whether this is maximizing utility or the Kantian respect for persons) is applied to concrete moral situations with the expectation to derive concrete answers leaves no room for the rich diversity and complexity of these situations and presents a very impoverished understanding of human life in general (Williams, 1985; Winkler, 1993; Arras, 1994) and of professional experience.

The second challenge relates to the precise working of the deductivist methodology. The application of one or the other of the two ethical theories in a particular moral situation presupposes, as a starting point, the assumption that one, rather than the other of them, is valid. But as John D. Arras blandly puts it, if after more than two thousand years of ethical debate philosophers haven't come to an agreement about which is the correct moral theory, it would be, to say the least, unreasonable to expect the consultant applied ethicist, employed to offer advice in the clinic or social work environment, to take a reasoned stance before they apply a theory to their particular dilemma (Arras, 1994). It would be even worse to expect the busy and morally perplexed practitioners to do so.

Principlism

The four principles approach or principlism, developed by Tom Beauchamp and James Childress in the late 1970s, was introduced with the intention to overcome both of these challenges. The principles of beneficence and non-maleficence (often considered as one principle), autonomy and justice were conceived as expressing fundamental values and providing a framework that could be used in practical contexts to guide moral decision and action. They were thought to be compatible with both Utilitarianism and Deontology, although some were more directly linked with one rather than the other (autonomy with Deontology, beneficence with Utilitarianism); at the same time, knowledge of these theories and commitment to one or the other of them was not considered necessary when invoking the principles in decision-making situations. They were thus understood as 'mid-level', occupying a level of generality and abstraction below the single overarching values of Utilitarianism and Deontology, and hence closer to the diversities of concrete ethical problems than these monolithic theories. Moreover, this understanding of them helped bridge the (often thought) undesirable gap between the two theories.

The more pluralistic approach of the principles (incorporating more than one value), together with the simplicity of the framework they were conceived to form (easy to teach and follow in practical settings) have contributed to the enormous popularity of this methodological approach, initially in medical ethics but subsequently in other areas of applied ethics, including social work ethics. In relation to the latter, principlism has been discussed and employed although not uncritically. For example, Sarah Banks puts it forward as a possible approach for social work ethics in the second edition of her book *Ethics and Values in Social Work* (2001), but becomes critical of it in the third edition (2006). She distances herself totally from it in her more recent book with Ann Gallagher, *Ethics in Professional Life* (2009). As in other practical areas, here too it has been articulated fully by explanations of its basic principles and by making connections with subsidiary principles central in social work practice, such as those of informed consent, truth telling, paternalism and confidentiality. Not unlike the case of the direct appeal to theories for advice, the use of principles in social work practice, as in all other practical contexts, became associated with the notion of the ethicist or ethics adviser as a moral expert: educated in moral philosophy, he or she utilizes specialist knowledge in order to select the relevant moral principles for a particular moral problem identified by the practitioner, which are then deployed to find an appropriate moral solution. (In the case of the direct appeal to theories, it is the appropriate moral theory, rather than moral principles, that is selected.) The two levels of operation, that of the thinker/philosopher and the doer/practitioner, are as evident here as in cases of the direct appeal to abstract moral theories (Loughlin, 2002).

Below is an example of how the framework of the principles is thought to be able to offer guidance, in accordance with the principles approach, using a case study from social work (adapted from Clark, 2000).

Case study 2.1

Mrs G, a lady in her early eighties who lived alone, was admitted to hospital after lighting an open fire in her front room, under the impression that her coal-effect electric fire was broken. The hospital doctor wished an early discharge as there were no acute medical needs, and the patient wished to return home. The house had suffered some damage because of the fire. The social worker found that although Mrs G appeared to be rational in many respects, the daughter and lodger whom she spoke about as waiting for her at home had died eleven and four years previously, respectively. Further investigation revealed several other serious health concerns.

Reflection point

What guidance could the social worker get from the principles? He might decide to allow Mrs G to return home – appealing to *the principle of respect for autonomy*, that the wishes of autonomous people should be respected. After all, Mrs G seems quite rational and competent and she might have simply lied about her daughter and lodger. Or he might decide that it is best for Mrs G to be rehoused, in view of the damage in her house and further health concerns – appealing to *the principle of non-maleficence*, that one ought to avoid doing harm. Alternatively, he might decide, in addition to rehousing Mrs G, to arrange for support packages, so as to contribute to Mrs G's quality of life – appealing to *the principle of beneficence*, that one ought to promote the well-being or benefit of others. Or, further, he might think about the issue of the just distribution of resources, for example whether Mrs G is in fact eligible for all the packages – appealing to *the principle of justice*, that equals should be considered equally.

Despite its widespread popularity, primarily in medical ethics and healthcare ethics more generally, but also in other areas, including social work ethics, principlism (sometimes appropriately referred to as 'the paradigm theory') is viewed by many as unsatisfactory. Specific reasons for this include the difficulty that arises when some of the principles conflict with others but also the inability of principlism to deal with the issue of moral status.

As the four principles are presented in no particular order of priority, conflicts of principles, such as when the choice of the autonomous service user (autonomy) is not in accordance with what the social worker considers to be in that user's best interest (beneficence), cannot be resolved within principlism. The practitioner or ethics adviser would have to appeal to resources beyond the principles, such as a theory (the need for which principlism was conceived to overcome) or intuitions, in order to find a resolution. Moreover, principlism has nothing to say about to whom its principles apply (Gillon, 1986, 1994), or what characteristics an entity must have in order to qualify for moral consideration. It is thus incapable of offering advice in areas of applied ethics where, for example, the issue of the value of the embryo or the treatment of severely impaired individuals (such as patients in persistent vegetative state or anencephalic newborns) is at stake.

In addition to the objections above, there is a more general concern that although principlism is more modest than, and hence an improvement over, the deductive, top-down orientation of the two theories, it is still top-down itself, in the sense that its principles are still too abstract to allow for the complexities of concrete moral problems and offer useful advice. Autonomy and beneficence may not provide sufficient guidance to the social worker in the case of Mrs G, as there may be important subtle issues that the invocation of these principles obscures, for example issues that have to do with the authenticity or inauthenticity of Mrs G's desire to return home (is this desire consonant with her current fears and uncertainties?) or how to understand Mrs G's refusal to go to a care home (is she testing the commitment of all those around her, her refusal in effect being a question in disguise – do you care for me? – see Arras, 1994). Even taking into consideration the improvement offered by the 'reflective equilibrium' methodology (Beauchamp and Childress, 2001), according to which principles are in some way modified or shaped in the context of the subtleties of concrete situations and by our 'considered' moral judgements and responses to ethical dilemmas, the concern is that principles still dominate, in a downward orientation, in ethical decision-making (Winkler, 1993; Arras, 1994).

A contextualized approach: virtue and care ethics

In view of difficulties such as the ones discussed above, the applied ethics model of moral reasoning, exemplified by both the theories and the principles approaches, has been recently falling out of favour. In its place, a more particularistic and contextualized approach has been rising, in which moral reasoning in general, and in specific professional areas in particular, is a multifaceted process. Rather than depending on the invocation of certain predetermined values expressed by theories and principles, it occurs within the context of the unique features of specific situations, their various particularities and contingencies. A discussion of a further, legitimate concern about the top-down methodology, which is moreover of particular relevance to social work ethics, will bring us naturally to an exploration of this rival approach.

This further concern is that top-down approaches focus on short-term 'ethical fixes', and fail to appreciate and address the underlying structural shortcomings responsible for so many difficult ethical problems (Moreno, 1999; Dracopoulou, 2005). Michael Loughlin unravels this problem in connection with both healthcare ethics in general and the ethics of health service management in particular (Loughlin, 2002). The scope of the predominant applied ethics model, he claims, is restricted to addressing ethical problems within a practice or context (whether cultural or historical or institutional) which is taken as 'given' and which is not subjected to moral questioning. So, for example, when the issue of healthcare rationing is debated, the assumption is that 'economic scarcity is a fact of life' and then solutions have to be found about 'who are singled out for inconvenience, suffering or even death' (Loughlin, 2002: 156–7). The underlying social and economic defects responsible for the existence of scarcity are not put to question. Rather than enlightening professionals who try to find answers to problems generated by their roles, the applied ethics model 'vindicates the roles themselves and the broader system of which they are part' (p. 148). The 'prevailing social and economic order', and the ideology that underpins it, remain intact (p. 149).

Merlinda Weinberg locates the same concern within social work ethics dominated by the applied ethics model (Weinberg, 2010). Although structural shortcomings – such as insufficient resources, problematic institutional policies, cost containments and broad patterns of social injustice more generally – are sometimes identified in discussions of ethics in social work practice, she observes, these issues 'are seen as peripheral rather than central' (Weinberg, 2010: 34). The focus on developing lists of principles and on how to deal with situations where they conflict ignores 'the influence of history and the contexts in which ethical dilemmas occur'; 'the field [social work ethics] is...based on the premise that the current social arrangements are equitable'; it 'seeks to comfort victims of social problems' rather than a critical approach that aims to bring fundamental changes to underlying social structures that are responsible for these problems (Weinberg, 2010).

To broaden the focus of ethics to take account of relevant contexts and underlying structural arrangements in practice areas such as healthcare or social work, the predominant applied ethics model must give way to a more contextualized approach. Loughlin implies this by redefining the role of philosophy in practical areas; rather than selecting or producing theories or principles which are then deployed in finding solutions to practical ethical problems, philosophy's role is to practise conceptual analysis and critical thinking, 'a method...which exposes fundamental assumptions and hidden commitments' (Loughlin, 2002: 193) and which enables practitioners to understand the true causes of their dilemmas by encouraging them 'to think honestly and critically about the roles they occupy and the forces and structures which shape these roles' (p. 148). Loughlin wants to see the division implied in the applied ethics model between the thinkers/philosophers and the doers/practitioners, and the accompanying notion of moral expertise (provided by the thinkers), collapse. A practitioner can of course be both a doer and a thinker. For example, he or she may be a social worker who has also had some education in philosophy and ethics. It should be replaced, Loughlin thinks, by the skill of critical thinking, practised by all, at all levels.

In a similar spirit, Weinberg encourages a 'shift' in social work ethics that takes into account 'the broader structures and paradoxes that shape and limit practice' (Weinberg, 2010: 40). She emphasizes the need for the professional 'to question continually the taken-for-granted discourses that frame the development of those structures'; rather than to focus on issues arising within the one-to-one relationship with the service user (which is the primary focus of the applied ethics model), such as autonomy or confidentiality, at the exclusion of fundamental social and economic problems transcending this relationship and being responsible for individual service users needing help (p. 35). She further emphasizes the need for 'self-reflexivity' in relation, for example, to how social workers, who depend on funding, benefit from maintaining the *status quo* – 'keeping the poor poor and the marginalized marginalized' (p. 40) – and from 'not questioning broader patterns of social injustice' (p. 35) and adopting an approach 'that seeks fundamental social change' (p. 34). This is a theme taken up by Pat Cartney in Chapter 5.

In both Loughlin and Weinberg, what is discerned is a direction away from abstract theories and principles and towards a particularistic and contextualized approach to moral reasoning and justification: ethical problems, whether in healthcare management or social work practice, must be seen in the context of their unique features and be addressed critically within the framework of a complex network of relevant social, cultural and institutional realities and their underlying shortcomings. As Loughlin explains, theories and principles do not have 'even the potential to influence practice in a any meaningful way because what individuals do in specific contexts where decisions actually take place is likely to be influenced by features of these contexts which are unique' (Loughlin, 2002: 209). But Loughlin goes a step further. Critical thinking and contextual awareness are supplemented by the development of 'the right sort of dispositions' or 'sound intuitive thinking' in people, enabling them to 'find good answers for themselves' (p. 24). A preference for 'virtue ethics' is evident in his work (Dracopoulou, 2005), which, although not necessarily suitable for all professional contexts (unlike Loughlin seems to think), may be thought to lend itself well to the caring professions, such as social work. This is especially so when care, empathy and concern for the needs of others are included in the list of appropriate virtues.

For virtue ethics, the focus shifts from general theories and principles to the particularities of character and dispositions or 'virtues'. The morally right action is not the one that is in accordance with certain principles, but what the virtuous person would do in certain circumstances (Hursthouse, 1999). From this follows the importance of virtue education in all contexts, including the context of the professions. As Loughlin says, 'the moral problems of practice become problems of education: how do we acquire the right sort... of instincts...?' (Loughlin, 2002: 24). In relation to the professions, it is interesting that many codes of professional ethics emphasize the kind of person a professional should be (Banks, 2006), while an emphasis on virtue has become prominent with the requirements of professional registration for social workers (Clark, 2006). Traits that have been traditionally regarded as virtues, following the views of Aristotle, include courage, integrity, honesty, truthfulness, justice and generosity. But the list of virtues has changed dramatically in more recent virtue ethics theories, with traits that are characterized by other-regardingness becoming more prominent (Banks, 2006, 2012; Banks and Gallagher, 2009). Thus care, empathy, trustworthiness, sympathy, respectfulness, discernment, compassion, sensitivity, conscientiousness, all figure, to different extents, in a variety of virtue ethics theories found in the literature today.

One of the advantages of virtue ethics is that, by focusing on the importance of cultivating virtues through education, it provides a reliable basis for morally correct behaviour. The compassionate social worker will always act in a compassionate manner, no matter what the circumstances. Interestingly, even Beauchamp and Childress, who developed the principles approach, admit, in the fourth edition of their book *Principles of Biomedical Ethics* (1994), that 'often what counts most in moral life is not consistent adherence to principles and rules, but reliable character, moral good sense, and emotional responsiveness' (quoted in Banks, 2006: 58). A further appeal of this approach lies in how we understand certain moral actions. For example, truly helping the service user with their problems involves careful attention, on the part of the social worker, to the subtleties of their situation and their very special needs, in order to determine the best way of helping them. But this clearly involves exercising certain virtues – a capacity for discernment, which in itself depends on emotional attunement and sympathetic understanding (Nussbaum, 2001; Mappes and Degrazia, 2005).

More recently, some have viewed the 'ethics of care' as a more appropriate approach than virtue ethics in the context of social work (Parton, 2003; Hugman, 2005a) and within the literature on feminist approaches (Orme, 2002; Rogers and Weller, 2013). The impetus has come from a general dissatisfaction about the predominance of the Aristotelian type of virtues (essentially indifferent to the other) in virtue ethics theories. However, although this predominance has now been reversed, most care ethicists have distanced themselves from virtue ethics. This is because even when 'care' is high on the list of virtues in a virtue ethics approach, it is 'care as a relationship', involving a 'displacement of interest from my own reality to the reality of the other' (Noddings, 2003: 14), that is at the centre of the care ethics view. The focus is on the recipient of care and the connection between the recipient and the one who cares, whereas, according to care ethicists (see also Held, 2006), the focus in care as a virtue is on the person who is caring, his or her motives and attitudes. So Noddings (2002) suggests that one may care truly in the virtue sense (have a disposition and motivation to do so) but be unable to connect with the person cared for. But as Banks and Gallagher (2009) argue, there is no reason why care as a virtue should be understood in this narrow sense. Taking into consideration Tronto's (1993) understanding of care as involving attentiveness, responsibility, competence and responsiveness, Banks and Gallagher are able to argue for an account of care as a virtue that is much broader and which accommodates some of what the care ethicists think is at the centre of care as a relationship. This broader understanding of care as a virtue, Banks and Gallagher imply, is in accordance with how we understand, for example, the (virtuous) caring practitioner. We would not characterize a social worker as caring if, although strongly motivated to give good quality care, they failed to engage with the service user because, for example, of their incompetence either in terms of communication skills or technically. It might then be the case that care ethics cannot sustain itself as essentially distinguishable from virtue ethics

Returning to virtue ethics

To return to virtue ethics, despite its recent popularity, especially in the context of the caring professions, this approach is not without its shortcomings. One of the problems is that the notion of virtues, and the accompanying understanding of the morally right action in terms of what the virtuous person would do, are not sufficiently clear, and the latter, ultimately, may lack justification. As the various proponents of the virtue ethics approach often differ in which character traits they consider to be central virtues, the question arises as to what the criteria are for the selection of certain character traits over others. Moreover, it could be argued that a certain conception of the morally right action is presupposed before this selection is made (rather than the other way around). So, for example, it is because the compassionate person is thought to always do the (independently established) moral thing that compassion is favoured as one of the virtues to be included in a particular virtue ethics approach. A response to this could be that, following Aristotle's view, what dispositions count as virtues is determined by what human beings need in order to have *eudemonia* or a flourishing life, a life of living well. But contrary to the thinking that this offers an independent, objective grounding of virtues, and therefore virtue-derived moral action, the notion of flourishing is a relativist notion – what counts as flourishing (and hence virtue) in one particular cultural or institutional or religious setting or tradition may not be what counts as flourishing or living well in a different context. Think of a community of blind people who are willing to use genetic engineering to produce blind children as a way of increasing the eudemonia of the community. The conception of flourishing, and hence virtuous action, in this community is unlikely to be shared by many outsiders. The problem with virtue ethics, it is often admitted, is its inability to overcome the charge of relativism.

This problem can be also be discerned in attempts to develop a virtue ethics approach in the context of the professions. In this context, it has been argued, following Alasdair MacIntyre's understanding of virtues as dispositions that enable people to achieve the goods that are internal to the roles and structures of particular practices (MacIntyre, 1985), that the relevant virtues are selected by taking into consideration what is appropriate or 'internal' to particular communities of practitioners or professions (see Banks, 2006). So, for example, by considering the 'internal' features of social work practice, such as the responsibilities of the social worker towards their clients, their colleagues, the agency for which they work and society at large (presumably consulting the code of practice for social work), we can determine the appropriate virtues for social work practice. The conventionalism and relativism that characterize this approach appear to be present here as much as in virtue ethics in general. The concern is that by defining and identifying virtues by reference to the practices of particular communities, no room is left for going beyond these practices and becoming morally critical of them. Yet, might it not be the case that our most strongly held moral views are the result of cultural or institutional blindness? Could it not be the case that what the virtuous person does is simply morally wrong?

However, despite the problems discussed above, the emphasis on virtue and moral character in virtue ethics approaches in general and in the context of the caring professions in particular is important, as even proponents of top-down approaches recognize (Beauchamp and Childress, 1994). It is significant that the service user is unlikely to be as appreciative of the care they receive if they know that the social worker merely follows certain rules and acts out the role of being kind, honest and trustworthy than if they sense that the help they get arises out of genuine, humane concern and a disposition to be good.

In the end, as Mel Gray (2010) suggests, the question that is of importance in relation to the caring professions in general, and social work in particular, is which approach holds better prospects for delivering quality outcomes for service users. Questions arise about whether theories and principles approaches can address the subtleties and complexities of the problems with which social workers are faced. Would virtue and care ethics be better placed in this respect? Perhaps what is important, as Gray, drawing on Nussbaum's (2001) work, points out, is that we inculcate compassion at both individual and societal levels, so as to ensure that we are disposed favourably to all those in need, and thus to humanize practice. Both virtue and care ethics have the resources to instil compassion through values education and involvement in caring relationships respectively. It is less likely that the top-down theories and principles approaches are equipped to instil compassion in a significant way.

Discussion point

How useful are virtue and care ethics compared with 'top-down' approaches (Deontology, Consequentialism) in enabling professionals to deliver quality outcomes for service users?

Chapter summary

In this chapter, I have endeavoured to offer a critical account of the main trends in applied ethics in general, placing particular emphasis on the ethics of social work. After a discussion of the nature of applied ethics and a brief account of its short history, including the development of social work ethics, the chapter focuses first on an exposition of the two dominant ethical theories, Consequentialism and Deontology, and their application to professional practice. Within Consequentialism the focus remains entirely on Utilitarianism, one branch of it. The challenges faced by these two top-down approaches to moral reasoning and justification, and how these can be addressed, leads on to a discussion of Principlism. In turn, the problems with this approach and with the top-down methodology in general prepare the ground for an account of a more contextualized understanding of moral reasoning in decision-making. Finally, virtue and care ethics in general and in the context of social work practice in particular are explored. Despite its considerable shortcomings, the appeal of virtue ethics is emphasized at the very end of the chapter.

The contribution of education and learning for ethical practice: situating ethics and values within the social work continuum

Trish Hafford-Letchfield and Jean Dillon

Introduction

In Chapter 1, it was suggested that an understanding of ethics and values, adopting an appropriate value stance and modelling of 'good' behaviour are integral to inclusive social work practice. Key ethical theories and issues were considered in Chapter 2, and this chapter continues with some of these themes. We begin by considering the importance of values and ethics in relation to your motivation to enter social work and how this develops as you continue your journey to becoming a registered and regulated professional. Drawing upon ideas related to lifelong learning and life course development, this chapter asserts and illustrates the importance of an understanding of ethics and values for inclusive practice within the continuum of social work. This starts at your point of entry to social work education and follows through to your continuing professional development in social work practice. Implicit within this chapter is a recognition of the 'experiences of being' (Dalrymple and Burke, 2006: 5), and 'becoming' a social worker. These are central concepts for developing and maintaining continuity and consistency in your attitude, behaviour and practice *vis-à-vis* inclusive practice and working towards principles of social justice within various social work contexts (Dunk-West, 2013).

As we saw in Chapter 1, successful engagement with social work values and ethics cannot be achieved by social workers in isolation, or by simply adopting formal codes of practice as you progress through the education process leading to a professional qualification. There are many different levels at which commitment to social work and its core values have to be reflected. Here, we have conceptualized these at three levels, termed the 'macro', 'meso' and 'micro'. First, if we consider the macro level reflected in government legislation, policy and professional leadership, your commitment will be reflected through key embedded messages received about principles and aims of social work and its governance. Second, at a meso level in relation to social work education, there are specific policies and agreed approaches in terms of how students are recruited, selected and supported, both in education and practice settings. Much attention has been given to the role of social work education in progression and continuing professional development, all of which are seen as essential for maintaining standards and promoting quality. Third, at the micro level, retention of individual social workers is promoted through valuing their unique identities, experiences and attributes as lifelong learners, as well as by giving attention to essential tools required to ensure that those already in the workforce are supported and developed. This latter issue has been one that social work has been grappling with for a relatively long time and significant research findings are now beginning to inform strategies around workforce development which pay attention to these issues (DCSF, 2009; Hafford-Letchfield et al., 2009). Coherence of initiatives at these three levels should work towards supporting social workers' roles in a way that allows fulfilment of expectations for the ethics and value frameworks explicitly stated by the profession. It is also important for you to be aware of how these inform your education and training.

The literature is relatively silent, however, on developmental stages for those being socialized into social work and how one might learn relevant values and ethics: this is one of the key purposes of this chapter. We hope to assert that in professional education, giving explicit attention to 'learning to learn' effectively plays an important role in imparting social work values and a sense of professional identity alongside essential knowledge and skills learned. (This theme is taken up and further developed in Chapter 4 by Linda Bell, who debates how values and ethics further shape our professional identity(ies)). Participating in your own educational journey contributes, in both intended and unintended ways, to socialization of students into professional culture(s) as well as contributing to the successful pursuit of career goals. Suffice to say here, becoming a social worker requires a high degree of intellectual ability, empathy, resilience and insight, and this particular combination is attributed to a degree of life experience and the ability to articulate and make sense of that experience when entering social work. Getting the right recruits and keeping the workforce motivated, resilient, up-to-date, trained and supported are powerful ethical issues underpinning workforce development strategies (DSCF, 2009). Importantly, those engaged in workforce development need to make links between this activity and the quality of support offered to service users and their communities in order to raise the standards of available services (Hafford-Letchfield et al., 2009).

Learning to be a social worker

Over the last few decades, debates about the role of social work education have usually been linked to adverse events in society, following which the public and the social work profession have called into question the quality, content and standards involved in educating social workers. However, each major review of social work education subsequently offers new opportunities for examining how 'learner' social workers acquire their professional identity(ies) and suggests changes in the wider context within which this education takes place. Social work is a profession, we would argue, that is committed to understanding that the social environment and cultural setting have an enormous impact on individual experiences. We also need to appreciate how social work scholarship assists us to frame the different roles that social work plays and the nexus between the personal, biographical, political and social knowledge covered. Dunk-West (2013) refers to the importance of student social workers being able to enter a period of time and space within social work education where they 'learn and fashion' their 'social work selves' (p. 9). She further emphasizes the active process of how learners interact between older ways of thinking and relate to newer ways that develop alongside their journey to becoming a social worker. We are writing this chapter in order to touch on some of these issues from a learner's perspective and to encourage you to think about a range of issues during your learning journey, including motivation, the purpose of learning, and the teaching and assessment strategies you may encounter. As a developing ethical practitioner, you are expected to engage in lifelong learning, particularly in the context of widening participation. A critical understanding and interpretation of ethics and values underpinning educational and social work reform, and the links between the two, reminds us that these are not just unrelated events going on around us, but that paying attention to what and how we learn is an ethical issue in itself and requires our active participation. In the USA, the National Association of Social Workers' Code of Ethics is clear on this ethical standard. For example, in its Standards for Cultural Competence in Social Work Practice (NASW, 2001), Standard 8 states:

> Social Workers shall advocate and participate in educational and training programs that help advance cultural competence with the profession. (cited in Coulter et al., 2013: 440)

In England, the Health and Care Professions Council's Standards of Proficiency (HCPC, 2012a) state clearly that social workers should be able to understand the key concepts of the knowledge base relevant to their profession by drawing on appropriate knowledge and skills to inform practice and to understand in relation to social work practice, social work theory, models and interventions, and to be able to change their practice as needed to take account of changing contexts. Therefore, a commitment to learning is a central value reinforced within professional development.

Shifting contexts of higher education

Social work has traditionally been a profession that attracts growing numbers of students from diverse social backgrounds, reflecting increased diversity among the student population as a result of a government education policy introduced mainly from 1997. This widening participation for 'non-traditional' students has intrinsic benefits as well as challenges for social work programmes because of the increasing rigour of professional entry requirements and the need to consider how these can be applied within a widening participation approach (Cunningham, 2005). In England, social work became a graduate profession (DH, 2002) and has since dictated very specific requirements in the recruitment process. More recent reforms assert that selection arrangements 'do not go far enough to ensure that all institutions are assessing candidates rigorously enough to ensure they have the right mix of intellectual and personal qualities to succeed as social workers' (DCSF, 2009: 18). The DCSF called for 'a mix of analytical skills, insight, common sense, confidence, resilience, empathy and use of authority' (p. 17) in social work recruits.

Taking forward these recommendations poses a key challenge in ensuring any entry criteria that are developed can balance academic requirements with more individualistic aspects of suitability for social work. Academic skills and 'potential' can be assessed, to some extent, by academic qualifications and examinations (Dillon, 2007). Personal characteristics and other social factors denoting suitability for social work are, however, far more nebulous, being more difficult to gauge and assess (Dillon, 2011). Given social work education's fundamental gatekeeping role to the profession, it is imperative that admissions criteria are not only balanced, but also permit a fair and rigorous scrutiny of non-academic attributes. As a social work student or graduate you will almost certainly have gone through these rigorous processes and be working within the notion of 'threshold criteria', which frames the stages in your future professional development (DCSF, 2009); you will also have your own views about the qualities that make a good social worker as well as the balance between academic and practice qualities and how you have to work harder at one or both during your learning journey. Different issues belie these ideas, such as motivation and equality of opportunities, which straddle the values of both education and social work. Being aware of your own motivation and autonomy of motivation has been shown to be associated with enhanced persistence in learning, more positive affect, stronger conceptual understanding, higher grades and higher levels of psychological well-being (Deci and Ryan, 2008). This makes it worth while to review and refresh your motivation from time to time, taking any actions to ensure that they are in tune with social work values and ethical approaches to your learning. We shall see in Chapter 5 that this is at the heart of critical reflective practice.

Motivation for entering social work within a values framework

Dillon (2007, 2011) identified the following themes in relation to motivations for entering social work while researching the influence of students' life experiences when enrolled on further education college 'Access to Social Work' courses. These were:

- Turning bad experiences into good
- Gradual recognition
- The philanthropic drive
- The education imperative.

Dillon has illustrated some experiences of students involved in her research in relation to these themes:

Case study 3.1

Esme
Esme had experienced severe depression in the past resulting in her being admitted to a psychiatric unit. This traumatic experience, subsequent voluntary work with young people with learning disabilities, and a growing religious faith, influenced her decision to become a social worker. (An example of *turning bad experiences into good*)

Precious
'I can't go anywhere [in my current job] ... There's no promotion but it's not really what I want with children. I want something I can work round my children and I've said to myself I've had enough now and I've spent eight years in Royal Mail and work in my church, I deal with the elders. And working with the elders in my church I see I can give more and I enjoy doing it.' (An example of *gradual recognition*)

Samuel
'When I was a young boy, I grew up to know my dad as a philanthropist within my local community back home in Africa. He kind of supported people around the community because he was a councillor and helped people, especially around big holidays like Christmas and New Year. He would buy gifts and give them to people who did not have enough and as I was growing up I began to copy him.' (An example of *the philanthropic drive*)

Sarah
'I was always educated ... like I was always in education. My parents always forced upon me to be educated; they've sent me to quite a good school as well, so I've never

like...it's just that I took a break from education to work because at the time I wanted to have some money, because also I was young, single and I just wanted to earn some-thing for myself before going back to college.' (An example of *the education imperative)* (Dillon, 2007).

Other research has identified similar factors that support autonomous motivation, particu-larly the influence of significant others (Rodriguez-Keyes et al., 2013). It may be useful for you to pause here and reflect on your own motivation for social work, which may be in tune with the above or illustrate something completely different.

Reflection point

Consider your own motivation for wanting to be a social worker.

- What were some of the key life course experiences that influenced your career deci-sions?
- How have these experiences formed your views of society and your future work with service users, carers, communities?
- What key messages do you take from these experiences in relation to key social work values and ethical stances?

If we also think about these questions in the context of life course theory, adulthood is associated with finding one's professional role or identifying the main source of income generation through employment. As we have begun to identify, negotiating this in times of change, shifting personal circumstance and economic hardship has a key influence on how we enter the social work profession and its meanings to both ourselves and others. Arnett (2000: 473) states that emerging adulthood is a distinct period of the life course characterized by change and exploration of possible life directions, which offers the most opportunity for identity explorations in the areas of love, work and worldviews. It is important for you as a social work student to understand these rela-tionships within the context of educational policy and social work reform and how you can capitalize on opportunities to work in a diverse community of learners. Career choices, according to Arnett's (2000) exploration of students' worldview, can be a time of both struggle and professional socialization. This supports the belief that values and ethics are important elements of teaching and learning during this potentially fruitful period. The merits of thinking through these issues in the context of the journey into and through social work education also helps us to acknowledge how we do not simply acquire 'appropriate' ethics and values from our training, but that we come with prior expectations that are influenced by a number of different factors: these include key life course experiences, the influences of religion, family members and previous work with particular client groups, to name just a few. Harnessing and reflecting these factors appropriately within the educational environment can reinforce the student's poten-tial commitment to core social work values such as social justice (Hafford-Letchfield, 2007; Dillon, 2011). As Dillon's (2011) earlier research examples suggested, social work students' life course experiences are a key influence on their motivations to under-take social work training, and can provide insights into socio-economic contexts of the issues frequently presented by service users. As social work students come from a range of different backgrounds, and have varied life course experiences, their trajecto-ries can be both non-linear and complex.

Widening participation, equality and social work education

Government policy in relation to widening participation in higher education (HE) has also responded to historical concerns about underrepresentation of students from less privileged social backgrounds, notably students from low-income families, particular minority ethnic groups, those with disabilities and women (Dearing Report, 1997; DfES, 2003). Despite encouragement of underrepresented groups into HE and particularly into social work education, those from less privileged social backgrounds and black and minority ethnic students are still underrepresented in the older, elite universities (HEFCE, 2009; Dillon, 2011). In the context of social work education, '24% of undergraduates enter undergraduate programmes via access to HE routes' (Social Work Reform Board, 2010: 52). However, they also tend to experience differential outcomes in access, progression and attaining their degree (HEFCE, 2006). While social work education is attracting increasing numbers of black and minority ethnic students (Hussein et al., 2009; Bernard et al., 2010), they disproportionately experience progression problems compared with their white counterparts, being more likely to defer, to have academic work referred (e.g. for not achieving a pass grade) and, together with disabled students, they also have higher withdrawal rates regardless of age and gender. Dillon's work (2011) highlights potential for growing educational inequalities in the face of insufficient recognition of life course experiences denoting suitability for social work, rising tuition fees and subsequent vocational stratification; diminished opportunities to enter the profession have the potential to mirror external environments regarding the experience of those on the receiving end of social work intervention. These are some issues you might also consider when working with different students during your training and education as a social worker and the contribution that you, from whatever background, make to a learning environment that is open to different ways of learning together, as well as about each other. Motivation to succeed and to go on and seek further educational experiences in adult life, particularly for mature-aged students, can be determined by a variety of external factors, including teachers, peer support, cultural values, financial and family pressures, among others (Calder, 1993; Hafford-Letchfield, 2007; Dillon, 2011). We all have an ethical responsibility within learning environments to recognize these findings and the complexities of developing diversity and equality within social work through training. We will now look at some ethical questions that illustrate challenges within the educational environment itself in relation to dilemmas or conflicts that students and their facilitators might face, including within the formal educational setting as well as practice education.

Dunk-West (2013) has written about the idea of the 'everyday' in social work and asserts that in our contemporary, everyday life, we are faced with a number of ethical-related dilemmas (p. 93). She also highlights the relationship between our personal and emerging professional self regarding ethics; how to make ethical decisions and what is required in order to justify such decisions. This also involves being aware of values as they relate to ourselves and how these are influenced through our own biography and broader socio-cultural context. We saw this reflected in the earlier statements about assessing your motivations for entering social work. Social work students frequently juggle a number of competing priorities during their studies, and more often than not demonstrate resilience and determination in the journey towards achieving a social work qualification.

An exploration of students' unique trajectories, insights gained from key life experiences, and intrinsic beliefs and developing value commitment within the learning environment, therefore, has potential to encourage greater inclusivity and group cohesion, more empathetic work with service users, carers and communities, as well as promoting

reflexivity. It may also set the foundations for more supportive learning cultures to facilitate students' progression and achievement.

Dealing with ethical conflicts in your learning journey: Albert's dilemma

Your tutor or practice educators have the additional role and responsibility as gatekeepers
to safeguard the profession by assessing your ongoing suitability for social work, especially in relation to regulation and approval of training by the statutory bodies (Bell and
Villadsen, 2011). The following case study is an example of an everyday issue that may arise
in social work education.

Case study 3.2

*Albert, aged 38, is on the MA Social Work having achieved a previous degree in Engineer-
ing in Ghana. Since living in the UK and being unable to get work as an engineer, he
gained valuable experience in a community project with older people living with complex
needs, which motivated him to explore an alternative career as a social worker. Albert is
eligible for a bursary for his final year and up until now has been working two evenings
a week and on Sundays to keep the family going and to contribute to their (very much
reduced) income. With two months to go in his first year, his 16-year-old son, who has
been experimenting with drugs, took an overdose. Albert has been trying to keep this confidential from his peers, tutor and practice educator, as his son has also recently come
out as gay; this has had repercussions in Albert's own family and community networks.
Albert also fears that some of his fellow students might be very judgemental, given some of
the homophobic comments he has heard on occasions in the classroom over the past year.
Also, he doesn't want to jeopardize his placement, which has, against all odds, gone really
well this year and he knows that some members of the team are really relying on him to
complete work with a family that is just coming to conclusion. In order to get some breath-
ing space, Albert decides to call his tutor and tell her that there has been a bereavement in
the family and he needs a two-week break from practice.*

Reflection point

Ethical dilemmas involve making 'a choice between two equally unwelcome alternatives'
(Banks and Williams, 2005: 1006). Before thinking about what frameworks can help social
workers and their peers to resolve ethical dilemmas, we invite you to first consider the conflicting sides of the debate leading to Albert's decision and to weigh these up.

In the case of Albert, you might consider the following statements apply (A):

- Albert's decision is understandable given his difficult circumstances and the discrimination and oppression he is facing and he made this decision in good faith.
- The real issue is that of homophobia in the classroom, which has not been tackled by
  the institution.
- If Albert's tutor and practice educator had established genuine rapport with him, then he
  need not have deceived them.
- No one has been explicitly or seriously harmed by Albert's decision.

Or, you might think (B):

- Albert needs to be more assertive and learn how to deal with difficult situations given that he is training to be a social worker.
- Albert is colluding with his homophobic peers and needs to take responsibility for challenging this.
- If Albert is not able to be honest and disclose difficulties now with those assessing him, how is he going to deal with increasingly complex and serious dilemmas in the future?
- Albert has clearly breached the social work code of ethics by telling lies and his actions will inevitably lead to harm of service users, which is more important than anything else.

If you were Albert's university tutor or practice educator, you would need to use both ethical theories and ideas about equality, diversity and human rights, as well as relationship-based practice in this situation to justify your chosen course of action.

In the preceding chapter, we saw that a *utilitarian approach* would focus us on the outcome of actions for the greatest good and move us towards balancing out the arguments so that the least harm is done. Similarly, a *Kantian approach* to this situation would highlight one's duty towards others, taking into account Albert's own need for support, the circumstances of his son (who is also a service user) and Albert's duty towards his own service users from his practice placement. Kantian ethics asserts the importance of trust in working out the long-term issues in order to resolve the situation and stresses the importance of taking a moral stance in doing so.

Virtue-based ethics would require the tutor or practice educator to confront the situation and exercise their authority as 'virtuous' educational professionals, which is likely to have a more adverse impact on Albert. The aim would be to help everyone involved through negotiation and reflexive thinking and to emphasize the complex interactions between Albert and others involved in his situation and context. They may also use their knowledge of social work theories to evaluate the situation and to contextualize and select different ways of working with Albert. For example, if they were to take a social justice approach, their initial understanding might emanate from the positions embedded within the first set of statements (A); this awareness might form the basis from which they can find a way forward to address those structural barriers and issues that are contributing towards Albert's unethical behaviour.

So we can see through closer consideration of Albert's dilemma that while education plays a critical role in shaping students' attitudes and behaviours towards diversity, ethics and values, *self-awareness* remains a powerful influence.

For example, there are numerous challenges for social work education that are central to the above situation, when explicitly considering and addressing anti-heterosexism in the academic or practice curriculum (Cocker and Hafford-Letchfield, 2010) as well as examining heteronormative models of care used to frame certain events such as puberty, cohabitation and parenthood (Jeyasingham, 2008). Similarly, learning strategies within social work education at pre- and post-qualifying levels should assist in developing a more critical awareness of frames of assessment and how these impact on the personal lives of students from diverse communities (Hafford-Letchfield et al., 2009). As a student, you are expected to interact with and challenge social work curricula, which if not critically interrogated, can reinforce frames of reference and knowledge that then become part of your professional repertoire. Some research has demonstrated that notions about citizenship, social inclusion and respect for diverse lifestyles and cultures are primary social and political discourses that are not always given priority within social work education

(Cocker and Hafford-Letchfield, 2014). Recent reviews of the roles and tasks of social work have cited the following as key areas of knowledge and skills within the profession: commitment to putting into practice equalities and diversity principles, recognizing and dismantling barriers, and challenging discrimination against people using services, carers, families and fellow workers (TCSW, 2011). These have to be achieved in a way that integrates individual, family and community dimensions in a creative balance. Being aware of what you bring into the learning arena is very important, as well as the way in which you present yourself. In the case of homophobia, Jeyasingham's (2008) critique provides us with an imperative to address ways of 'not knowing' or continuing 'ignorance' within social work education, which fundamentally ignore the operations and consequences of homophobia and which can spill out into students' personal lives, as illustrated in Albert's case.

Social work education: an ethical journey

Earlier we referred to the importance of individuals who deliver social work programmes harnessing students' differences as a resource for learning, as this has been shown to have a positive impact on progression rates and facilitating students being more positive about their learning experiences (Hafford-Letchfield, 2007, 2010b). This also aims to encourage you, the student or learner, to reflect around your own ethical journeys in line with core underpinning social work values. An important aspect of learning and teaching strategies is support given by educational staff (including the modelling of professional social work values), which helps students to articulate their individual or group experiences, and use of teaching methods that facilitate the sharing and interrogation of students' own oppression towards a better informed understanding of those they are frequently working with in practice. Giving and receiving constructive feedback within the opportunities presented by those facilitating learning is something you can directly contribute to help mediate and reinforce positive values.

In one study, Hafford-Letchfield (2007) documented expectations of students on a social work degree programme versus the reality of their actual experiences. She found that this was a frequent source of social work students' anxiety affecting their perceptions of themselves and their social work identities. This uncomfortable juxtaposition of their feelings of anticipation and excitement about achieving a place on a social work degree with the fear and anxiety experienced during the process highlighted questions about whether there are sufficient structures and support for students to express these in a safe and supported way. Fear and lack of self-confidence have a real impact on the quality of the student learning experience and can affect the learning process (Dillon, 2011). Leathwood and O'Connell (2003), writing from the perspective of learning theories, talk about pervasiveness of shame inherent in learning experiences, particularly for students from working-class backgrounds entering HE for the first time, where they experience the constant fear of 'never getting it right'. Acclimatizing to student life, having a new or different identity and being able to manage studies with other demands on their lives, such as child care and other caring roles outside the university, were cited by the working-class students. A resurgence of fear about academic competence and what it means to be a student working in a professional arena in particular can be a further challenge for students in general but particularly for 'non-traditional' and mature students. The culture of the learning environment, including supportive learning cultures, and reinforcement of different and flexible learning styles are therefore vitally important for their potential impact on social work students' identities, past and present, and their developing ethical stance once they are on a social work programme (see Linda Bell's discussion about identities in Chapter 4).

These issues share a commonality with the principles and values underpinning social work practice, including respect for the person, individual choice/responsibility and the right to receive help/support, and respect for diversity and difference (Banks, 2004; Dillon, 2007). Given the significance of the Human Rights Act 1998, our understanding that people ought to be treated with respect and dignity as a fellow individual is key and is one of the underpinning philosophies to user involvement in social work education. So often in social work, service users' issues are externalized and language that we use enables us to attribute their experiences as 'an other' when they are in reality much closer to our own experience, as seen earlier in the case study of Albert. The final part of this chapter briefly revisits some common themes in social work education that you may find familiar and draws out some issues when grappling with ethical, moral and value stances that characterize professional social work.

Themes in social work education to support the development of ethics and values

Mirroring values in learning methods

Promoting a safe, supportive environment where students can address their individual learning is crucial in social work education, although learning theories confirm that a process of traumatic learning is normal (Atherton, 1991). This is where the role of your tutor can provide conditions that at least hinder these anxieties. The challenge is also there however for you as a learner to be willing to venture out of your comfort zone and into a process of open critical enquiry. The discomfort that such thoughts engender in some students often prevents them from pursuing controversial topics and arguably perpetuates oppression or injustice through silence. Coulter et al. (2013) refer to a 'pedagogy of discomfort' model, where the design of the teaching inputs facilitates the psychological process of entering into emotionally laden material but which is supported through warm-up exercises, facilitation of personal reflections and applying the learning to practice through case studies. Engaging in group work can expose you to a variety of views and inputs and synergistically increase learning. Similarly, discussions between students and practitioners and/or service users and carers can expose you to the realities of ethical issues in practice, particularly where these come from diverse backgrounds, demographics and theoretical orientations (Kjellberg and French, 2011). Inter-group contact theory (Pettigrew, 1998) is a theoretical approach that suggests that increased contact with individuals in other groups, more personalized relationships with individuals in other groups, and a view of the 'out group' as being relatively equal in status to the 'in group' can lower the level of prejudice or bias towards members of minority groups. (Some of these themes will be picked up in the discussion on critical reflection by Pat Cartney in Chapter 5.)

Reflecting on your role as an active learner

This may be an opportune moment to make a few notes about your current learning styles and to reflect on what would be needed for you to 'engage' with any 'discomfort' felt necessary for deeper learning.

Discussion points

Here are some questions to get you going:

1 What are your responsibilities as a student when learning with service users/carers?
2 Who from your current programme of study or practice placement is part of your network? How active are you in seeking the views, experiences and knowledge of those who are not in your current learning circle – and what would be the most ethical and sensitive way of engaging with them to establish such a relationship?
3 How do you use your tutor or practice educator to reflect on or engage in reflective conversations about the terminology used in your study in relation to ethics and values? Are there areas or questions that you have not yet felt comfortable discussing? What can help to make this happen?

Sharing values with service users through a co-productive approach

Service user involvement is now firmly embedded in important aspects of social work education, given that the everyday experiences of service users are fundamental to equipping emerging social workers with key aspects of knowledge and expertise, particularly early on in their training (Coulter et al., 2013). There are many ways in which involvement can promote ethical practice in social work, including the contribution of service users' narratives to the curriculum, and their contribution on an equal footing to the co-productive design, delivery and assessment of learning and pedagogic approaches drawing on students' lived experiences.

An ethical approach to service user involvement in your learning should avoid a tokenistic approach and facilitate a transfer of power that explicitly acknowledges service users' own expertise. (Some of these issues will be discussed further in Trish Hafford-Letchfield's discussion of power and relational power in social work in Chapter 6.)

It is also important to consider the skills and support needed by both students and service users when learning together. For example, Wright et al. (2006) and Branfield et al. (2007) have developed the following pointers, suggesting that students need to:

- understand what participation means and why it is important;
- understand the potential impact of participation (on service users and the organization);
- have an opportunity to explore attitudes towards participation and working in partnership with service users;
- have knowledge and experience about different methods that can be used to involve user groups such as children, older people and members of marginalized communities;
- develop communication techniques that enable the involvement of all service users;
- be responsive and sensitive to service users' individual needs when they are involved in learning;
- have the opportunity to develop imaginative and creative techniques;
- have knowledge about how to work with service users safely and establish appropriate boundaries for their involvement.

In turn, service users need to:

- understand what participation means for them and why it is important;
- understand the potential impact and limits of participation;
- have an opportunity to explore attitudes to participation and working in partnership with workers;
- have knowledge about different methods that might be used;
- have an opportunity to explore how they would like to be able to participate and what they would like to see changed;
- experience team-building activities that enable the development of such skills as listening, being responsive to others, taking responsibility for specific roles, debating, communicating;
- have the opportunity to develop confidence and skills in expressing their own views as well as those of other service users.

Relationship-based teaching and learning

A key theme in this book is the notion of relationship-based practice. In relation to the second and third discussion points above, some more obvious things you may have thought of include engaging your tutor in discussing critical incidents during practice learning and the proactive use of learning contracts, planned reviews and making reference to clear policies and procedures to manage problems to ensure equity in the process. Some students, especially those previously educated in a different culture, find adjusting to a different type of relationship than was expected or previously experienced as difficult, for example where tutors are not just regarded as 'guide, philosopher and friend' (Elsey, 1990). In contrast, Channell (1990: 73) quotes the perspective of tutors who 'set boundaries on what you can and will do for them. Demands and expectations otherwise become limitless.' Several ethical issues can arise in relation to the power dynamics encompassed within your student–tutor relationship; in particular you look to your tutors not only for academic support but for empowering approaches that relate to 'professional' development. The importance of role modelling and the centrality of your relationship with your tutor is not only necessary to facilitate effective communication skills, emotional containment and development of your own self-awareness and confidence, but is also linked to learning about how to become a professional (Bell and Villadsen, 2011).

Woodward and Mackay (2012: 1099) demonstrated that although most students understand the dominant nature of societal values, they still observe discriminatory views on class, gender and race as not in keeping with social work's value base. They hoped that social work education would help them develop their political awareness and the confidence to challenge the *status quo*, but felt that some criteria for practice learning assessment only encouraged them to 'churn out' standards rather than develop as creative practitioners. Terminology remained unclear to some, which reflects the elusiveness of values (Banks, 2008: 28) and they wanted more opportunities to discuss and debate the knowledge, skill and value base with staff, service users, carers and each other. These examples only serve to highlight the extent to which wider economic, social policy and managerial constraints make it difficult for values to be applied in practice. These challenges highlight how important it is for learners to be active in the learning contract and co-creating opportunities for exploring values.

Finally, engaging in peer support, group work, formal or informal mentoring can provide complementary or alternative mechanisms for getting support and learning how to develop relationships. Development of peer support systems during social work training is valuable not only for academic issues but for sharing of biographies and raising conscious-ness within peer relationships to provide mutual support for issues such as child care and finance.

Some researchers argue that creativity contributes to academic achievement (Gould, 1996; Goldstein and Ford, 2001). Learning activities that emphasize finding out or inventing such as 'discovery learning' can be more effective than traditional methods (Cropley, 1992), with beneficial effects on learners' motivation. Conventional educational methods may not develop the skills, attitudes and motives necessary for coping with change and uncertainty, particularly in areas that confront negative aspects of cultural or family upbringing. In social work education, there has been increasing criticism that students can be limited to acquiring only the skills needed to produce orthodoxy and that associated attitudes, values, motives and self-image remain unchallenged. Transformational learning (Mezirow, 1991) emphasizes the importance of making a new or revised interpretation of experience, thus avoiding orthodoxy or taken-for-granted frames of reference.

Learning as a source of power

Students who are relatively new to social work have often described the quality of prac-tice learning experiences as crucial to being able to connect critical social work theory with everyday practice. Learners with substantial practice experience often highlight how beneficial it would be for the types of discussions that occur in their continuing profes-sional development to be mirrored in practice. This feedback resonates with critical social work scholars' assertion of a 'disconnect' between navigating ethical difficulties on the one hand, and institutionalized approaches to 'social work ethics' on the other (Dunk-West, 2013; Cocker and Hafford-Letchfield, 2014). The critical theorist Foucault (1983) used the metaphor of navigation to describe efforts to live an ethical or just life. In this conception of ethics, as learner social workers we would need to govern our lives at all times in relation to particular and contingent norms about what constitutes justice, acceptable behaviour, integrity, and so on. Dunk-West's work (2013) on understanding how we 'become' social workers notes that behaving and living ethically as a social work professional is always contingent on one's particular circumstances and therefore should not be approached exclusively through abstraction, from books alone or through expectations that our tutors and practice educators will tell us what to do. As we shall see in Chapter 6 on power, Fou-cault (1997: 229) suggested that how those in power or at the top of institutional hierarchies, such as government, universities or organizations in which we work, navigate their lives is the 'hinge point' between ethics and social justice.

We have seen in this chapter how social work education and commitment to lifelong learning have roles to play in shaping students' experiences of institutional oppression. From a critical perspective, we are also interested in how you as students need to interact with these systems to engage in deconstructing everyday experiences in order to learn about ethics and values for social work.

Chapter summary

If you are a social worker or a social work student, this chapter will have encouraged you to think about how ethics and values in social work are situated within your own journey to 'becoming' a practitioner; this is not independent from your own learning towards becom-ing a social worker and the identity(ies) you bring with you, as well as the identity(ies) you will develop throughout your training (see also Chapter 4). Learning theories underpinning social work education often have an emotional dimension and the value of reflection and reflexivity, as featured in the detailed case study of Albert (above), illustrates that it is not always the subject of learning that is a priority, but that the process of learning is an important professional self-development tool (this is further illustrated by Pat Cartney in Chapter 5). Learning about values and ethics in social work requires honesty and confidence in handling one's own experiences, being able to use them positively within the reach of one's professional intelligence. Having good support and structures and a safe learning environment can promote ethical learning, particularly around how to handle challenges to one's authority or judgement, and in relation to issues that touch on one's own professional or personal values. Making explicit links to professional codes of conduct or using service users' knowledge can offer richer learning around dilemmas professionals may subsequently face in practice. Involving service users in the design, management or evaluation of your own learning can add more dimensions and help you to identify the differences between theories and the realities of service users' lives. This chapter has attempted to open up a discussion about a relatively poorly documented area of social work ethics and values, that is, the experiences of you as a student or learner on social work programmes in the context of diversity and widening participation and some of the issues encountered throughout your learning journey. Both are underpinned by government policy and principles of equality. It has been important to acknowledge not only how access and recruitment to social work tries to respond to these external drivers but also to suggest exploring your own ethical journeys as a 'learner'. We have tried to demonstrate how the learning of appropriate ethical, moral and value stances are inevitably linked to the socio-economic contexts and key life course experiences of an individual and group before and during training and how these insights can inform their professional practice. This necessitates an active exchange between yourself as a learner and those supporting your education, training and development and which also emulates the social work practice environment.

Key points for social work practice

Practical, financial and emotional challenges facing social work students from diverse backgrounds should not contrast with but complement the philosophy and value base of social work and social care where all domains form a holistic understanding of a person's experience. We leave you with the following key points for your own lifelong learning:

- An exploration of students' unique trajectories, insights gained from key life experiences and intrinsic beliefs and developing value commitment within the learning environment has potential to encourage greater inclusivity and group cohesion, more empathetic work with service users, carers and communities and promotes reflexivity.
- Learning about ethics and values is an iterative process that involves the creation of opportunities for personal and wider reflective practice and reflexivity and active engagement.
- Theories about life course theory and lifelong learning are important precursors for understanding your commitment to developing your knowledge, skills and ethical behaviour essential to quality services.

4 Ethics, values and social work identity(ies)

Linda Bell

Introduction

This chapter explores the relevance of ethics and values to the construction of 'professional' identity(ies) in social work. It examines recent literature relating to 'professional' identity(ies), including how these may be constructed and maintained, drawing on broader approaches to identity and professionalism (Dent and Whitehead, 2002; Jenkins, 2004). This chapter first takes the position that professional identity(ies) are (re)constructed in practice rather than being completely fixed and unchanging. Through this approach we acknowledge, following Jenkins' suggestion, that identity(ies) in general are necessarily 'interactional accomplishments' that can 'only be understood as process, as "being" or "becoming"…never a final or settled matter' (Jenkins, 2004: 6). The first section of the chapter will explore how professional identity(ies) in social work relate to individual practitioners as well as to collectivities; we also consider whether there can be a single social work identity, or whether there are several. We connect these processes to issues of ethics and values, ending the chapter with a discussion of social work identity(ies), ethics and values in international contexts.

For some, the *individual practitioner* is where any links between *identity* and *values* should begin: this focus on the attributes of the individual practitioner and their fitness to claim a professional or occupational identity connects mainly to a perspective that philosophers would call 'virtue ethics', as we will discuss in the following section (Clark, 2006; Gray, 2010). An alternative but similar approach relates to an 'ethics of care', a model that emphasizes responsibility and caring relationships rather than more abstract ideas about rights, justice, virtues or outcomes. As we saw in Chapter 2, however, there are various approaches to applied ethics that can be relevant to social work, including the two dominant theories in the Western philosophical tradition (namely, Consequentialism and Deontology) as well as the more recent developments of Principlism, 'virtue ethics' and 'ethics of care'.

As well as the individualized focus of 'identity', we need to consider its more collective aspects, emerging within interactions and relationships, in collectivities, groups or organizations constituted of individuals (Frost, 2008). It is important, in other words, not to focus only on 'identity' as an individualized attribute, but also as a collective concept. As the sociologist Jenkins points out, 'identity' is 'one of those rare concepts that make as much sense individually as collectively' (Jenkins, 2004: 24).

Even if we start with the individual practitioner and consider their behaviour and beliefs in terms of *values*, we will not get very far if we do not also consider the influence of the settings in which social workers actually work or learn. As we saw in Chapter 3, it is first of all within social work educational settings that what we might now specify as a professional identity comes into play. To recap, it was suggested in that chapter that when you are learning to 'become' a social worker, key issues that will affect the construction of your professional identity(ies), especially in relation to values and ethics, include:

- The 'culture' of the learning environment (how you are 'learning to learn').
- Your relationships with your tutor or practice educator, especially as role models.
- How your tutor or practice educator act as 'gatekeepers' to continually assess your suitability for social work. (This is important in relation to the regulation and approval of training by the statutory bodies, but also includes suitability in terms of professional codes of ethics.)

Even before starting your social work education there will have been other aspects of your own sense of 'identity' that connect with the motivations that may have encouraged you to seek a social work training in the first place. Some people work for many years in 'care' settings before training professionally, while others seek to train more quickly soon after leaving school, college or university; whichever of these situations applies to you, some reasons will have emerged to motivate you towards taking up a career in social work and these will almost certainly be related to your own sense of 'yourself', your identity(ies).

Discussion points

1 Before you began your professional training, were there important aspects of your own sense of 'identity' that you thought you could bring with you to your professional work?
2 What were these aspects?
3 Were they related to what you would consider to be your 'values'? If so, how?

The educational setting where you are learning to become a social worker has an important place in the development of each worker's own sense of professional identity and therefore, some would argue, their 'moral' development as a social worker (Clark, 2006). Placement (work) settings are an integral part of social work education; it is here that everyday relationships and day-to-day practice will also begin to contribute to these processes of identity construction. For some people, this suggests developing a social work 'identity' that reflects mastery and control over their own 'ego'. In this model, theoretical knowledge, for example, is supposed to relate to the social worker's acquisition of relevant skills and these can help to manage their anxiety when dealing with 'others'. This ' identity work' should in practice exemplify social work values such as being ' non-judgemental' or displaying 'empathy' (Memmot and Brennan, 1998; Gerdes and Segal, 2011). Miehls and Moffatt (2000) offer an alternative approach that involves working reflexively on the 'self' in relation to others. They suggest that instead of trying to manage the 'ego' by acquiring knowledge and skills in this way, social workers should allow the 'reconstitution' of their identity to happen 'in the presence of the other', since this will promote healthy change:

> The social worker identity is based on a relationship of reflexivity through which the construction of identity is made present through working on the self. Self-care is not an isolated, individual or narcissistic process but one in which the social worker must be open to the influence of the other in the creation of enhanced practice. (Miehls and Moffatt, 2000: 346)

To recap, we can see from this approach the importance of relationships to social worker identity(ies), and how this could link their *values* to ethical models relating, for example, to 'virtue' or to 'caring'. However, as Dracopoulou has already suggested in Chapter 2, there are many other aspects of ethics relevant to social work and these can also relate to identity construction.

In now briefly introducing the idea of ethical codes of practice, we should note Whittington and Whittington's later discussion about professional values and professional ethics in Chapter 7. They suggest that professional *ethics* in social work are typically expressed in professional and regulatory codes and provide both a guide to expected conduct and standards of accountability. Professional ethics are the active form of professional values. These professional and regulatory codes will surely have an impact on social workers from the beginning of their formal social work education, and will often have helped to shape that education. How much these codes and regulations will impact on direct aspects of social work practice, as social workers are learning from experience and constructing their own professional 'identity(ies)' in the process is, however, an open question. Papadaki and Papadaki (2008), for example, in a study of Cretan (Greek) social workers, report that their respondents did not generally use the formal Greek professional ethical code to guide their practice and none reported consulting the Code of the International Federation of Social Workers (IFSW, 2000).

As we have already implied, on the level of direct contact between people, relationships that individual social workers engage in involve recognizing, respecting and valuing the identities of others. As we will see later, it is also within the practice of these relationships that individuals will identify *boundaries* and *boundary processes* between themselves and others (Barth, 2000; Jenkins, 2004). Following Barth (2000) and Wallman (1986), Jenkins suggests that:

> Boundaries are to be found in interaction between people who identify themselves collectively in different ways, which can in principle occur anywhere or in any context…Identity is about boundary *processes*…rather than boundaries: it is a matter of identification. (Jenkins, 2004: 102–3)

Jenkins refers to these boundary processes as 'temporary checkpoints rather than concrete walls' (p. 103). In other words, they are points at which where there is the opportunity for an individual to construct identity(ies) in different ways on different occasions. Possibilities for 'professional' identity construction may therefore be strongest exactly where social workers' *values* towards service users, other social workers, managers, other 'professionals', and so on emerge and are acknowledged during social work practice. We have already noted that the emergent or constructed professional 'identity(ies)' that you recognize as part of becoming and being a social worker can therefore be not only individualized but also collective. Jenkins has suggested that in broad terms, 'Collectivities and collective identifications are to be found, in the first instance, in the practices of the embodied individuals that generate or constitute them' (Jenkins, 2004: 133).

Collective identifications can also be drawn out from, for example, practices within educational settings where social workers are trained, as we saw in Chapter 3, or in relation to codes of ethics or expectations within organizations employing social workers, whether formal or informal (e.g. expectations related to 'continuous improvement' cited by managers involved with training of staff in local authorities, as discussed by Bell, 2007).

These collective identifications also emerge across broader, international arenas related to social work that occur in different social and cultural contexts (see, for example, Hugman, 2005b, 2009; Frost, 2008; Chu et al., 2009): Frost (2008), for example, draws our attention to the 'top-down' differences in policy and history occurring as differing national expressions of 'social work' occupation(s) within Europe, compared with the 'bottom-up', enacted practices of 'social workers' in those varied settings; all these social workers are simultaneously sharing and developing certain 'social work' values and collective identities.

Yet most people would acknowledge that the concept of 'identity' still encapsulates ideas about who we are individually, as people, and that this may thus go much deeper than everyday adherence to a specific occupation. For example, in a recent Canadian study of social workers who were highly rated on 'subjective well-being', Graham and Shier (2010) describe how some of their respondents made a deep connection between their identity as a 'professional' social worker and their personal selves. The significance of reflexivity in constructing identity(ies) should also not be overlooked (see Miehls and Moffatt, 2000). Let us now look more closely at this key concept of *professional*.

Professional identity(ies), organizations and social worker characteristics

Dent and Whitehead (2002) are among those who have indicated that notions of the 'professional' have shifted in recent years. They suggest that we should question the whole idea of 'professionalism' in terms of it representing ideas about an occupational identity based on 'fixed' expertise and status:

> One of the anchors of order has been 'the professional': someone trusted and respected, an individual given class status, autonomy, social elevation, in return for safeguarding our well-being and applying their professional judgement on the basis of a benign moral or cultural code. That professional no longer exists. They have gone, swept aside by the relentless, cold, instrumental logic of the global market, and with it the old order has been upturned. (Dent and Whitehead, 2002: 1)

Looking more closely at this quotation, perhaps this situation only reflects a demonstrable loss of, or challenge to, professional power of occupational elites? Taking doctors as an example, Dent and Whitehead seek to demonstrate how 'elite' professionals face these challenges, whether through 'marketization' or the rise of patient or service user advocacy/ involvement in services. A question arises here:

Discussion point

Does this kind of situation also apply to social workers? Do you think social workers could in any sense be regarded as a powerful elite?

Dent and Whitehead go on to state that in organizational terms there has recently been a 'blurring of boundaries' between 'professionalism' and 'managerialism', suggesting that now there is often little distinction between 'professionals' having specific expertise and the cadre of managers or bureaucrats. What implication does this have for professionals' *values*?

Taking this point further, for many years theorists (including Weber) have discussed the potential for *conflict* between *loyalty to an employing organization* (especially if it is a bureaucracy) and *loyalty to a profession*; this conflict might be even more likely where practitioners are perceived to be elite or 'autonomous' (such as doctors or lawyers). Although this professional–bureaucratic conflict model is somewhat out of vogue now, Wallace (1995), for example, has re-examined it using lawyers as her example. She suggests an 'adaptation' theory, in contrast to Dent and Whitehead, arguing that in recent years, 'professionals have *adapted* to their new and changing employment situations and have maintained control and autonomy over their professional work' (Wallace, 1995: 230; my emphasis). Wallace strongly emphasizes that the settings where 'professionals' work, and the nature of their employers, will potentially influence the construction of their identities in those settings. This is so even if we reject relatively simplistic theories like the professional–bureaucratic conflict model. I would add that professional identities of related occupational groups within the work setting are also potentially influential. We might therefore ask at this point:

Discussion point

Do you as a social worker experience conflicts between your values and the occupational identity(ies) in the organizational setting in which you operate? What effects might this have on your sense of professional identity(ies)?

Some research, including an American study by Carpenter and Platt (1997), has suggested that this does happen and that social workers can experience strain between personal and professional values, depending on their work setting. Papadaki and Papadaki (2008) also suggest that there could be fundamental conflicts between what their Cretan social workers saw as their 'moral duty' to help clients and the work setting, with its lack of resources. They comment: 'Having the responsibility to help people in need without having sufficient resources in order to respond to the increasing demand for services made social workers feel powerless' (Papadaki and Papadaki, 2008: 176).

In a British context, Preston-Shoot (2010) argues for greater emphasis on promoting social work values via a focus on law and the relevance of professional codes of conduct as a basis for social work(ing) as carried out in pursuit of 'social justice'. ('Social justice' being a key value said to be espoused by most social workers internationally.) This raises further questions about the perceived power, status and autonomy of social workers as 'professionals' and the kinds of identities they may develop. This will be addressed further in Chapter 6.

Discussion point

Should we think of social workers as having and needing to maintain a collective identity as a single profession?

We might imagine that social work is a 'single' occupation (and it has recently acquired a 'protected title' in the UK); but even a cursory glance at the history of social work in the UK since the nineteenth century reveals that, according to some commentators, there have been many, related occupations coming under the umbrella of 'social work' (Burt, 2008). This might suggest the development of 'multiple identities' within the occupation(s) of social work, as well as complex linkages between individual practitioners, the organizations in which these 'social workers' are employed and the 'other' professionals with whom they come into contact. As reported by Whittington and Bell (2001), when 481 individuals who had recently qualified as 'social workers' (including probation officers) named 'other professionals' with whom they had the most contact, 35 per cent of respondents cited other 'social workers' (including, for example, residential social workers and care managers). This was the fourth most frequently cited occupational category by these respondents after police officers, solicitors and health visitors. Processes of identification can also involve 'merging' of individual occupational identities and managerialist agendas within organizations; for example, identification with a profession or with the employing organization itself may shift if an individual acquires a management position in the organizational hierarchy (see Ford and Harding, 2004).

Against this view, however, there are some very strong narratives arguing the case for a core, stable professional identity already being attached to social work, albeit one that may be perceived to have 'lost its way' (Dominelli, 2004; Stevenson, 2005). These debates have been taking place within the increasingly important contexts of 'inter-professional' practice and learning (see, for example, Whittington and Bell, 2001). A recent study (Bell and Allain, 2011), based on earlier work by Hean et al. (2006), challenged student child and family social workers with 'stereotypes' relating to their own occupation and to other occupations/professions. Bell and Allain found that their social work students held both positive and negative assumptions about specific occupations/professions (such as medicine), including their own. These assumptions acted as a tool for reflecting their views of social work identity(ies). These authors argue that this exercise identifying stereotypical assumptions about 'others' could encourage construction of a positive sense of social work identity, and that this should be dynamic and responsive to changing contexts.

Baxter and Brumfitt (2008) have further suggested that health or social care practitioners will 'have adopted the values, norms and stereotypes held by members of their particular profession as part of a process of professional socialization' (p. 4). For student professionals, this may extend in certain circumstances to building their own sense of identity, partly by making comparisons between their own characteristics and those of other professions (Hean et al., 2006). Adams et al. (2006) have suggested that even at the start of professional education, different professional groups may demonstrate different degrees of professional identification. In a study of 1254 students, these authors identified that physiotherapy students displayed the 'highest level' (strongest) professional identity, and social work students the lowest level, compared with other groups in their study. There was a sampling bias towards nursing students who made up 48 per cent of the sample, compared with social workers, who accounted for 5 per cent. Results were based on self-report measures. In relation to social work values, Jensen and Aamodt (2002) have suggested, in a Norwegian context, that 'moral motivations' for entering social work may have shifted over time, with greater emphasis now being placed on 'finding oneself', rather than on earlier ideas about changing society (see also Miehls and Moffatt, 2000; and the 'final reflections' in Chapter 3 by Hafford-Letchfield and Dillon).

In terms of a knowledge base, do social workers still need to maintain certain kinds of expertise, in order to construct a sense of 'social work' identity? How would this expertise dovetail with the expertise or characteristics of other professionals working in the same organizations (see Hean et al., 2006; Baxter and Brumfitt, 2008; Bell and Allain, 2011)? It may also be suggested (e.g. by Bisman, 2004) that a focus on values may have been 'hidden' by an alternative focus on the development of the professional 'knowledge' base.

There have also been attempts recently (for example, via specific projects within some London boroughs) to 'reclaim social work' as 'the profession' its exponents believe it to be, and to strip away what are perceived as 'non-professional' tasks carried out by social workers within the employing organization (Ferguson, 2008). This seems to be an attempt to remove some of the 'newer' managerialist aspects of social work identity with a return to an 'older' notion of identity(ies) based on occupational/practitioner expertise (Clarke and Newman, 1997; see also Bell, 2007: 289–90). This brings us back again to Dent and Whitehead's point about the potential 'loss' of professional expertise: but here is an attempt, in other words, to reclaim social work as a fully fledged profession.

In a recent study of social work student support in the UK (Bell and Villadsen, 2011), social work tutors were interviewed about the support given to students working on placements in organizations, some of whom were local authority employees and some of whom were 'college based':

> This social work tutor suggested that tensions between the identities of 'student' and 'worker' would cause issues for those who already saw themselves as 'professionals' through working in an organisation, as well as those college-based students who had yet to acquire this persona:

> *'I think it is quite important as well to talk about organizational issues if that's what they want [in student groups], because it, again, I suppose it's like I was thinking in the beginning, the university academic bit meeting the practical bit and that is about the students' coping with two separate identities, I suppose, their working identity and their student academic identity . . . some of the students are already employed by Local Authorities and they have that, they see themselves perhaps as more, as being that professional person and going to work and the course is part of that, so then I'm aware that some students are college-based and maybe don't feel necessarily that professional identity as marked as others, so there is a balance to be had.'*

Davies (1996) adds another strand to these arguments by considering the relevance of social worker characteristics, and specifically *gender,* to professional identity(ies). We know that social work is an example of an occupation that has been heavily (and is increasingly) dominated by women: 84 per cent of social work students on the UK BA social work degree since 2003 have been women (according to Hussein et al., 2009). Davies (1996) points out that if, for example, we consider the professional–bureaucratic conflict model in relation to gender, it is the similarities rather than the differences between 'profession' and 'bureaucracy' that become obvious. Davies' arguments suggest that bureaucracies 'create a stable and predictable order in which the interests of men as hostile strangers are tightly controlled' (Davies, 1996: 667). In these circumstances, there would be no place for emotions and the hierarchy ensures loyalty is due to the offices people occupy, rather than to individuals. Davies further suggests that women are not so much *excluded* as professionals in these types of work settings, but *included* in ill-defined support roles; established professions may therefore be seen as *gendered* and represent, to a large extent, masculinity. She suggests that this could have had positive results since managerialism has 'coincided with feminisation, in the sense of growing numbers of women in professions and in management, a wider acceptance of feminist ideas' (p. 673).

Morley (2003) has noted similar *gendered* processes at work in higher education, although her assessment of resulting power structures appears less positive than that of Davies (see also Kemp and Brandwein, 2010). Berg et al. (2008) have also noted that some (mainly female) social work managers in England and Sweden appeared to feel comfortable dealing with management tasks such as budgets, contrary to other research. These managers enjoyed the autonomy this gave them in their relationship with their subordinates, whom they respected as colleagues. These social work managers also regarded the knowledge gained from their position as managers as transferable to other areas of public and private sectors, thereby opening up new career opportunities.

Perry and Cree (2003) have suggested that in the UK in the recent past there has been a good deal of interconnectedness in social workers' backgrounds between gender, ethnicity and class structures. They suggest that social workers have therefore tended to be 'white, middle-class women' and it appears that in the UK at least, (female) gender remains the predominant defining characteristic of social workers, even if the ethnic and class backgrounds of social workers may be changing (Panaser, 2003; Graham, 2007a). According to Gibelman (2000: 462), using 1998 statistics, women also make up the majority of social workers in the United States, most of whom are also ethnically white. Pease (2011) also recently discussed whether a greater presence by men in social work would challenge discriminatory processes and occupational segregation. He suggests that it is unlikely this would necessarily support alternative masculinities that will challenge gender inequalities, unless a pro-feminist commitment is evident (for examples of practice related to issues of *gender*, see Chapter 8). These characteristics clearly have implications for the kinds of identities social workers construct, as well as the values they espouse when working with their clients and their colleagues (Graham, 2007a), to which we now return.

How does the construction of social work identity(ies) relate to 'ethics' and 'values' in international contexts?

We now revisit the potential relevance of social work identity construction to values and ethics, while also considering international perspectives on social work more specifically (Frost, 2008). In a recent critical commentary, Banks (2008) refers to 'social work ethics' as a specialist area of professional ethics that is aspired to, as well as enacted, by social workers (Banks, 2008: 1238). (We should also reiterate here the distinction made between ethics and values by Whittington and Whittington in Chapter 7.)

As Banks (2008) points out, there has also been a significant increase (internationally) in the amount of literature relating to social work ethics, including revisions, or re-draftings, of codes of professional conduct, particularly in places where 'social work' is a relatively new occupation. Nevertheless, ethical codes seem to have had little impact on social work practice in some cases (see, for example, Knezevic, 1999; Papadaki and Papadaki, 2008).

Professional codes may be linked explicitly, if only in theory, to notions of 'professionalism'. Professionalism 'entails holding on to the extant values of the profession as outlined in a professional code and accepted by the current community of practitioners. Ideal professional integrity involves holding on to a more timeless service ideal of what the profession should be at its best' (Banks and Gallagher, 2009: 207). In making a case for the importance of 'virtue ethics' in this context, Banks (2008) has argued for closer links between social work ethics and politics, suggesting that ethics is not only about decision-making in 'difficult cases' but is also reflected in social workers' motives, professional wisdom, qualities of character and moral perceptions (Banks and Gallagher, 2009). As we saw in Chapter 2, there are different perspectives on the relevance of different kinds of theories about values and ethics to social work that influence how we might think about the construction of social work identities.

Wilks (2005), for example, asserts the apparent centrality of 'values' for all social workers, but recognizes that these values can be grounded in very different theoretical and ideological perspectives. Clark (2006), however, suggests that there is no room for public service professionals to be 'value-neutral', and that the requirements of the social work role include demonstrating a 'virtuous character'.

When considering *social work values* and *ethics* as potentially unifying factors, from international perspectives, the meaning of these terms may in fact appear highly contested. Frost (2008) has drawn attention to what she perceives as the potential for a 'European' social work identity based partly on shared ideologies or theories (especially those derived from Freud and Marx) as well as focusing on shared values or principles. As already noted, however, Frost (2008: 348) also suggests that while 'top down' differences in policy and history result in different (national) forms of social work occupation(s), it is the shared values, ideologies or principles emerging from social work in practice that produce a shared sense of how 'social work' is defined.

Both Hugman (2009) and Chu et al. (2009) draw our attention to the need to look further afield when considering the nature of social work and the kinds of identity(ies) emerging among social workers internationally. In addition to debating social work's uncertainties, these authors suggest that social workers should take account of 'global' influences from the global 'South' or 'East' as well as the Northern, European heritage as discussed by Frost (2008).

Many other commentators already make the case for social work and social work 'values' to be considered in both international and situated, 'local' contexts:

> social work is both an international social movement, concerned to promote social justice across the world, and a situated practice that takes place in a context of national laws, policies and cultures... (Banks, 2008: 1243)

> Social work is a contextual profession... an activity which varies considerably given the cultural context within which it operates... (Taylor, 1999: 310)

From a globalized perspective, the significance of values and ethics can be highlighted as a way of linking together professional social work identifications occurring within welfare regimes internationally (Hatton, 2001; Papadaki and Papadaki, 2008; Chu et al., 2009; Hugman, 2009). A paper by Hatton (2001) sheds light, for example, on values espoused by Danish social workers, this time comparing their value system directly with that of their colleagues in the UK. Hatton suggests that Danish social policy has emphasized social solidarity and equality, and that these values have on the other hand tended to obscure a recognition of differences between service users. (It may be that a description of very recent attempts to include service users in social care decision-making in Denmark [Hòjlund, 2009] is an attempt to redress this balance.) Hatton (2001) describes UK social workers' value base as being focused, in contrast to that of their Danish colleagues, much more on the recognition of 'differences' and that UK social workers would therefore be expected to challenge discriminatory practice(s). By suggesting the 'translation' of these two sets of social work values from different contexts, Hatton draws attention to the significance of values and ethics as a way of linking together professional social work identifications occurring within welfare regimes internationally (even where value systems themselves appear to differ).

Knezevic's (1999) Croatian study draws comparisons between 'values' attributed to people who are motivated to become social workers and those who take up other career paths; the study draws methodologically on the long-term research of D.E. Super about the importance of work (see also Super and Šverko, 1995). Knezevic also sets reports of individualized student motivations within changing political and economic contexts (in Croatia), important since social work as a 'profession' is relatively new in Croatia. Knezevic suggests why social work education, and the profession more broadly, has developed in the way(s) they have in Croatia is linked to the 'crucial [political] differences' between this country and others in the (Eastern) socialist bloc. Western expertise and influences from European and American social work education models have, according to Knezevic, come 'quickly to Croatia and... had a tremendous impact' (p. 420), not least on the individuals who have been motivated to choose social work as their occupation. Furthermore, the 1990s war in the former Yugoslavia has meant that social work is seen as a very significant occupation, since 'Croatian social workers have taken over a huge burden of refugees and the displaced' (Knezevic, 1999: 420). This has reportedly increased the reputation of social work in the region. Knezevic's study identifies some key work values espoused by those entering social work compared with other students, in particular 'altruism', which was much more highly rated by social work students in a hierarchy of 19 key work values. While 'personal development' was rated most highly by all students, altruism was rated third by social work students and fourteenth by other students.

Hòjlund's (2009) study of Danish welfare related to older people's services takes us into very different social work contexts. He suggests that Danish welfare has changed in the past decade, during which policy changes have meant recipients of welfare have become more active consumers. In describing the processual detail of older people's welfare services, using a systems-based approach, Hòjlund describes how assessment of needs is highly standardized and based on checklists and schemes of observation. (This suggests potential for the use of 'consequentialist' ethical reasoning, for example.) The specially trained expert (a 'social worker') is supposed to demonstrate professionalism when using these assessment tools: 'In a more symbolic way, the technology empowers the assessment expert: one could say the formal declarations and checklists underpin his or her status as objective and professional' (Hòjlund, 2009: 424). In considering the values of these professional 'social work' experts, Hòjlund describes how:

> The expert must be dedicated to the aim of determining the particular needs of the person visited. The expert is expected to present himself or herself not only as an expert acting on behalf of a formal service system, but also as a person dealing with private matters. There is a certain intimacy in dealing with persons in need, and this intimacy must be reflected in the professional identity of the expert. (Hòjlund, 2009: 424)

Chapter summary

In this chapter, we have explored the relevance of ethics and values to the construction of 'professional' identity(ies) in social work. By examining recent literature relating to 'professional' identity(ies), organizational issues and professional practice in various settings, including internationally, we have highlighted the complexities involved in the construction of social worker identity(ies) and the fragile and contested nature of these forms of professional identification. This raises many questions for social work practitioners and students as well as for those from other professions:

Key points for social work practice

I leave you with some further questions that will help you focus your own reflections on social work identity(ies):

- Is 'social work' (or other professional role) an important part of your own identity(ies)? What part do you think ethics and values play in the construction of your identity(ies)?
- Do you see your social work/professional identity as mainly fixed/fundamental or fluid and (re)constructed through daily practice?
- Can you identify any areas of your own work setting(s) that may have influenced your sense of identity as a professional?

5 Links between reflective practice, ethics and values

Pat Cartney

Introduction

The starting point for this chapter is to build further on some of the key themes relating to values and ethics identified in earlier chapters and in doing so to 'problematize' the nature of professional knowledge and 'know how' in social work. The complex, multi-layered knowledge held by practitioners is presented and explored and practice knowledge is conceptualized as incorporating elements of both formal and informal knowledge. The chapter also makes links to the literature on reflective practice and the relationship between 'internalist' ways of knowing and more 'externalist' ways of justifying our actions, for example by drawing upon evidence-based research. The nature of this tension currently in social work is explored and the chapter goes on to suggest that a more holistic, nuanced understanding of the nature of practice knowledge is required. Such understandings are of particular relevance in the field of applied ethics and values as professional judgements in this arena are often particularly complex.

A case study exploring a particular practice issue is presented to encourage you as learners in social work to make a contextualized exploration of how reflective practice can facilitate consideration of ethical action. Locating this debate in a specific practice context allows for a detailed exploration of the subtleties and complexities of some of the problems social workers grapple with and their multifaceted nature to emerge. Discussion focuses on utilizing contextualized approaches to moral reasoning and ethical practice where reflection on the agency context and broader social and structural issues is encouraged – alongside the development of critical thinking and self-awareness. As noted in Chapter 4, these issues are increasingly being argued as important in the move away from abstract ethical theories and principles towards a more contextualized and specific approach to moral reasoning within social work. Reflective practice is utilized as a vehicle for exploring these issues.

Setting the context for exploration

As shown in Chapter 2, debates about how we come to know what we know have been the cornerstone of a great deal of philosophical discussion over many years. Our task here is not to engage in complex philosophical analysis but to consider this question in relation to its importance for social work practice and in particular to the application of ethics and values in day-to-day professional work. The questions we are particularly interested in exploring are:

- How do you know what you know?
- How do you apply your knowledge in practice?
- How does social work as a profession engage with different ways of knowing?
- Why are these debates of particular relevance in relation to ethics and values?

These questions form the backdrop to the issues discussed in this chapter.

Reflecting on practice

Throughout this book the relationship between ethical practice and social work values is highlighted and discussed. As we have already seen, Part 1 of the book focuses on key contextual issues, such as the nature of applied ethics in relation to social work (Chapter 2), motivations to enter social work (Chapter 3) and the construction of social worker identities (Chapter 4), and their relationship to the continuum of social work practice. In this chapter, we will focus on how seeking to adopt a reflective stance in relation to practice can open up opportunities to engage with the complexities and dilemmas that may be presented when seeking to act in an ethical and value-based way in social work. We will look at how some of the tools of reflective practice can aid such engagement.

The contribution of reflective practice

A huge body of literature exists in relation to what reflective practice is and how it can be developed. Knott and Scragg (2010) note that most public service professions are committed to promoting reflective practice. The Social Work Reform Board (SWRB) incorporates 'reflective practice in action' (Knott and Scragg, 2010: 13) as an underpinning component of the newly developed professional capabilities for social workers. Elsewhere in their report, the SWRB state that, 'Reflective practice is key to effective social work' (p. 27).

The term 'reflective practice', however, has been the subject of some criticism and debate in recent years. Ixer raised questions about whether there was any agreed definition about what the term actually means, suggesting that 'reflective learning has come to enjoy something of a cult following amongst curriculum planners and those responsible for professional education' (Ixer, 1999: 513). He questioned whether social work programmes should be attempting to assess such an ill-defined term. The key thrust of Ixer's argument, however, appeared not to be against reflective practice *per se* but about how it is defined and assessed.

Rushton and Suter argue that a proliferation of books, journals, training packages, etc. in recent years 'work, re-work and re-work again reflective practice in the apparent pursuit of a holy grail of reflective practice' (Rushton and Suter, 2012: 2). The authors criticize the 'over-theorization' of reflective practice, which has led to a proliferation of multiple models and frameworks that result in confusing and demotivating practitioners. Rushton and Suter (2012) are, however, strong supporters of the need for practitioners to develop reflective thinking – their criticisms relate more to the tools that are purported to aid such reflection.

The argument being expounded here is that it is wise not to become too wedded to any term, as this can promote the 'cult following' approach Ixer (1999) warns us against. It can also lead to the creation of a proliferation of models that may end up bemusing rather than enlightening those who attempt to use them in practice. In the complex arena of professional practice, criticality needs to be maintained – even of the terms that set out to encourage critical awareness.

The suggestion here, however, is that the term 'reflective practice' should not be abandoned in social work, as that would be akin to throwing the proverbial baby out with the bath water. The complexity of daily social work and the importance traditionally afforded to process as well as outcome in practice means that social work is a natural companion of reflective practice. How social work is practised – in an ethical, enabling manner in line with our value base – has always been part of our professional identity alongside our focus on outcomes. Recent work in relation to developing relationship-based practice has also revived and added new life and meaning to how social workers can use reflective practice to develop a deeper appreciation of the multi-layered nature of practice. Wilson and colleagues argue that reflective practice is 'an integral part of relationship based practice' (2011: 12). They see the two processes as being inextricably linked, as both:

- Promote thoughtful, risk – tolerant practice where workers are able to tolerate the complex emotional dimensions of practice
- Recognise the uniqueness and complexity of the service user
- Utilise the role of 'the self' as a social work resource. (Wilson et al., 2011: 18)

So what is reflective practice?

Given the argument explored so far, you will probably not be too surprised to learn that a universally agreed definition of what reflective practice consists of is rather hard to produce! At this point, it is helpful to try to identify some key underpinnings of reflective practice.

Discussion point

We start by asking you to consider what you understand by the term 'reflective practice'?

Clearly, there are many different ways you could respond to such a question. For many people, however, understandings around reflective practice draw upon ideas about:

- thinking things through in depth rather than accepting situations at face value;
- considering a range of alternative possible explanations for an event;
- being able to stand back and think about what is happening almost as it happens;
- avoiding blanket solutions to problems or standard responses to people and situations that are in essence unique and complex;
- being aware of emotional as well as cognitive impacts of your work on – and from – yourself as well as others;
- being able to tolerate anxieties created by uncertainty and complexity;
- demonstrating an understanding of self and the impact of who you are on what you do.

I have argued elsewhere (Cartney, 1998) that engaging in reflective practice makes demands on social workers. It is an active and interactive way of being in the world and to practise in this way requires practitioners to demonstrate their willingness to:

- admit to and experience uncertainty
- focus on means as well as ends

- engage openly and honestly in a search for meaning
- expose feelings and critically examine values
- unlearn as well as learn
- foster a sense of curiosity about themselves and the world around them. (Cartney, 1998: 53)

Donald Schon differentiated between reflective practice and technical-rational approaches to practice. In a famous passage, he argued that:

> In the varied topography of professional practice, there is a high hard ground overlooking a swamp. On the high ground, manageable problems lend themselves to solutions through the use of research-based theory and technique. In the swampy lowlands, problems are messy and confusing and incapable of technical solution. The irony of this is that the problems of the high ground tend to be relatively unimportant to individuals or to society at large, however great their technical interest may be, while in the swamp lie the problems of greatest human concern. (Schon, 1987: 3)

We explore Schon's ideas a little further and devise a basic typology to highlight the differences between a technical-rational approach and a reflective approach to practice. This is illustrated in Table 5.1.

Table 5.1 A basic typology of the differences between a technical-rational approach and a reflective approach to practice

Technical-rational approach	Reflective practice
Theory, knowledge and necessary skills agreed: define situation and prescribe action	Theory is critically evaluated: 'fit' with specific service user and situation explored
Human behaviour is seen as predictable and certain. Common case used in assessments	Human behaviour is accepted as unpredictable. Uniqueness in assessment accepted: 'universe of one' is understood
The worker is the expert who identifies the problem and prescribes the solution	Worker and service user work in partnership: negotiation is important

Life on the high ground and in the swampy lowlands

Although Schon was not writing about social work, his ideas have often been applied to the arena of social work practice. Before we do this, however, it is helpful to pause and reflect on your own perceptions in relation to some of the key issues raised so far.

Discussion point

Where do you see the 'high hard ground' of social work practice and where do you see the swampy lowlands?

Having asked this question to many social work practitioners for the past twenty years, in this author's experience, most social workers respond that legislation, policy, research and theory form part of the high, hard ground for social work. Together these provide an overt framework to instruct or inform practice. When pressed, however, debates often ensue about the complexity of even the highest hard ground within social work. Legislation requires interpreting and policies need to be assessed in relation to their application to specific situations (e.g. judgements need to be made about whether service users meet particular legislative or policy thresholds). Research is a key underpinning for knowledgeable practice but its findings need to be interpreted in relation to its applicability in any given situation. Research may suggest, for example, that it is usually best practice to place siblings entering foster care in the same placement; in the uniqueness of practice, however, there will be times when this general rule would not apply in a specific case. Theoretical knowledge is also a key underpinning for informed practice, but skilled practitioners draw discerningly on theories, assessing their applicability in specific situations rather than viewing theoretical knowledge as being 'off the peg' and applicable in all situations. In this sense, theory acts more as a map for social workers rather than a detailed procedural manual.

In my own experience, most practitioners identify day-to-day social work practice as involving a considerable amount of swamp dwelling where problems are indeed complex, multi-layered and not amenable to a 'one-size-fits-all' blanket solution. Schon's idea that we all live 'in a universe of one' (1983: 105) appears a helpful starting point in highlighting the uniqueness of each individual and their particular lives. Professional judgement is always a requirement for skilled social work practice and reflection on whether the general rule for the many does – or does not – hold in the specific instance for the individual is an essential component in decision-making. Skilled practitioners draw on a range of different sources of knowledge to assist them in making such judgements, and we will explore this further.

Recently, some commentators have argued that social work attempted to move away from its roots in appreciating process and reflection and sought to adhere to a more technical-rational outcome focused mode of practice. Increasing bureaucracy, financial restrictions, emphasis on targets and performance management in practice, all have been suggested as being partly responsible for this shift (Ferguson, 2008; Ferguson and Woodward, 2009). In the field of child care, Ruch (2007: 660) argues that 'child-care social work has witnessed the steady emergence of technical-rational approaches to practice, which are risk-averse and bureaucratic in nature. These approaches have emerged in a wider social and political context that privileges economic efficiency and effectiveness'. While promoting economic efficiency and effectiveness are goals most would aspire to, the suggestion here is that these have been seen in an overly narrow manner where effectiveness is judged primarily in relation to performance targets and financial measures of success as opposed to a more complex understanding around the measurement of effectiveness in relation to social work outcomes. In later work, Ruch offers an alternative to such a model where she comments on 'the risk-ridden, uncertain and anxiety-provoking context of child-care social work where "the person is the product" and reflective practice is a central feature of professional interventions' (Ruch, 2011: 2).

In the field of social work and criminal justice, Gregory (2010) refers to the development of 'punitive managerialism', a term originally coined by Cavadino et al. (1999), and suggests that social work in this context is increasingly operating in a 'new penology' with management rather than transformation as a key task. Gregory argues that this is 'a setting that is now dominated by a technical-rational approach in which practice is managed within a routinized framework' (2010: 2281). Interestingly, Gregory's primary research here found that practitioners within this context continued to draw upon reflective practice as a way of processing and coping with the changes in their working environments. She found that:

> Ultimately, what seems to sustain the resistance of these participants in what is clearly a difficult and uncomfortable work environment is their ability to think critically and reflexively...As they reflect upon practice encounters, the value base that the participants continue to deploy, in the face of working practices that do not facilitate or support it, is essentially an ethic of care. (Gregory, 2010: 2280)

These arguments are important within contemporary social work and although it would not be appropriate to explore them in depth here, they are part of our recent history and have led to increasing debates about the very nature of what social work is. Reflective practice is a topic that is interwoven and intrinsic to these debates and, as noted earlier, is embraced by the new developments in relationship-based practice. The recent Munro Review looking at child protection services also adopted an approach to practice that is far removed from a bureaucratic, technical-rational understanding of social work. Munro proposed a more sophisticated and nuanced understanding of the complexity of social work decision-making and urged the development of 'a system that values professional expertise' (Munro, 2011: 91). Munro's argument that social workers need to utilize 'intuitive expertise' (ibid.) most clearly locates social work within the arena of reflective as opposed to technical rational practice. This influential review is highly critical of the over-bureaucratization of recent social work practice and highlights the need for 'appreciating the importance of both logical and intuitive understanding and the contribution of emotions' (ibid.). The suggestion here is that both types of understanding are important in competent social work practice.

Such comments highlight the complexity of understandings we need to draw upon in social work and the range of different 'knowledges' that underpin effective social work practice. Skilled social workers are required to draw upon formal and informal sources of knowledge. Formal knowledge is often written down and publically accessible in a 'codified' form that is available for others to read and judge its merits (e.g. knowledge demonstrated in assignments on social work programmes or outlined as part of the evidence drawn upon in court reports). In contrast, informal knowledge exists in a more private arena, and contains personal knowledge a practitioner has from his or her own life experiences. This knowledge is also supplemented by the more public knowledge gained from undertaking the day-to-day responsibilities of social work practice. Elements of this knowledge base comprises our 'practice wisdom' – a 'know how' that has developed over time. Informal knowledge is often not written down or codified in any way and is known mostly to the person who possesses it. Whereas formal sources of knowledge may be part of the high, hard ground in social work, appreciating the importance of informal knowledge places social work more firmly in the terrain of the 'messy' swampy lowlands. For a fuller discussion of these issues, I refer you to Cartney (2011) and Eraut's (1994) work on knowledge elucidation.

So far we have discussed what reflective practice is and highlighted its importance in relation to social work, including contemporary practice developments. We will now turn to exploring the relationship between reflective practice and social work ethics and values. Using a case study, we will explore how adopting reflective practice as a starting point can be particularly helpful when seeking to navigate the complex terrain of values and ethics, and how examining issues from a reflective standpoint is likely to bring issues of ethics and values into the foreground.

Case study 5.1

After qualifying, Mary spent five years employed as a social worker in a voluntary community action project working with women who were leaving situations of domestic violence. Mary was knowledgeable about working in this area. She possessed both formal sources of knowledge in relation to certificated courses she had attended about working with survivors of domestic violence; she was up to date with current legislation and research in this area and had a firm grounding in social work theories. In her practice, she frequently drew upon ideas from psychodynamic thinking to help her to make sense of some of the complex emotional issues involved in this area of work. Psychodynamic theoretical understandings helped Mary to reflect on both the conscious and unconscious elements involved in her practice and to be attuned to the emotional context of the situation. She also had a wealth of informal knowledge derived from her own life experiences alongside her 'practice wisdom' that had developed over time from the many different situations she had been involved with as a worker.

Six months ago, Mary moved house and was successful in being appointed to a post as a social worker in a statutory children and families team. She was allocated the case of Ann, a 26-year-old white woman of Irish decent and Siobhan, her 18-month-old daughter. Ann was referred to the service following several incidents of domestic violence, which had been reported to the police by neighbours. In the final incident, the neighbours reported that Siobhan had been heard crying while Ann's ex-partner Paul had been hitting Ann and smashing furniture in their flat. There was no suggestion that Paul had physically harmed Siobhan but the local authority was concerned about the emotional impact witnessing such abuse could have on the child. After Mary's first visit to the home Ann stated that she had asked Paul to leave, as she was worried his presence in the home would result in Siobhan being taken into care. Mary had not met Paul when she visited. Paul was Siobhan's natural father and Ann said he was the only boyfriend she had ever had. Siobhan had been examined by a doctor and was physically unharmed and Mary noted a warm attachment appeared to be present between Ann and Siobhan. The health visitor had also confirmed that Siobhan was meeting – and in some instances succeeding – the developmental milestones for her age. Siobhan seemed contented and Ann appeared responsive to her needs.

Mary gave Ann advice about her legal rights and suggested she contact a solicitor to discuss obtaining a Restraining Order in case Paul returned to the flat. Ann initially seemed interested in doing this but never seemed to be able to find the time to make the appointment with the solicitor. Mary also discussed with Ann her rights as a tenant and how she should discuss changes to her tenancy with the local housing department. Mary also informed Ann that the housing department should be able to help by fitting additional security adaptations to her flat, such as alarms. Again, Ann had professed interest in doing this but had not pursued it. Mary suggested to Ann that she might want to attend the local community Irish Women's Centre as a way of making new friends, as she did not know people in the area. Ann had not done this.

Mary visited Ann on a number of occasions and sought to support her both emotionally and practically. Ann did take up some of the practical support Mary offered (e.g. Mary was able to secure a small amount of funding to support one day a week child care for Siobhan). Ann did not want to discuss her experiences of domestic violence with Mary, however, and only superficially engaged in any discussions about how she might be feeling since Paul had left the home. Ann maintained that Paul was angry when she asked him to leave but he had not tried to make contact with her since.

Drawing on her previous work experiences, Mary suspected that Ann may have been finding things more difficult to cope with emotionally than she was disclosing (Kearney, 2001). Mary thought leaving violent relationships was often a process rather than a single event and that reunions with abusers were not uncommon in the early stages of separation. Some researchers suggest that on average women leave violent relationships five to seven times before they finally separate (www.domesticviolence.com.au). Mary drew upon formal sources of research knowledge to support her thinking and informal sources of knowledge from her own experiences that this was often the case in practice. Mary was also concerned that women are often most at risk when a violent relationship has ended, as the perpetrator may return. Research suggests that women are at the greatest risk of being killed at the point of separation (Lees, 2000; Walby and Allen, 2004). Again Mary drew upon a combination of formal research-based knowledge and her own practice wisdom here. Ann maintained she did not miss Paul in her life and felt no ambivalence about her decision to ask him to leave the home. Ann also said she had no worries that he would return to their home and commit further acts of violence.

While respecting Ann's right not to discuss such issues beyond addressing questions about Siobhan's safety, Mary was concerned that Ann appeared to be constantly suspicious of her reasons for asking questions and Mary's answers all seemed geared to assuring her of Siobhan's well-being with no reference to Ann herself. Mary also wondered whether Paul was still a frequent visitor to the home; a suggestion denied by Ann. Drawing on Munro's (2011) concept of 'intuitive expertise', Mary was aware of feeling uneasy about the situation. While her role in the family was clearly focused on ensuring Siobhan's safety, she also wanted to support Ann but felt Ann saw her as simply visiting to assess her parenting and her care of Siobhan. Mary wondered how far she was being presented with a staged version of reality where elements of the situation were being consciously obscured by Ann.

Mary raised these issues in supervision with her line manager. As a way of highlighting the processes involved here, we will imagine that Mary's line manager introduced a model of reflective practice in order to help them both think through the implications of Mary's experiences. Using this model is also a way of contextualizing some of the ethical issues Mary was grappling with in this instance.

Using a reflective practice model

There are many models available that set out to help practitioners think reflectively about their social work practice. Most of the models employ a triadic structure around thinking, feeling and doing (Ruch, 2002) with interconnections between these being a primary focus of analysis. In this chapter, we will draw upon Smyth's (1989) Framework for Reflection on Action as a way of highlighting the ethical and values issues in the above case study alongside issues around how different sources of knowledge may be used to reflect on the complexity of the situation. This helpful model, outlined in Table 5.2, draws attention to the wider structural and power issues involved in analysing practice.

We will now explore possible ways that this model could be used in practice to help Mary to reflect on her experience and to raise issues around ethics and values in this process.

Table 5.2 A Framework for critical reflection

Activity	Cues
Describe	What did I do?
Inform (Analysis)	What does this mean?
Confront (Self awareness)	How did I come to be like this?
Reconstruct (Evaluation and synthesis)	What do my practices say about my assumptions, values and beliefs?
	Where did these ideas come from?
	What social practices are expressed in these ideas?
	What is it that causes me to maintain my theories?
	What views of power do they embody?
	Whose interests seem to be served by my practices?
	What is it that acts to constrain my views of what is possible in my practice?

Source: Adapted from Smyth's (1989) Framework for Reflection on Action

Describe

The first stage of the model seeks a description of events. At this point, using this model required Mary to detail the reason for the referral to her agency and the planned focus of her work. As Mary worked in a statutory setting, she described relevant legislation and policy that had guided her initial interventions. She noted the number of visits she had undertaken and said what happened on each of these visits. Mary described what she had done to ensure that Siobhan appeared to be safe and well cared for. She also described how she had sought to support both Ann and Siobhan, highlighting what she *did* in this process (e.g. how she had advised Ann to see a solicitor and to contact the housing department). Mary also outlined how she had sought to work with Ann to support her (e.g. by accessing funds to support childcare for Siobhan). The focus at this stage was on Mary detailing what had been said and done.

Inform (Analyse)

This is a crucial stage of the model, which encouraged Mary to revisit her experiences and ask herself *why* events might have happened in the way they did. She moved away from describing events and was encouraged to stand back and consider their meaning at this point. Mary's line manager suggested a helpful initial starting point was for Mary to address this first from her hypothesis that Paul was still in contact with the family and that Ann was refusing support on this basis. Mary began by detailing her evidence to support this way of thinking (e.g. Ann not pursuing contact with solicitors and the housing department). She detailed Ann's reluctance to speak about any ambivalent emotions she may have felt, having asked Paul to leave and how unusual such feelings seemed to be in relation to Mary's experiences working with other women in her previous role. Mary suggested that Ann's concern to reassure Mary that she was taking care of Siobhan could be interpreted as a defensive stance on her part and evidence of Ann's desire for Mary to leave and close her case. If Paul was still involved, Mary hypothesized that Ann would be relieved when her visits ceased.

Mary and her line manager explored the meaning of events from Mary's initial hypothesis. Mary's line manager, however, suggested to Mary that engaging in a fully reflective stance meant that Mary should be encouraged to try out different meanings for the events she had described rather than simply exploring one hypothesis. Mary was encouraged to consider the additional questions raised in Smyth's framework as a way of pursuing potential alternative explanations and raising additional ethical issues.

Confront/Self-awareness

It was helpful for Mary to answer the question, 'how did I come to be like this?', as this provided a focus for exploring her own role in her interaction with Ann – what *she* brought to that encounter. Considering how who she is impacts on what she does and what lens she brings to her work opened up another source of rich information for Mary to consider. Reflecting on her own life and work experiences led Mary to acknowledge that at least part of her uneasiness with Ann may have emanated from this.

In Mary's previous experience working in the voluntary sector, her relationships with the women she worked with were developed in a particular practice context. Her role was not as a statutory social worker and the focus of her agency was explicitly to provide support for women leaving violent relationships. The role she occupied may have encouraged women to trust her more easily and to feel they had permission to discuss any fears they had in relation to their own or their children's safety. She was not in the role of having statutory responsibility in relation to the safety of their children. Where women maintained an emotional attachment to the person who had abused them, they may also have felt more free to discuss this and to work through the emotional complexity and the pain involved in leaving the relationship. Mary's theoretical understandings from psychodynamic theory may have encouraged such exploration and hopefully offered understanding and containment in this process.

The formal and informal knowledge Mary gained in the process of her previous work experience was a key factor Mary reflected on when answering the question, 'how did I come to be like this?' This was helpful in encouraging both her self-awareness and an appreciation of the context in which she was using 'self as resource'. Mary was also able to reflect more clearly on the importance of context in relation to her practice.

Reconstruct

Having reflected on how she came to think in the way she did, Mary could then helpfully return to her analysis of the situation with Ann and Siobhan. It was helpful for her to clearly articulate the new statutory role she worked in and to consider the impact this may have had on the interactions with Ann. Ann's primary concern may have been to demonstrate to Mary that there were no concerns in relation to her care of Siobhan, as she would be aware Mary had statutory powers of removal if she was concerned about Siobhan's safety. Any fears Ann might have about renewed violence if Paul returned may have been withheld from discussion on this basis. Ann may have felt concerned that going to a solicitor or the housing department would provoke a violent response from Paul but she may have felt unable to discuss these concerns with Mary in case Mary decided that the implication of this was that Siobhan was not safe in Ann's care. Ann may have felt disempowered by her experience of violence and unable to take these important steps alone but may have been afraid to ask for Mary's help in case she saw this as a sign Ann was not coping.

Mary reflected on her own position and saw that her beliefs about how women might act in circumstances similar to Ann's had emerged in a very different context. Ann's reluctance to accept the support Mary was offering may have been misinterpreted on this basis. Reflecting on the social practices and power positions at play here also raised value and ethical issues for Mary to consider. Mary questioned whether although it appeared on the surface that Ann was being offered support as a woman who had experienced domestic violence, in practice Mary's statutory role in relation to Siobhan may have meant that Ann may have been reluctant to avail herself of the help offered and thus she was not being provided with a service. This raised both ethical and values issues for Mary to reflect on. Mary had always tried to work to support women who had been abused but started to see how her statutory role to protect Siobhan may leave Ann feeling unsupported and subject only to statutory surveillance. This led Mary to consider that seeking to work in an empowering way as a statutory social worker in this context needed her to think through the impact of her role in some depth and not to assume that Ann would feel able to automatically avail herself of the support Mary was seeking to offer her.

Mary began to consider how Ann's reluctance to engage with her had left her in a dilemma about whether Siobhan was safe or whether Ann's reluctance to engage was putting Siobhan at risk, as Ann may not have been open with her about her concerns or her circumstances. Starting to reflect in more depth on these issues raised important ethical issues and presented uncomfortable questions for Mary to consider. The issues Mary debated here could be seen as lying in the realm of meta-ethics – conceptual analysis of ethical concepts of 'rights', 'responsibilities' and 'professional integrity' (Banks, 2008). Mary was aware of Ann's rights in terms of autonomy but also aware of her responsibilities to ensure the safety of Siobhan. Was Ann's reluctance to engage with a statutory social worker likely to lead to closer surveillance and suspicion? If this was the case, how would this impact on Mary's own feminist values and her conceptions of professional integrity? The available evidence appeared to suggest that Siobhan was safe and there was no need for statutory intervention, but feelings that Ann was not being open had left Mary feeling uneasy about closing the case.

Smyth's final question was an interesting one for Mary to consider further in this case. Smyth asks us to reflect on 'what is it that acts to constrain my views of what is possible in my practice?' Thinking through the ethics as well as the statutory limits of her involvement in this situation encouraged Mary to reflect on the tension between the right to privacy and non-intervention that social workers need to balance alongside the need for intervention. Mary was aware that in Beauchamp and Childress's (2001) four principle approach to applied ethics the principle of respect for autonomy was the first ethical principle. This principle could suggest that Ann's wishes not to avail herself of the support offered by Mary should be respected and her decision not to see a solicitor, etc. accepted as her right to make this choice as a rational and competent person.

Social workers often walk a tightrope of conflicting values, however, in relation to child protection. Munro (2011) acknowledged that a high value is attached to the autonomy and privacy of family life. Parton explored the philosophical tensions experienced in this arena, noting that there are 'Problems on the one hand posed by the contradictory demands of ensuring that the family is experienced by its members as autonomous and the primary sphere for rearing children, while on the other recognizing there is a need for interventions in some families where they are seen as failing in this primary task' (1991: 44). Beauchamp and Childress's (2001) two principles of beneficence were important ones for Mary to think about here. Did the principle of non-maleficence suggest that in order to avoid doing harm she should close the case and respect Ann's autonomy, or was she adhering more closely to this principle if she kept the case open on the basis that closing it may promote future harm to Siobhan and Ann? Would utilizing the position of privileging beneficence over autonomy result in paternalistic practice? Did the principle of beneficence – that one ought to promote the well-being of others – suggest she should struggle to engage further with Ann? Mary wondered whether there was an ethical tension between the different principles in this particular situation.

Mary reflected on how much she could trust her 'intuitive expertise' in this circumstance where her previous knowledge may have skewed her perceptions about how she experienced Ann's lack of engagement. She may have been expecting Ann to behave in the way women she had worked with previously had done, although Mary was now aware that her own changed role as a statutory worker may have inhibited this. Mary also acknowledged that emotionally she may have felt rejected and de-skilled by Ann's reluctance to engage with her. Mary discussed with her line manager, however, about how safe it would be to ignore her sense of uneasiness and the feeling that her visits could be being stage-managed. Mary explored further what constraints there might there be on acting on this feeling of unease and discussed whether there might be alternative ways of seeking to address these issues.

Mary raised all of these issues in supervision with her line manager. Her manager encouraged her to move from a principles approach to understanding her practice ethically, as the conflict between the differing principles did not appear to be helping Mary in her desire to act ethically. Her manager encouraged the reflective approach Mary had taken to this situation and recommended that she continue exploring a contextualized embedded approach to her ethical practice where the unique factors in this particular situation were thought through and its particular features explored. Her line manager suggested that Mary's thinking about this situation appeared to sit more closely with virtue ethics and ethics of care as discussed in Chapter 4. These 'new' approaches to social work ethics pay attention to 'the situated nature of values and conduct, as embedded in families, relationships, communities and cultures, and take account of commitments to specific others, motivations and emotions' (Banks, 2008: 1243). Her line manager suggested that Mary's concerns were connected with questions of virtue ethics – what would a 'good person' do in this situation? Was Mary being a 'good person' with appropriate virtues in relation to her approach to Ann and Siobhan? Her line manager also suggested that the concerns expressed by Mary could be understood in the context of ethics of care, as Mary's concern for Ann and Siobhan was based not just on feelings around responsibility and duty but also a sense of compassion and care which is fundamental to effective social work.

Such discussions enabled Mary to fully contextualize her analysis of the situation and to reflect on the differing ethical issues she had been grappling with. After discussing the options available with her line manager, Mary decided to visit Ann again and to speak openly with Ann about her concerns and her feelings of unease. Truthfulness is a key virtue associated with virtue ethics in social work (Pullen-Sansfacon, 2010). Mary intended to be explicit about her need to monitor Siobhan's welfare and the need to work alongside other professionals to do this. She was keen to frame this conversation in a facilitative rather than accusatory manner and to acknowledge to Ann why she thought Ann may be reluctant to seek her support. She decided to share with Ann her previous work experiences and her knowledge about helping women leaving abusive situations. Mary wanted to encourage Ann to talk with her about her experiences of their work and whether there were things Mary could do that would be more helpful to Ann. This could be a way of both openly addressing the complexity in their work together within a framework based upon the ethics of care and potentially offering a way forward for future work.

Mary also discussed with her line manager the possibility that Ann could be offered alternative support in her own right and be given a referral to a support agency that did not have direct statutory responsibilities. While such agencies would be expected to report child protection concerns in the way any other community agency would, the lack of direct statutory responsibility and the need to have a primary focus on the welfare of the child could potentially change the dynamics of the relationship between Ann and the worker. In this way, Mary could be alerted if major child protection concerns arose but Ann may also feel she had more freedom to discuss her fears and emotions more openly.

Evaluating the model

Smyth's model raised some interesting questions in relation to the case study and quickly engaged us in discussions focusing on the search for meaning and analysis. It also raised questions about self-knowledge and the need to consider thoroughly what we bring to a situation from our own knowledge – both formal and informal. Questions about how we know what we know and how such knowledge influences how we see the world were raised in this process. Such reflections led us into pertinent discussions about values – the social worker's, those of her agency and the wider society we live in. Addressing questions of values also moved us into the terrain of considering the ethical basis for practice and the limits and opportunities for action.

It was the intention to use the case study and Smyth's framework to illustrate how reflective practice can assist workers to think more deeply about their work and to consider the multi-layered aspects involved. In a profession as complex as social work, questions relating to values and ethical positions usually surface relatively quickly in this process and their role in the decision-making process can be clarified more transparently. The questions raised through using the model did not, of course, lead to clear prescriptions for action and one set of questions often led to another. Using the questions raised in this model, however, did clearly highlight the uncertainty involved in the decision-making process and the potential for a range of explanations to be feasible. The need to accept and manage the anxiety created by uncertainty was demonstrated in this example.

Chapter summary

This chapter set out to prompt consideration of issues of values and ethics by 'problematizing' the nature of professional knowledge and drawing attention to the different sources of knowledge social workers draw upon in practice. The place of reflective practice was discussed and presented as an alternative to the technical-rational approach that has emerged in some areas of social work in recent years. A case study from practice was presented and a model was used as a way of highlighting how reflective practice can assist social workers to think more deeply about their experiences, considering both the complexity and impact of their different sources of knowledge. Thinking reflectively about practice effectively ensures consideration of issues of values and ethics, as both in essence run through the day-to-day experience of engaging in social work practice.

Part 2

Themes for social work practice: 'Power', 'Social justice', 'Partnership', 'Diversity and difference' and 'Relationship-based practice'

6 | Power

Trish Hafford-Letchfield

Introduction

Power is a challenging concept to operationalize or define within social work practice, especially given the strong steer by government exercised through its extensive legislative, policy and procedural guidance. The nature of 'power' or 'empowerment' also raises fundamental questions about the very purpose of social work itself and what it aims to achieve (Smith, 2008: 2). Questions have been raised about whether social workers can be truly anti-oppressive in their practice given that they inevitably bring more power to their interactions with service users than vice versa (Sakamoto and Pitner, 2005; Cocker and Hafford-Letchfield, 2014).

This seemingly discordant relationship with power has been illustrated in a developing sense of helplessness in the face of increasing managerialism in social work, in which professional expertise has been usurped by increasing actuarial activities (Bar-On, 2002; Harris, 2003; Hafford-Letchfield, 2010a). Despite a plethora of government policy directives that seek to promote the rights, citizenship and empowerment of different service user groups, some of the assumptions underpinning these policies have directly contributed to tensions for social workers in their everyday practice. An all-party UK parliamentary inquiry into the state of social work (BASW, 2013), for example, noted that the effects of well-intentioned new government policies have negated many of their intended outcomes. The extent of subsequent macro- and micro-management from above was identified as instrumental in hindering any potential for facilitating a solution-led focus closer to where practice actually takes place.

Within this environment, diverging demands about how to effectively share and distribute power therefore necessitate that social workers develop both insight and a better understanding of discourses about power in order to engage with it effectively. This chapter aims to look closer at how these tensions are acknowledged and worked with. Through the examination of two key scenarios we will consider some of the challenges in relation to exercising power ethically and the dilemmas faced in staying close to the values of social work in its everyday context. How you understand power in different contexts and engage and interrogate with power dynamics is a crucial part of your learning to become a social worker.

This is all, of course, easier said than done. Ethical and practical dilemmas for social work practitioners will arise whenever power is present, and this may occur at a number of levels in your relationships with service users, with other professionals or within your own organizational hierarchies. Debates about social work's use of delegated authority, power and decision-making alongside the roles, responsibilities and expectations of other stakeholders are regularly scrutinized in the media regarding risk and protection of vulnerable people as well as being documented in highly publicized serious case reviews (Laming, 2009; Munro, 2011; Lundberg, 2013). Playing these debates out in the public arena exerts a powerful influence on the way in which the social work profession is positioned, accompanied by a corresponding increase in closer surveillance and defensive practice. These events inevitably divert attention away from examining power in its socio-economic and political context in relation to the reality of structural issues affecting the lives of service users. Here lies the real irony, since although having limited capacity to exercise change, as holders of statutory authority social workers are also expected to exercise further control and constraints over those already perceived to be oppressed. It is hardly surprising then that social workers are sometimes uncomfortable with the phenomenon of power.

Let us start by focusing on the concept of 'professional' by theorizing competing discourses of empowerment in social work and its key concepts, drawing in particular on the explanatory powers of critical theorist Michel Foucault (1991). We will then problematize the concept of power by explicitly drawing on both users' and carers' accounts from the literature to demonstrate different external and internal influences on the root causes of disempowerment. In this chapter, we will focus specifically on everyday issues around 'safeguarding' and 'vulnerability' in relation to how different service users are supported to make decisions about their own care and support. 'Empowerment' is not something professionals just 'do' to people but is a reflexive activity or process initiated and sustained by others as well as by service users. Empowerment requires an appropriate climate, relationship, resources and procedural means through which people can enhance their own lives. Core aspects of this model derive from both a value base concerned with social justice, self-determination and self-actualization, and a theory base emphasizing the significance of power in social relationships. Some of these issues have been aired in other chapters relating to social justice and relationship-based practice. In this chapter, we will encourage you to consider more creative approaches through the use of narrative, and relationship-based approaches that emphasize the centrality of experience, critical reflection, meaning-making and the importance of flexible and facilitative relationships within social work practice.

Theoretical aspects of power

Power can be defined as the ability or capacity to act or to exercise influence (Lukes, 2005), and the most significant contribution to the study of power is provided from sociology. In social work and social care, however, while power is frequently alluded to in theory and practice, empirical studies and in-depth analyses tend to be more of a rarity. As a field of practice, Webb (2010) argues that social work itself is constituted as a complex hierarchy of material and symbolic power relations. Its attempt to redistribute power, particularly through activities of assessment and service provision, guided by statutory, political, social and economic frameworks, is also driven by professional values such as the recognition of cultural diversity and the promotion of person-centred approaches. Further layers are introduced through the role that social work plays in relation to the Welfare State, as well as and complicated by the direct role that the state itself plays in structuring power relations. According to some perspectives, social work is a major social institution that legitimates the power contained in modern democratic capitalist states, which Webb (2010a: 2369) revealingly describes as being 'complicitous, as a functionary apparatus, but also decidedly hostile to its machinations'.

Typologies of power

Power can operate in various ways, including personal, dispersed, relational and dispositional power (Lukes, 2005). Within social work, power is also frequently discussed in relation to its abuse (as illustrated in serious case reviews). Lukes' typology (2005) refers to the different dimensions of power, such as coercion, influence, force, authority or manipulation. According to Smith (2008), these go beyond the overt authority by one individual over another to one that is contextual or institutional. Among the most widely used conceptualizations of social power is the five-fold typology developed by French and Raven (1986). They identified several sources that are useful to consider in everyday social work practice:

- *Referent power*: this refers to situations in which you may identify with an individual or group – for example, someone who has a strong leadership style or skills and thus has influence over others because of the respect they command. Alternatively, you may comply with your managers' requests because you respect their leadership and expertise even if you don't necessarily agree with all of their decisions!
- *Expert power*: this source of power comes with the authority and skills attributed to substantial knowledge and expertise. A common example is the authority attributed to doctors and psychiatrists within an inter-professional team or in relation to your own power, as a qualified professional over service users. Recognition of the expertise and knowledge of service users is essential to the principles of co-production where people and professionals combine their expertise and experience to explore problems and collectively find appropriate solutions.
- *Reward power* lies with those who have the ability to provide incentives and rewards. For example, within assessments of carers for adoption and fostering, the social worker holds power in determining the nature of exchange and type of information required. In order to be 'approved', foster carers may comply with how they think the social worker wants them to be perceived. Hicks (2014) has highlighted how social work can make powerful claims and decisions about families and, at times, concerns have been raised about the possibility of oppressive and damaging practice, especially in relation to black, gay, lesbian or single-parent families.
- *Coercive or punishment power* exists where there is an ability to impose force or punish others. This may be subtle, such as through peer pressure within teams where conforming prevents social inclusion, such as not 'coming out' as gay or lesbian in a predominately heterosexual team. It may also be present within supervision, such as accepting a further allocation of work beyond what you can manage because refusal might lead you to be perceived as inadequate. The principal aim of coercive power is compliance, and at an organizational level it is to be found in the unquestioning compliance with excessive recording requirements related to government time-scales. Another example is illustrated in the case prior to the introduction of the Mental Capacity Act (2005) and Deprivation of Liberty Safeguards (2009), which provide statutory guidelines in relation to decision-making on behalf of vulnerable adults unable to provide informed consent. Before their implementation, coercion in its most friendly guise was common custom and practice when admitting or detaining vulnerable adults in a residential home in the absence of any statutory guidance with occasional consequences for human rights abuses.
- *Legitimate power* refers to sources of authority generally accepted because of one's position or accepted ways of working. Working to social work legislation confers legitimate power and also the normative acceptance of social workers' professional code of practice. Managers, for example, have legitimate power derived from their role in the organizational hierarchy.

As organizations have become more integrated at a structural level, subsequent inter-professional working has revealed continuing undermining or diffusion of professional power. Government's emphasis on even further integration (DH, 2013) cites the need to create a culture of cooperation and coordination between health, social care, public health, other local services and the Third sector to provide the basis for an aspirational culture in which individuals can gain greater control. Putting social workers on a par with other professionals has also achieved the potential for a much richer knowledge and evidence base, which is still growing. However, both the unforgiving scale and pace of these reconfigurations of care provision and social work services have ironically led to social work having a much weaker and often insufficiently negotiated presence in some of these organizational structures and less of a voice. The importance of building partnerships and alliances with service users to pioneer new and different approaches to providing individual and collective support for them has therefore never been greater. The introduction of personalization into social care (HM Government, 2008) has brought into question the various core functions of social work assessment, advocacy and brokerage, safeguarding and capacity, which according to some contain elements of conflict and incompatibility (Lymbery and Postle, 2010). The future for social work in this policy area runs a strong risk of becoming both fragmented and isolated. Similarly, within the literature on user participation, for example, there is tension expressed between a fear of possession of power and a fear of loss of power (Pinkey, 2011), which speaks of the difficult and sometimes uncomfortable relationships resulting from the possession and use of power when intervening in service users' lives (Carr, 2007; Pinkey, 2011). Evidence from service users' narratives (Hafford-Letchfield, 2011) contradicts social work's own mission and values, supposedly to be profoundly shaped by notions of enabling, empowering and participatory ethics. When viewed through these different lenses, we can see how power is constituted at many different levels, including between government and professionals, within organizational hierarchies, between different groups of professionals, and between professionals and service users. We will now turn to the language of power, another means by which this is expressed.

The language of power

As a concept, the definition of power remains contested, as it is so critical to everyday life and innately value-dependent and linguistically problematic (Bar-On, 2002). Much has been written about the impact of language in preserving professional power and resources. For example, certain terms used to describe service users have been claimed as a political endeavour (Heffernan, 2006: 140). Evolving terminologies such as 'client', 'consumer' to the current 'service user', reflect political ideologies influencing the overall provision of social care services. The concept of choice has played an important role in the neoliberal agenda and remains a mantra within the UK Coalition government where choice of provider, for example, is seen as the mechanism for increasing the quality and efficiency of services through conceptualizing individuals as discerning consumers (Stevens et al., 2011). Making ourselves aware of these debates about terminology enables us to be more critical about the potential use of labelling, which may be stigmatizing. The provision of direct payments and individualized budgets both stress the importance of the interaction between the person receiving and the person providing support. This shapes services users' own determined outcomes and aims to alter the power dynamic by delegating control (Glendinning, 2009). There is controversy, however, in relation to potential conflicts that arise from the focus on choice for unpredictable inequities. Research by Leece and Leece (2006) demonstrated how these might favour people with existing financial and social capital who are both able to make best use of resources and to combine them with their own at the expense of other groups and concerns. However, giving services users more of a role in assessing their own needs and in making choices about the kinds of services they want to 'purchase' will hopefully challenge existing power relationships with social workers and other professionals. Gate-keeping roles will also remain as a means of assessing eligibility and negotiating resource allocation, as well as concerns about managing risk where services may not be regulated, resources misused or vulnerable service users are at risk of abuse or possible harm through exercising their choices, 'wisely' or 'unwisely'. As both a policy requirement and social work value, choice will always be associated with restraint because of its association with the use of public funds and legal frameworks. As both a policy requirement and social work value, choice will always be associated with restraint because of its association with the use of public funds and legal frameworks. Research by Leece and Leece (2011) has demonstrated that public mandates enshrined in personalization, for example, will lead to social workers continuing to exercise control over what is accepted as legitimate ways of spending public welfare funds and creating a built-in power imbalance. They suggest that concepts of power and autonomy are fundamental to our understanding of service users' perceptions of personalization and social work.

As social care is concerned with both individual people and wider society, particularly those deemed 'vulnerable', standpoint theory provides us with a useful tool to help analyse power relations. One example is how we work with older people by being tuned in to both the adverse effects of the ageing process on the individual (critical realism) and taking account of how this interacts with other complex social and economic problems and political ideologies about later life, such as those enshrined in the concept of 'structured dependency' (Townsend, 2006). While policies and practice with older people may on the one hand appear to be promoting empowerment and self-directed support, they may also be subject to increased rationing and changes in resource allocation thus giving rise to priorities that are increasingly oriented towards contradictory economic, biomedical and professional determinants of care. Grenier and Guberman (2009) identify a number of different types of social exclusion and thus powerlessness arising from the direct effects of government policies and organizational practices. These, they assert, work to deprive people of the capacity to exercise their rights or participate in activities that might normally be taken for granted by ordinary citizens. Their framework provides a valuable means to critically analyse service users' situations and for articulating the ways that policies and practices operate (e.g. institutional, social and political), not only to limit older people's participation but also their expressions of identity and personhood. Let us now look at how we might conceptualize the different types of exclusion identified by Grenier and Guberman using the case study of Olga.

Case study 6.1

Olga is an 84-year-old Polish woman living alone since her partner died nine months ago. She has a history of schizophrenia and depression. She recently spent four weeks in hospital following a stroke and undertook a short period of rehabilitation. Since discharge from hospital she has been relatively confined to her home most of the week. Only a year beforehand, Olga was active in the local Polish Women's Labour Association. She was told by the hospital staff that it could be very risky for her to now go out alone but at the same time she was assessed as not meeting the eligibility criteria thresholds for support with meeting her 'social' needs. Olga relies mostly on her state pension and is reliant on a range of prescribed medications. Olga has however chosen to reduce some of her medications, as she is concerned about high prescription fees. Olga has a carer who comes in to assist her with her personal care. Although the carer is kind and reliable, Olga is somewhat reluctant to ask her to do anything extra for her while there. Her overall feeling is one of intense gratitude for the help she feels she is getting, since others of a similar age and situation might not be so fortunate. Sometimes the carer will do her a 'special favour' as she recognizes how 'vulnerable and frail' Olga really is.

Reflection point

Consider ways in which Olga's case demonstrates exclusion.

When thinking through Olga's situation, we can identify 'symbolic exclusion' via the sense of deservedness that Olga perceives through her identity as an older person in society. Older people are often problematized in policy terms, for example, as a potential drain on the public purse and older people may internalize these discourses. Exclusion on the basis of Olga's 'identity' is likely to arise in situations where carers and other professionals have explicitly identified her as frail or dependent or gear their responses to this common form of identity. This can shift the focus of care relationships to looking just at basic needs and in Olga's case may serve to overlook her identity as a Polish woman with a personal history in which she has made a meaningful contribution to society and one she can continue to make if the circumstances allow her to do so. Olga might be described as a 'schizophrenic' rather than as a person living independently with mental illness. The classification of Olga's needs into eligibility for certain services further leads to 'institutional exclusion' whereby Olga is subject to professional assessment of what she can or cannot do safely. Care is then allocated on what is determined at an institutional level rather than on Olga's own lifestyle or personal preferences. This obscures any appreciation of Olga's strengths and potential. Furthermore, 'economic exclusion' has resulted from Olga's limited financial leverage to make real choices about, for example, her medication or getting out and about in the community. These limitations often contradict the stated intentions of care and in Olga's case may actually compromise her health and quality of life. The final area of exclusion identified by Grenier and Guberman (2009) relates to someone like Olga's exclusion from meaningful relations where the dominance of meeting her personal care needs at home in turn monopolizes her time and actually has the effect of limiting her opportunities for pursuing leisure or social interaction. Hafford-Letchfield (2011) has documented this common experience of older people who had previously led active lives but following an acute illness or new disability were confined to their own homes and subject to care regimes over which they had no control. Olga's forced withdrawal from the Polish Women's Labour Association ignores the psycho-emotional aspects of her support needs. As Olga has recently experienced grief and loss, this short-term approach to meeting her support needs could lead to longer-term adverse consequences.

The issues arising in Olga's situation illustrate the various levels and dynamics around how power is asserted or expressed within what might seem to be on the surface a very straightforward or uncomplicated situation. Being sensitive to the power inherent in Olga's care arrangements points us towards a need to assert social work values that promote a co-productive approach. Co-production defines the contribution of service users in policy terms (Needham and Carr, 2009). For social care it means involving service users in collaborative relationships to tackle issues together with more empowered front-line staff able and confident to share power and accept user expertise in developing appropriate support. For example, how far is the carer able to value the strengths that Olga has in order to find appropriate solutions? Theorists of social work with older people (Scourfield, 2007; Lymbery, 2010), for example, have criticized the underpinning consumerist, entrepreneurial assumptions that older people are expected to share more responsibility and manage more risk in return for much greater control over resources and decisions. Co-production requires highly effective channels of communication between users, practitioners, commissioners and service managers and is very important in the front line of delivering support, as Olga's relationship with her carer illustrates. For example, empirical research by Glendinning et al. (2006) using postal surveys and case studies in six localities identified that those outcomes identified by older service users themselves are not consistently related to the aims of services currently constituting the bulk of care provision. They found that services prioritize older people's basic needs with less attention to keeping them active and sustaining social contacts, as Olga would have experienced. Qualitative research by Qureshi and Henwood (2000) into what older people define as a 'quality service' identified that the commissioning of outcome-focused services for older people requires a broader approach attending to leisure, learning and community cohesion where older people might be active participants and volunteers. Their recommendations stressed the importance of facilitating outcomes that address the *process* of seeking, obtaining and using services, as these enhance or undermine the impact of services overall. Outcomes on the process of services included feeling valued and respected, and having an individual say or control over how services are provided. What these accounts did not acknowledge is that it is not only health and welfare services that play a part in older people's well-being but also the effects of structural inequalities and material well-being. Olga's own individual identity and social capital may need to be explored in terms of her expectations and ability to exercise a real sense of agency when taking risks and finding a new role for herself.

Structured and institutional power

Foucault's (1991) notion of 'governmentality' offers a valuable theoretical perspective for understanding some of the power and rules within social care, as featured in Olga's case study. Foucault asserted that the state should normalize the way it governs through its institutions, in which social work plays a significant part. According to Epstein (1999), social work influences and motivates people to adopt normative views by enabling service users to accommodate to the *status quo*. However, social work can also be seen as challenging the *status quo* by trying to bring about social change enshrined in its ethics and value base, which highlights the dissonance intrinsic to the nature of social work. Governmentality refers not only to the institution or political powers of the state but to how individuals are active in their own government. For example, feeling anxious and needing to be able to fix things is something we all face in social work practice, but also being willing and supported to explore problems in partnership with service users can help us move away from the more technical approaches that are often encouraged or expected. These essential steps may have been missed in Olga's case. Within social care, self-esteem and empowerment are increasingly seen as ethical obligations of citizenship and matters of personal and social responsibility.

To unpick further how power operates, Foucault's conception of discourse and discursive formation enables us to question how service users and carers are represented in government policy and how policy shapes our understanding of social care users. Alongside perspectives of its 'subject', one can anticipate a dialectical relationship between power and resistance where neither is passive nor in complete control. More fundamentally, Foucault alluded to the transformative potential of his ideas by illustrating through careful exposure that many discourses about institutions are not inevitable or absolute. Change can come from the realization of the precarious nature of established ways and by inviting the development of alternatives. In summary, we learn from Foucault that social workers who become socialized to professional practices often lose the stronger challenging voice they expressed when they first entered the field. In order to maintain that voice, they have to actively resist the acquisition of a more distanced professional language and the corresponding skills.

Building on Foucault's work, Chambon (1999: 78) recommends that 'ethical' social workers might utilize the following building blocks and ways of conceptualizing power by:

- Allowing oneself to be 'unsettled' to move away from pre-established models and open up new avenues of questioning practice.
- Historicizing our understanding of reality by retracing how particular practices and forms of knowledge have been created and adopted over time and not accepting these as absolute truths. The voices and narratives of service users are crucial here.
- Examining 'practices' (accepted ways of doing things) and 'texts' (such as policies or procedures) in a detailed manner to reveal hidden patterns and effects on practice. This helps to enhance our grasp of the different ways in which power is manifested and concurrently to consider the multi-functionality of practices and discourses.
- Linking subjectivity to actions and knowledge to help us better understand how social work activities create and sustain the distinctions between 'user' and 'professionals'. This also involves conceiving of different forms of knowledge, practice and their systems of rules as those that can be modified and transgressed. Different types of knowledge such as tacit, experiential or user-led knowledge are important to recognize here.
- Exploring new possibilities through the use of critical reflection.

Opportunities within social work practice such as within supervision, team work and the everyday use of advocacy can help you to raise issues and questions that are more curious about than accepting of policy and practice. Having a confident grasp of the issues impacting on practice is essential before being able to tackle broader bases of power as the next section illustrates.

Radical social work and power at the structural level

Social work has attempted to grapple with the concept of empowerment through the development of theories on power influenced by features of Marxist, socialist and radical ideologies, structural/sociological understanding of interesting oppressions, and emancipatory and feminist perspectives (Ferguson and Woodward, 2009). Based on these, power is mostly conceptualized within institutional and macro levels of society and manifest through its power structures alongside individually focused practice. Radical social work has called for a more conceptual model for understanding multiple layers of oppression, privilege and power dynamics and how they impact on the individual as well as how to engage with these in everyday practice.

More recently, some argue that due to the limitations of radical social work, it has received limited support amongst front-line practitioners or it has been incapable of offering practitioners tangible, pragmatic or sustainable ways of meeting the needs of service users at the micro level (Carey and Foster, 2011). Ferguson and Lavalette (2004) have sought to demonstrate the relevance of Marx's concept of alienation to inform the development of critical or emancipatory social work practice. While the grand narratives of

Marxism or feminism are now marginalized within social work theory and practice, they remain useful in illustrating the sense of powerlessness that can emerge during difficult socio-economic climates. This is at the heart of Marx's theory of 'alienation', which Ferguson and Lavalette (2004) argue still has considerable relevance in explaining the rise of individualism and the downplaying of structural oppression experienced by service users. For example, in relation to the impact of marketization in social care, many commentators have reflected on the increased proceduralization of assessment and care provision and the application of eligibility criteria. Ferguson and Lavalette refer to the act of commissioning care as an 'alien' object where the welfare state has retreated in the face of the developing industry around social care. This has had the effect of distancing social work with less control over both scarce resources and the process of providing support. Other examples of where social work skills have been subordinated to managerialism were exemplified in the UK Social Work Task Force Report (DCSF, 2009), which documented a number of challenging issues. For example, there was frequent reference to the excessive use of electronic information systems where loss of control over process was replaced by ever increasing administrative demands. Faced with these working conditions, social workers expressed how they felt their values and ethics were being compromised with the resultant loss of professional discretion and the jeopardizing of the personal and therapeutic relationship with service users (Munro, 2011). Dunk-West (2013) discusses these dilemmas in relation to how social workers need to focus on reflexivity. She asserts that the choice of words and the way we frame social work, while influenced by historical, social, cultural and political contexts, should never dictate what social work entails. Instead, she stresses how the 'social work self' can be nurtured towards commitment to the purpose of your work with others and careful consideration of ongoing interactions between yourself and those you work with, including your colleagues, employers and service users. This interactionist approach should enable you to move between these different modes of power. We will explore this notion of the role of personal power and identity in the next section.

Personal power and the role of identity

As we saw in Olga's situation, feeling empowered or powerful has an ontological nature as well engendering a sense of self-worth, a process that may fluctuate throughout the life course or as a result of external and internal influences (Phillipson, 2000). Those theorists interested in the concept of 'agency' or identity politics (Fraser, 1996) argue for more humanistic and interpretive forms of theory about power, based on biographical or narrative perspectives. This allows empowerment to be examined not only through the proposed transformation of society as discussed earlier, but also through the creation of shared meanings and the establishment of positive social identities. The 'sociology of childhood', for example, describes children as agents with a capacity for competence and children being perceived as citizens both in the current and future context (Pinkey, 2011). The increased use of life course and attachment theory in social work with adults can prompt different and more rounded understandings of harm and abuse and lead to more holistic responses that explore the problems from the point of view of experiences of both 'victims' and perpetrators. Bowes and Daniel (2010) remind us that safeguarding work is explicitly associated with power dynamics between service users' interpersonal relationships and the powers used by professionals to intervene. The recognition of agency and resilience are therefore useful concepts that can be contextualized to explore different types of abuse and their construction as social problems. We will use some of Bowes and Daniel's ideas to explore the power dynamics in the following case study.

Case study 6.2

Chen is a 36-year-old Nigerian man who has been living in Wales for eight years. Chen has two undergraduate degrees in engineering and management and a postgraduate diploma in human resource development. He has not been able to capitalize on his qualifications and is currently working as a security guard in a local factory. He is married to Bola, a 28-year-old woman who he met in his Nigerian home town ten years ago and who only recently came to the UK to live with him. Her citizenship status is not yet secure. Bola has recently been diagnosed with bi-polar disorder as her behaviour became very unpredictable. Bola is also in the early stages of pregnancy and this is a cause for concern as their living accommodation is unsuitable, they have several debts and no family living close by. Bola is reluctant to take any medication for fear of jeopardizing her pregnancy.

Chen is very dominant in the relationship and appears to be very controlling. Recently, he has been physically aggressive towards Bola, with neighbours reporting domestic violence on two occasions. Chen then assaulted Bola very badly following an occasion when she spent a lot of money they didn't have on some new clothes. Bola was admitted to hospital and nearly lost her baby. The police are taking steps to prosecute Chen although Bola returned home to him. As a result of a case conference, the social worker was asked to undertake an assessment under the Mental Health Act, as Bola is becoming severely depressed, is refusing ante-natal care and neglecting herself and possibly her unborn child.

Reflection point

Consider what power dynamics are at play in the case of Chen and Bola.

It is useful to stand back and consider the presence of different power relations in this case study and to identify where the power is potentially located, including how it is manifest at both structural and individual levels. Although the safety of Bola and her unborn child is absolutely paramount, the situation remains very complex at a number of levels. It is clear that a sense of powerlessness prevails for both Chen and Bola if one considers the issues of poverty, ill health and other psychosocial frustrations likely to be present. We know from research that these different indicators are likely to contribute to individuals or groups behaving in violent or anti-social ways. Serious consequences may result if intervention does not take place in a timely or sensitive way. Within the field of domestic violence, the attention given to power and control within violent intimate relationships has provided clear directives for how social workers might initially work with this family and the approaches evidenced to address issues of safety and human rights.

There are also implications for how social work explains and supports the different relationships present. For example, by reducing the individualistic conception of power within the relationships between Chen and Bola to the interpersonal level, social work may act to obscure some of the other power discourses present in society. These might be manifest in the institutional racism experienced by Chen and the potential consequences for Bola and her unborn child if she becomes compulsorily detained using mental health legislation. Once the social worker intervenes in this family, the question remains as to how broader social change can be achieved and more holistic solutions found to the challenges faced by the family. This particular case study captures some important power discourses about the underlying socio-economic problems and cultural barriers faced by vulnerable and hard-to-reach groups. At a broader level, you may ask how far social work can penetrate beneath to analyse the underlying socio-economic relations and the context in which support is subsequently provided. Any broader strategies within safeguarding work similarly have to recognize the value of preventative work with families and community development approaches and the role that social work can play in improving service users' material circumstances and in giving marginalized communities a sense of their own power, choice and control.

Similar to the issues raised by the case of Olga, the experiences and views of different minority groups may be fundamentally influenced by social exclusion, which results in a lack of access to services, lack of support for family carers and lack of choice. Strategies that maximize participation can value any approaches that are based on their strengths. These illustrate that interventions need to address users' needs beyond safeguarding work and to promote human rights. Responding accurately and holistically to discrimination and oppression are highly relevant, as illustrated in the case of Bola and Chen and suggest that harm and abuse are issues that, according to Bowes and Daniel (2010), resonate far beyond the approaches that social workers currently use specifically to address them.

Research by Pinkey (2011) into power relations contained within the participation process highlight three levels of anxieties commonly invoked in work with children and families. First, there are the anxieties and stress of the welfare institutions themselves as they try to balance the competing rights of parents, children and professionals. Second, there is the anxiety and stress experienced by individual professionals within those organizations that are working directly with children and trying to balance children's rights within a complex field of rights. Third, Pinkey referred specifically to the concerns of children and young people of participating in decision-making processes that relate to their lives. This research makes visible some of the difficulties of working with these complexities and is clearly a dilemma for Bola and Chen's social worker. Pinkey talks about understanding the emotional dilemmas for professionals within participatory policy and practice with children, young people and their families. This entails moving beyond the current state of play where many people report not feeling listened to, being taken seriously or having their views heard. Understanding some of the challenges and resistance to change involves further research and insight into the different ways that adults and professionals negotiate and enact participation and the challenges faced in doing this effectively (Pinkey, 2011: 45). Within inter-professional work, the phenomenon of power is perhaps more commonly and comfortably discussed in terms of authority, status, territory or influence. While inter-professional work projects the notion that all professions have an equally important role to play in the delivery of care, there is still a great deal of evidence that demonstrates how some professions continue to protect exclusive areas of knowledge and work practices which monopolizes specific areas of knowledge and expertise.

The positive use of power: exchanging power ethically through user narratives and pedagogies

As discussed earlier in this chapter, organizations are powerful sites for influencing social work practice, where the organizational systems enable professionals to distance themselves from the people they are working with. Much has been written in social work about defensive anxiety and the elaborate guidelines and procedures that constrain the way individuals work. Welfare organizations working in high-risk areas, such as child protection, where the highest anxiety is aroused, expect high degrees of accountability from staff. However, the institutional response is one that, it has been argued, can lead to defensive, procedural, checklist regulation and control-driven practice. The importance of emotional literacy, which engages with ethics and values as well as professional competence in being able to communicate with service users about difficult and sensitive issues, illustrates the importance of participation as part of a process rather than a one-off event that is 'done to' a service user.

We end this chapter by turning to the potential of participation in rebalancing power relations at different levels and promoting empowerment. We have identified some of the potential contradictions that policy imperatives regarding participation have posed in their actual implementation. Seeking to improve participation and involvement can also draw on an alternative body of critical educational literature informed by historical materialist theory and socialist politics (Freire, 1972). Social work could engage with this in order to enter debates about service users' own empowerment through increased participation and the skills and knowledge required to participate effectively. For example, some researchers have asserted that social pedagogy (Hafford-Letchfield, 2010a, 2011), its provision and support should recognize the importance of informal, incidental and embedded learning that occurs in settings such as families, communities and social movements. Social care environments play a significant part here. Achieving recognition requires the development of appropriate pedagogical solutions for policy-makers, professionals enacting policy in social care practice environments as well as for service users themselves. Habermas's (1984) and later Mezirow's critically important distinction between instrumental and communicative learning is relevant here. For example, Mezirow utilized Habermas's third domain of emancipation, which involved:

> becoming critically aware of how and why the structure of psycho-cultural assumptions has come to constrain the way we see ourselves and our relationships, reconstituting the structure to permit a more inclusive and discriminating integration of experience and acting upon these understandings. (Mezirow, 1981: 5)

Through their relationships with service users, practitioners might equip themselves with the power of criticism and create opportunities for the development of critical consciousness for transformative action (Mezirow, 2009). Service users need opportunities to engage in processes wherein dominant social and political ideologies can be deconstructed. Mezirow (2009) referred to emotional aspects of living, making reference to emotional intelligence and to understanding the cognitive domain of learning and different levels and forms of reflective activity. However, this assumes that professionals are themselves critically reflective and we refer back to the pointers given by Chambon (1999) earlier that facilitate the conceptualization and analysis of power through the provision of more enhanced opportunities. Within social work education and practice there are a number of mitigating cultures and tensions in encouraging mutual interaction between professionals and service users. These assert task-focused orientations in practice, with a dominant procedural culture where professionals seek to 'fix things' and the perception that professionals must remain 'objective'. In their professional code of practice, social workers hold strong beliefs about not engaging in self-disclosure with service users. These conditions not only directly discourage critical reflection but may also create conditions that make it more difficult (Fook and Askeland, 2007). Nevertheless, empowerment-based practice within social work practice recognizes the importance of linking micro-educational and practice methodologies to theories of social change. If the development of critical consciousness within the service user movement is an important precursor to critical action where the self is a key site of politicization, different approaches will need to be developed and fostered. It is suggested here that adopting a learning and educational approach within social work practice might be one aspect that could provide people with scope to extend their understandings of themselves and the contexts from within which a more liberating approach to self-directed support and a person-centred approach could be developed.

Chapter summary

This chapter has looked at some of the dynamics involved in the way in which power is conceptualized within social work practice and has made particular reference to the shifting priorities of government policy and its resultant political, socio-economic context. The implications would appear to have shifted social work away from more radical and critical theoretical interrogation of power towards a more individualized approach in which power is used uncritically to manage the everyday lives of services users. The ideas of Foucault are useful in analysing the discourses, ruling practices and moral imperatives that influence the way in which social work enacts power, which tends to be more technical rather than ontological. Some of these aspects were illustrated in the two case studies in which we examined different ways in which social exclusion might be perpetuated. Identifying the causes and effects of power can take us some way to becoming more reflective and proactive practitioners and calls for more imaginative use of tools, techniques and interventions that resonate with the aspirations and potential of those we work with.

Key points for social work practice

- Power can be conceptualized in different ways within social work and it is essential that you are able to interrogate power critically to identify how to use it positively in practice.
- Having a good theoretical knowledge of power can help to deconstruct its enactment and to exert influence that accounts for and works positively with power at both the structural and individual level.
- Using opportunities to be a curious, reflexive and proactive practitioner in a way that revisits social work ethics and values will facilitate more user-centred and authentic practice.

7 Partnership working, ethics and social work practice

Colin Whittington and Margaret Whittington

Introduction

Partnership is a 'virtue' word, potentially loaded with positive meaning. Consider the following: 'The essence of partnership is sharing' and is marked by 'respect for one another' (cited in Taylor et al., 2006: 1). The description conveys not only that partnership is virtuous but also that it is about relationships, another virtue word in contemporary Western social work, where 'the relationship' is presented as 'central to good practice' (Ruch et al., 2010: 244). Although not all relationships are partnerships, all partnerships involve relationships, and the two ideas serve up a compelling combination in social work. Consider also the antonyms of partnership, such as 'antagonism', 'discord' and 'estrangement'. How could social workers and others in care services countenance these alternatives in their work? (Westen, 1985; Walton, 2005).

If these features of partnership tend to make the familiar injunction to 'work in partnership' an inherently persuasive one, the persuasion does not stop there. The idea of partnership has become politicized: an orthodoxy woven into policy and political rhetoric. Partnership has been a component of social policy for over 40 years and, along with the closely related idea of 'collaboration', has grown in the vocabulary of policy-makers since the late 1980s (Whittington, 2003a; Whittington et al., 2009a).

These observations on the semantics and politics of partnership are an important alert to practitioners: while the ideas of partnership and collaboration are well embedded in policy and social work practice and have much to offer, their power as 'virtue' words should not induce unthinking acceptance. We shall return to these issues. For now, we will set out the areas to be considered.

The chapter has four main components:

- an exploration of aspects of partnership and its place in policy and practice agendas, together with examples of evidence on partnership working;
- a consideration of ethics and values in social work and the location of partnership ideas within them;
- a discussion of practice scenarios, explored through the narrative of a single 'case', in which we identify particular spheres of partnership and collaboration, raise ethical issues relevant to partnership and suggest responses to them; and
- a concluding summary of the chapter's main points and some final issues for reflection and discussion.

Partnership and collaboration

Social workers participate predominantly in two dimensions of partnership: first, partnership in direct work with service users and carers in relation to particular services and support; and second, partnership working among and between teams, professions and organizations, arrangements that are often underpinned by strategic agreements (Whittington et al., 2009b). There is a third dimension of partnership, in which service users and carers cooperate with a social services organization in the development of services (Warren, 2007). However, we shall focus on the first two dimensions.

Working definitions

There have been many attempts to capture the concept of partnership outside of a strictly legal account, but no single definition prevails (Balloch and Taylor, 2001; Douglas, 2008). Our own working definition conceives it as the more formal of *two* key elements of the field of practice known as 'working together'. When a service user and a social worker, who is normally acting on behalf of the worker's employing organization, agree together a plan for services, they embark on a form of *partnership*. Similarly, when two or more agencies establish an agreement to work together – for example, to set up safeguarding arrangements – this, too, represents a partnership (SCIE/PLASED, 2011). In each case, the partnership has to be made to work by those involved. This is where the second element, *collaboration*, comes in. It represents the active, day-to-day form of working together. Collaboration is the combination of knowledge, skills and values that are used to translate commitment to work in partnership into real outcomes (Whittington, 2003b). To define them:

- *Partnership* in social work represents an agreed, cooperative relationship, carrying explicit or implied rights and obligations and possible imbalances of power, which may be formed with service users and carers, and among and between teams, professionals and organizations; partnership is a particular state of relationship.
- *Collaboration* is the active process through which the parties bring about the goals of the partnership; it is partnership in action.

The reference to 'possible imbalances of power' needs comment. Accounts by service users convey two principles, which are transferable to the other partnership relationships described above: first, that relationships are rarely symmetrical and some service users have an acute sense of their relative lack of power in relationships with social workers and other professionals (Beresford et al., 2007; see also Chapter 6 in this book); and second, that even where power is unequal, it is possible to work with commitment on all sides to form a productive partnership (Gosling and Martin, 2012).

The lexicon of partnership and collaboration contains several other terms related to cooperation between professionals (for example, multi-disciplinary and inter-professional collaboration) and between organizations (such as multi-agency, inter-organizational and inter-agency partnership). We shall use terms with the prefix 'inter', which we associate with greater *inter*-action and engagement of the parties than conveyed by the term 'multi', which places the emphasis on plurality.

The discussion above indicates that partnership and collaboration may involve a variety of people and organizations. We have previously used a 'model of practice and collaboration' to help clarify and manage the complexities that arise (Whittington, 2003b; Whittington et al., 2009c). We shall refer in particular to the following spheres represented in the model: the service user and carer sphere and the organizational, inter-agency and inter-professional spheres. (We use the terms 'organization' and 'agency' interchangeably.)

Partnership working: policy and evidence

Earlier, we cautioned against unquestioning acceptance of the idea of partnership. It is important to ask how the idea of partnership has achieved its established place in policy and practice and whether this position is justified. In short, what are the main policy 'drivers' and what is the evidence for and against partnership working? We begin with the policy drivers: they consist, on the one hand, of government attempts to improve service efficiency and effectiveness by getting professionals and agencies working together; and, on the other hand, a growing policy commitment to user-centred services.

Partnership in government policy

Modern care services are complex. They involve many organizations and employ a wide range of staff and professions. This complexity creates a problem – how to limit inefficiencies, fragmentation and the confusion of service users that complexity can create. One possible solution, promoted by successive UK governments from the 1980s, is partnership. The policy case for partnership gained weight from a number of sources, including: the drive to control service costs and improve efficiency; a history of inquiries where failures of coordination were blamed for child or adult deaths; and movements for consumer rights and service user empowerment (Whittington, 2003a). When New Labour came to power in 1997, ideas of partnership and collaboration were no longer new and became central to the Blair government's plans to 'modernize' care services. During the following decade, inclusion of these ideas in social policy and legislation was virtually automatic and gave, among other effects, significant support to those lobbying for the teaching and practice of inter-professional and inter-agency collaboration (Whittington, 2007).

There were important shifts over time, however, as Labour policies that had focused on strategies for coordinating organizations and professionals re-focused on giving people greater choice and control over how their individual service needs were to be met (DH, 2005; Newman et al., 2008). The change was driven in part by service user movements and is summed-up in the idea of 'person-centred support', which includes 'personalization' and 'person-centred planning' (Warren, 2007; DH, 2010; Beresford et al., 2011). Person-centred [...] eople who use services to plan, with necessary support, their [...] he services they need (Dowling et al., 2006). Personalization is [...] mmonly means tailoring support to individual requirements and [...] ference to personal budgets and direct payments (Glasby and Littlechild, 2009; Needham, 2011).

By the arrival of the Conservative–Liberal Democrat Coalition in 2010, the idea of partnership working had become mainstream, commanding fewer headlines in policies. The Coalition's flagship themes included *Open Public Services*, the *Big Society* and the reform of care and support described in the White Paper, *Caring for our Future* (Hurd, 2011; Minister for Government Policy, 2011; DH, 2012). The *Open Public Services* White Paper divided services into three types – commissioned, individual and neighbourhood – to which the five principles of increased choice and personal control, decentralization, delivery through regulated market competition, fair access and public accountability would be applied (Newton, 2011).

Some of these key ideas, such as decentralization and individual and neighbourhood service types, suggest policy continuity with the aim of the *Big Society* for a 'massive transfer of power from Whitehall to local communities' (Hurd, 2011). However, according to critics, this aim foundered in the first two years of government because the *Big Society* ideas remain vague (Williams, 2012) and, ironically, because the government not only cut funding destined for the voluntary and community sector but also failed to establish the partnerships with the sector on which the *Big Society*'s ostensible aims depend (Slocock, 2012).

There is also continuity of *Open Public Services* themes – namely, access, choice, personal control and care markets – in *Caring for our Future*, which invokes the principle of care and support delivered 'in partnership' between a care workforce and individuals, families and communities (DH, 2012: 18). As in the *Big Society*, the community is allocated an important if vaguely specified role. This is seen again in the Care Act, 2014, alongside policies for person-centred services, care markets, prevention and integraton, which are to be facilitated by partnership at all levels (Department of Health, 2014). These flagship policies may be read in two ways: as part of a populist project for freeing individual citizens, promoting independence and releasing the potential of communities and civic participation (HM Government, 2014); or, more critically, as intensification of a neoliberal agenda to reduce the role of the state in services and transfer responsibility to markets, individuals and volunteers, redefining partnership and the interests it serves (S. Hall, 2011b; Beresford, 2012; Bunyan, 2013; see also Chapter 10 in this book).

The partnership injunction plainly remains embedded, inhabiting the plans of successive governments while traversing established policy, law and statutory guidance on services for all groups from children and families to older people. It is reinforced in the procedures that social workers and others are expected to follow, recurring widely in policy-making and implementation (Whittington et al., 2009a; Local Government Group, 2011; DH, 2012; HM Government, 2013). Accordingly, there is a strong imperative to work in partnership and, in the last analysis, potentially serious consequences for service users across the age range, and for practitioners, where joint working fails, especially in safeguarding work (Haringey LSCB, 2009; Scragg and Mantell, 2011). However, to say that the drivers of partnership have been policy-led tells only part of the story. The ideas embodied in policy come from a variety of sources and take root in particular contexts. The important and growing influence of service user and carer movements contributes both support for, and critique of, policies. For example, Beresford (2008) distinguishes the 'liberatory' and the 'managerial' forms of personalization.

Partnership and evidence

An important potential driver of partnership working is the evidence that service users and carers seek a partnership relationship with social workers and want it included in social worker training (Sadd, 2011). There is also evidence to show that service users value a social work approach based on 'partnership, involvement, er equality', seeking interventions that are 'co-produced' by themse (Beresford et al., 2008: 1405). Among practitioners who are cor practice, these expectations represent an implied ethical obligati

Service users and carers also want social workers to engage in effective inter-professional and inter-agency collaboration (IPIAC) with others who provide services, and to seek better integration of services (Beresford and Andrews, 2012). Professionals and agencies in complex modern services are interdependent in achieving care objectives, and research shows the advantages reported by service users and carers when IPIAC is done well, and the problems when it is not (Whittington et al., 2009d; Harris and Allen, 2011).

In safeguarding practice, failure by agencies and professionals to share information and communicate effectively is reported time and again in public inquiry reports where death has occurred. Effective information-sharing requires more than a partnership protocol and procedures. An active, *collaborative* process is needed if the meanings and understandings of those involved are to be attuned, as shown in child safeguarding (Broadhurst et al., 2010). Similar principles apply in adult safeguarding, where staff report many advantages of effective inter-agency partnership, such as consensual decision-making (Perkins et al., 2007). Research on multi-agency practice in services for families with disabled children has also found significant positive effects, particularly in providing focused support in managing the children's complex health care needs (Abbott et al., 2005).

There are downsides in the evidence, too. Most studies of inter-agency partnership record disadvantages, such as that joint working can take time, which may be in short supply, and may need considerable effort (Whittington et al., 2009d). Obstacles to effective partnership between agencies and professionals, which can impact service users, include: poor organization; conflict between professional models of practice; unequal professional power; clash of agency cultures that prioritize, respectively, care and control; and ethical incompatibility in relation to the sharing of information (Abbott et al., 2005; Lymbery, 2006; Perkins et al., 2007; Williams, 2009; Heath, 2010; Harris and Allen, 2011). Even where these obstacles are overcome, it should not be assumed that collaboration and partnership are uniformly beneficial to service users. For example, access to services may be improved by bringing social care and health into closer partnership, but if biomedical models and professionally led care cultures should predominate, valued *social* and *empowerment* models of care, health and disability may be diluted or lost (Johnson et al., 2003; Oliver, 2009). Furthermore, differences between agencies or professionals might represent useful alternative care strategies for service users or even signify that a misjudgement is being made by one of the parties about need or risk; it is essential that the goal of maintaining a harmonious partnership should not submerge such differences (Whittington, 2003a).

In addition to the evidence of downsides, there are warnings about the methodological difficulties in attributing improved outcomes to partnership arrangements (Freeman and Peck, 2006). Nevertheless, the formal policy imperatives to work in partnership remain strong, both at the inter-organizational level, between services, and at the inter-personal level, between service users and professionals. The demand for partnership working also remains strong both from service users/carers and social workers. However, as public expenditure cuts deepen, interpretations of person-centred support may narrow further, reducing personalization to financial transactions and classing social work in adult social care as an optional extra, with damaging consequences for service users (Commons Health Select Committee, 2012; TCSW, 2012a). In this event, some formal ethical codes would require social workers and their representatives to mount a challenge to the policies in question (TOPSS England, 2004; BASW, 2012). We turn now directly to ethics and values.

Discussion point

The foregoing section began by stating that it is important to ask how the idea of partnership has achieved its established place in policy and practice and whether this position is justified. Weighing the arguments presented, and your own experience, do you think that agencies and professionals, including social workers, should continue to be expected to work in partnership with one another and with service users and carers?

Professional values and ethics

Professional *values* enunciate beliefs about morally good or bad conduct (Clark, 2000), for example in stating that social work is committed to human rights and the promotion of social justice (BASW, 2012). Professional *ethics* in social work are typically expressed in professional and regulatory codes and provide both guides to expected conduct and standards of accountability. Professional ethics are the active form of professional values. The expectations and standards of professional codes address, in particular, the relationship between the practitioner and service users and carers. However, examination of social work ethical codes and the values that shape them show that other relationships are implicated too, such as the relationship with the social worker's employing organization, and of the social worker with other professionals and organizations (Whittington and Whittington, 2007).

Ethical codes and statements

From early in the twenty-first century, there were three primary statements of values and ethics directed to UK social work. One was issued in 2002 by the four national councils for social care and social services in the UK as Codes of Practice, using a common template (GSCC, 2010). Pre-dating this by over 25 years, and periodically revised, is the British Association of Social Workers' code (BASW, 2012). The third statement was embodied in national occupational standards (NOS) for social work (TOPSS England, 2004).

Early in the second decade, a new *Professional Capabilities Framework* (PCF), which includes 'Values and Ethics', was formulated for social work in England (TCSW, 2012b). The framework has a distinctive provenance. In the aftermath of the death of baby Peter Connolly, the Labour government set up the Social Work Task Force to produce comprehensive recommendations for front-line social work in children's and adults' services in England (Haringey LSCB, 2009). In January 2010, the Social Work Reform Board was established to lead the national reform programme, developing the PCF, which was introduced from 2012 by the new College of Social Work (TCSW). From August 2012, responsibility for regulation of social work in England transferred from the General Social Care Council (GSCC) to the Health and Care Professions Council (HCPC). At the same time, the cross-national Codes of Practice and newly revised NOS for social work (CCW, 2011) ceased to apply to social workers in England but continued in Wales, Scotland and Northern Ireland; and the HCPC Standards of Proficiency (HCPC, 2012a) and Standards of Conduct, Performance and Ethics (HCPC, 2012b) became standards for social work in England. These standards set out, respectively, the expectations for safe and effective practice required to enter and remain on the professional register, and the conduct required of registrants, while the more comprehensive and tiered standards of the PCF state expectations at different levels of experience and achievement. Later, a separate Code of Ethics for membership of the College of Social Work was published, incorporating elements of the original cross-national Code of Practice template (TCSW, 2013).

In addition to the codes and statements referred to above, other expressions of values exert an influence on social work practice. Among them, notably, is 'person-centred support', which is promoted in particular by service user groups and is included in a description of the values component of the PCF (Challis, 2011). A national project on person-centred support consulted a wide range of service users and social care services, and found that person-centred support was, for most people, primarily a 'values-based' concept (Beresford et al., 2011: 48). Person-centred support was viewed as a way of working based on values of inclusion, respect, independence and choice, rather than a set of techniques. Beyond the UK, the International Federation of Social Work (IFSW) and International Association of Schools of Social Work (IASSW) also seek jointly to exert an influence through consultation and development of their definition of social work and the statement that 'it is the responsibility of social workers across the world to defend, enrich and realize the values and principles reflected in this definition' (IFSW, 2013).

Streams of values

We will not analyse partnership in terms of broad schools of ethical thought (Banks, 2012) but will focus instead on the main streams of values in social work and on the UK ethical codes. Analysis of the professional values and ethics expressed in the codes and statements cited above, including person-centred support, suggests that they embody aspects of the following 'streams' of social work values (Whittington and Whittington, 2007):

- a 'traditional stream', grounded in beliefs about serving and protecting our fellow human beings and the intrinsic worth of every individual, as articulated originally in the Judaeo-Christian discourse that so strongly influenced the development of professional social work in Europe and the USA – its chief principles include respect, individualization, acceptance, self-determination and being non-judgemental;
- an 'emancipatory stream', founded in reformism, rights-based approaches and socio-political critique and articulated in commitment to empowerment, anti-oppressive practice, alliance with service users and accountability to them;
- a 'governance stream', originating in a compound of 'new managerialism', outcome-quality audit and consumerism, which is manifested in the values of organizational accountability, service effectiveness, consumer participation, risk management and formal partnership.

The three streams converge in the idea of partnership, in a confluence of respect for people, self-determination, anti-oppressive principles, user empowerment, and goals of service effectiveness and consumer participation.

Discussion points

1 Social workers in different countries are bound by the ethical expectations and codes of different regulatory and professional organizations.
2 Which particular organizations and codes set the ethical standards that must govern and guide your own practice?
3 What examples of traditional, emancipatory and governance values are you able to identify among them?

Partnership in social work: values, ethics and collaborative practice

The exhortations in social policies to work in partnership and the representations of service users are highly compatible with methods of social work that employ ideas related to partnership, such as the relationship, participation, contracts and working agreements (Healy, 2005; IFSW, 2013). These ideas resonate positively with the traditionally rooted social work value of self-determination, the emancipatory commitment to empowerment, the governance values of accountability and partnership, and the methods of client-centred and person-centred practice built, for example, on the work of Karl Rogers (Rowe, 2011). Accordingly, there are direct expectations of partnership working in the BASW code and, arguably, implicit expectations in the four UK national codes, although it is noticeable that only partnership with other professionals is *explicit*, even in the most recent variant (TCSW, 2013). However, national bodies supplement their codes with clear expectations of partnership with people using services, as in the Care Council for Wales' 'citizen-centred' social work (CCW, 2014). Similarly, the expectation is endorsed in the TCSW *Professional Capabilities Framework* (PCF), where two 'domains' require, respectively, partnership with service users and carers and inter-professional and inter-agency collaboration. Again, the expectation is stated in the HCPC proficiency standards, is present in the revised NOS for social work and some person-centred approaches, and is central in person-centred planning (DH, 2001a, 2001b). The BASW's principles of ethical practice see partnership working as key in the development of professional relationships. Social workers, the code says, 'should work in partnership with individuals, families, groups, communities and other agencies' (BASW, 2012: 12). This and similar injunctions related to partnership are disseminated across the codes, standards and framework cited, which we have analysed. The result is collected in the list below, which summarizes their main, partnership-related ethical expectations:

Partnership-related ethical expectations:

- engage in partnership work with service users and carers, eliciting and respecting their needs and views and, wherever possible, ensuring their informed consent and participation in decision-making;
- recognize the effect of one's professional and organizational power on the partnership with service users and carers;
- protect privacy, promote trust and use in a competent and ethical way confidential information shared across agencies and professions;
- be able to justify, explain and act appropriately when the right to privacy is overridden by professional, organizational or legal requirements or accountability;
- inform one's own understanding and practice through partnership work with service users, carers and professionals;
- understand, value and respect the contribution and expertise of colleagues from other professions and agencies, working with them cooperatively and challenging them if necessary;
- inform service users of other services and work with other professionals to improve services;
- do not discriminate and challenge unjustifiable discrimination by others;
- understand and manage the limitations of partnership as well as the benefits.

How to demonstrate partnership-related values and translate them into collaborative practice

Although social work ethical codes refer to a number of partnership-related expectations as described, the codes do not aim to provide a detailed, ethics-based agenda specifically for partnership working with service users and carers. Therefore, as a prelude to our case scenarios section, we draw on the codes together with service user accounts and social work theories, to outline below how partnership-related values are demonstrated and may be translated into collaborative practice (Healy, 2005; Beresford et al., 2007, 2011; Doel and Best, 2008; Clifford and Burke, 2009; Whittington et al., 2009b; Gosling and Martin, 2012):

- Listen in a way that acknowledges and reflects the person as a whole and not only as a service user or carer.
- Build a relationship of confidence and trust through, for example:
  - acknowledging and discussing confidentiality and information-sharing;
  - demonstrating the knowledge and skills necessary to access resources and information;
  - being reliable; and
  - focusing on each individual's capacity and abilities and recognizing where these can be used and strengthened.
- Identify where support is needed in order to maximize independence and to manage risk
- Recognize that there are inequalities and differences in power and control in partnership relationships between service users and social workers and discuss these openly.
- Work in an enabling and empowering way with a flexibility that:
  - maximizes control and choice for the service user;
  - accepts that the social worker or others may need to provide extra support at times of crisis or particular difficulty.
- Communicate effectively and honestly with service users and carers and with other professionals and organizations in order to build positive, trusting partnerships and ongoing collaborative relationships.
- Understand that service users and carers may have needs or interests in common but that this must be verified not assumed.
- Ensure that practice is based on anti-oppressive and anti-discriminatory principles and that unjust policies or practice and discrimination are challenged in collaborative work with others.
- Appreciate that differences of professional perspectives are both essential assets and potential challenges; sometimes, inter-professional disagreement is unavoidable and social workers must be able to manage it.
- Understand that partnership with service users and carers and other agencies and professionals is not an end in itself, to be preserved at all costs, but a valued means.

Case study 7.1

The following case, which is informed by a strengths-based, person-centred approach, illustrates some of the ethical issues that can occur in partnership working and collaborative practice. It focuses, in stages, on the following spheres of practice and collaboration: the service user–social worker sphere; the social worker–organization sphere; and the inter-professional sphere. Issues will be raised for you to consider and responses suggested. The case is illustrative; actual local service arrangements may vary.

Scenario 1: Service user–social worker sphere
Mrs H is a 74-year-old 'white British' woman who is severely disabled as a result of a stroke 8 years ago. She is a wheelchair-user living in her own home, which has been adapted for her needs. She is a retired teacher and is active in her local community as a school governor and a charity committee member. Mrs H's husband, who was her full-time carer, died suddenly a month ago. As a temporary emergency arrangement, Mrs H's son, John,

came to stay but he has a demanding job and a young family and needs to return to his own home, which is a four-hour drive away. The son was alarmed to find the full extent of his mother's physical needs and realizes that his father may have been struggling to care for her. He has persuaded Mrs H to ask the local authority Adult Social Services for a full assessment of her needs and is wondering whether his mother will need to move into residential care. However, Mrs H wishes to remain at home. She wants to have as much control as possible over her care and support and to maintain her involvement in the community.

The social worker assesses Mrs H's needs by listening to her explain her day-to-day routine and clarifying the tasks and activities with which she needs support. The assessment emphasizes what Mrs H is able to do, with and without assistance. Account is taken of her bereavement, which is still very recent and has left her without her husband's companionship, emotional support and twenty-four-hour physical and practical assistance. Time will be needed to establish a relationship of trust with Mrs H. She has not had recent contact with social services and is apprehensive about the assessment, the quality of services she may receive and the control she will have over how they are provided. She has particular concerns about confidentiality and the sharing of information by the social worker with the other professionals and agencies who may need to be involved.

The beginning of a partnership between Mrs H and the social worker is signified through their agreement on a care plan, which includes:

- *Mrs H's eligible needs, using Fair Access to Care criteria (SCIE, 2013);*
- *goals of the care plan, which include enabling Mrs H to retain as much autonomy and independence as possible while ensuring her safety and well-being;*
- *how Mrs H would like her needs to be met, initially, through care from a local domiciliary care provider, so that her son can return home and, in the longer term, using a 'direct payment' to employ a personal assistant;*
- *identified risks and how they will be managed;*
- *Mrs H's expectations of the social worker and their respective commitment to work in partnership;*
- *Mrs H's access to support from family and friends;*
- *other assistance received by Mrs H, such as from NHS community health services, that may have implications for the care plan.*

The social worker obtains departmental management approval for the care plan and for the direct payment within a personal budget for Mrs H (SCIE, 2013). For the care plan to progress, information about Mrs H needs to be shared and discussed by a number of people. The social worker has to refer Mrs H to the local voluntary 'brokerage' organization, which is funded by social services, to set up the temporary care service and arrange subsequent recruitment of a personal assistant. She also wishes to establish Mrs H's health needs, which means communication with the GP and with the community nurse, who already visits regularly. In addition, the social worker suggests that the occupational therapist be asked to reassess Mrs H's needs for aids and equipment now that she is living alone. However, Mrs H is very reluctant for these contacts to be made and for her details to be discussed. This presents a dilemma for the social worker.

Reflection point

If you were to take up the narrative, how might you describe the dilemma being resolved? The aim would be to maintain the partnership commitment on both sides and respect Mrs H's wish for privacy, while allowing the social worker to work in partnership with other professionals and agencies whose knowledge and resources may be critical to supporting Mrs H successfully.

Suggested response to Scenario 1
The social worker understands and respects Mrs H's wishes. They discuss, with advice from the social worker, what information needs to be shared, with whom and why, in setting up Mrs H's care arrangements and ensuring her well-being and safety. They agree that only this key information will be shared. Mrs H consents to the care plan being passed to the voluntary brokerage service. Mrs H decides that to retain some control she will, herself, review her health needs with her GP and tell the social worker. They agree a suggestion that the social worker should arrange to visit her jointly with the community nurse and the occupational therapist so that Mrs H can explain her needs and concerns and be assured that information they share is focused on achieving a coordinated outcome for her.

Scenario 2: Social worker–organization sphere

In the early contacts with Mrs H, the social worker forms the view that a period of ongoing social work support may be necessary. This view is informed by Mrs H's recent bereavement, her apparent level of need, her desire for independence at home, and her son's concern that she may be in need of residential care. However, the social worker has not suggested ongoing support to Mrs H. It is departmental policy that social worker involvement normally ceases once the process from assessment to briefing of the brokerage organization is complete. This policy reflects a management approach to personalization that increasingly emphasizes goals of 'choice and control' and 'self-directed support'. While the social worker agrees this is sufficient in some cases, the approach is narrower than the scope of person-centred support, which is more holistic and takes account of the crisis of significant loss and change Mrs H is facing.

Reflection point

Is the social worker right to question the organization's 'self-directed support' view of 'personalization', which in this case does not allow for the ongoing partnership relationship with the service user in supporting a successful outcome? Take up the narrative and think how the social worker might respond to the conflict between the expectations of her employing authority and her own set of broader professional values.

Suggested response to scenario 2
The social worker decides she has an ethical obligation to raise the issues with her supervisor, rather than simply accepting the standard procedure, and puts forward her case for offering a period of ongoing support to Mrs H. The social worker knows that this has been an issue in some other cases and has been debated in the department and at national level (TCSW, 2012a). She has researched her arguments for continuity of support of older people, particularly after major life events, and the central place in this of the relationship with the social worker (SCIE, 2011). She is later given the go-ahead for a period of up to three months' contact, to be reviewed monthly in supervision.

Scenario 3: Service user–social worker sphere, continued

Mrs H responds positively to the social worker's suggested period of ongoing support and they agree a partnership plan, identifying a number of areas for collaboration in which the aims are to:

- *assist Mrs H to access information on local services herself, so that she feels less dependent on the social worker's knowledge; specifically, she will seek specialist transport in order to retain her community involvement;*

- *arrange a joint social worker–occupational therapist–community nurse visit to assess together and, where possible, resolve concerns about risks to Mrs H as she adapts to living alone;*
- *help with Mrs H's feelings of vulnerability and loss as she accepts 'strangers' into her home and experiences an increased sense of dependency;*
- *monitor the care arrangements closely, as it was apparent during the assessment that Mrs H has a number of health problems, which may alter or increase her care needs, and meet with Mrs H and her son John together, as his understandable concerns about her ability to manage at home need to be fully addressed and discussed.*

Reflection point

The partnership plan between Mrs H and the social worker identifies several important objectives. Bearing in mind Mrs H's circumstances and the time-limit on the period for ongoing support, what factors should the social worker be including in her thinking about how best to facilitate the objectives?

Suggested response to Scenario 3

The social worker recognizes that the three months allowed her will pass rapidly and that the plan therefore needs to be timetabled and well organized, in agreement with Mrs H and others involved. The plan takes account of the strengths that each of the key parties brings to the situation but the worker's thinking also allows for the factors that may affect the time and energy people have for participation. Mrs H brings her knowledge, experience and a motivating desire for independence but her health problems and the effects of her very recent bereavement may affect her participation and the pace of progress. The time-table also has to accommodate the social worker's other work commitments. These various factors will be important features of the regular discussions with the supervisor and may necessitate a revised timetable and adjustment of objectives, possibly to include referral for bereavement counselling. A referral is not an explicit aspect of the partnership plan and people's wish for counselling varies, but the social worker has details of the local specialist service should Mrs H want it.

Scenario 4: Inter-professional sphere

Following Mrs H's discussion with her GP, the GP contacts the social worker to say that, without her husband's help, he doubts it will be physically safe for Mrs H to remain at home. The GP believes that her aim to manage with support is probably unrealistic, especially as her health needs are increasing. He and the community nurse have been contacted by Mrs H's son John and have confirmed John's impression that the situation was precarious before Mr H's death. The GP says the couple were unwilling to have outside help and had not wanted John to feel pressure to assist them. John subsequently contacts the social worker and says that, as both GP and community nurse doubt his mother should remain at home, the social worker should not support Mrs H's plan.

Reflection points

1 How do you think the social worker might respond to this pressure to change the empowering, rights-based approach of her partnership with Mrs H?
2 How can the social worker reconcile her support for Mrs H's autonomy and choice with the concerns both of the son and of the professionals who know Mrs H and whose opinions carry considerable weight?

3 The social worker is committed to supporting Mrs H's wishes, if possible, but also wants Mrs H to retain John's ongoing support and to maintain her own positive inter-professional relationship with the GP and community nurse. Is it feasible to achieve all these aims? How might the story continue?

Suggested response to Scenario 4
The social worker discusses the issues with her supervisor. Their view is informed as follows. First, the social worker is responsible for supporting a service user who, despite being in a vulnerable position, is assumed to have capacity and wishes to retain as much control as possible over her own life (DCA, 2007). Second, they think it important to balance the influence of medical, risk-focused presumptions about older people with disabilities with a 'social model' of disability, which, while recognizing health issues, also seeks to reduce disabling barriers to a 'normal' life (Oliver, 2009). Third, they agree that during the initial period after her bereavement, Mrs H should not feel pressured into making major life-changing decisions.

With Mrs H's agreement, the social worker telephones the GP and son John, respectively. She listens, acknowledges the risks and explains her own position. Eventually, after some tense exchanges, they all agree to wait until the joint risk assessment meeting of the occupational therapist, community nurse and social worker with Mrs H has taken place. In the event, despite the earlier misgivings of the community nurse, the meeting comes up with a plan to minimize and manage risks to Mrs H, which all four present think should enable her to cope at home, provided her health does not deteriorate dramatically. It is agreed that the situation will be kept under careful review and, with this clear proviso, the son and GP agree to support the plan.

Chapter summary

- This chapter has addressed partnership working in two main dimensions:
  - partnership in direct work with service users and carers in relation to particular services and support;
  - partnership working among and between teams, professions and organizations.
- 'Partnership', which is defined as 'a particular state of relationship', is the more formal of two key elements of 'working together'. The second element is 'collaboration', which is the 'active process of partnership in action'.
- Partnership and collaboration are deeply embedded in social policy and are expected of social work practitioners; research evidence shows they have much to offer but also involve recognized obstacles and limitations.
- The important and growing influence of service user and carer movements has been an important, constructively critical force in the promotion of person-centred and partnership values in policy and practice.
- There are three streams of values and ethics in UK social work – traditional, emancipatory and governance – and each is identifiable in official ethical codes.
- The three streams converge in the idea of partnership, in a confluence of respect for people, self-determination, user empowerment, anti-oppressive principles, and goals of service effectiveness and consumer participation.
- The injunction to work in partnership is stated or implied in official codes, standards, guidance and statements of professional values and ethics in UK social work.
- Social work ethical codes do not set out a specific, ethics-based agenda for partnership working with service users and carers, so we use an outline, together with examples from a single case, to illustrate how partnership-related values are demonstrated and may be translated into collaborative practice.

Discussion points

No single and realistic 'case' is likely to be able to illustrate and explore all aspects of partnership working and its ethical dimensions. Reflecting on the 'case', the discussion that preceded it and your own experience, consider which aspects of partnership and collaboration are not illustrated by the case scenarios? Think about the inter-agency and carer 'spheres of practice', other service user groups and the limits of partnership with service users. Some suggested responses are given below. You may think of others.

Suggested responses

A wider discussion of the different services that may support Mrs H would explore arrangements for partnership and collaboration between the agencies involved. Social work ethical codes and practice guidance attach the same importance to partnership between agencies (the 'inter-agency sphere') as to inter-professional working (Morris, 2008; Whittington et al., 2009e). Turning to the 'carer sphere', Mrs H's late husband had been her full-time carer. Her son, John, is an important source of support but neither of them views him as her carer. Other scenarios might have explored the definition of carers and their legal and ethical rights to their own assessment and support and, in some cases, entitlement to financial allowance (Carers Trust, 2013). Carers are frequently an essential element of the partnerships formed with the service users (Lee, 2009; Warren, 2007).

Key points for social work practice

- These scenarios focus on partnership-related values and ethics in relation to work with an older, white British woman who has become disabled following a stroke and is recently bereaved. However, partnership and collaboration are applicable to a wide range of service users and we might equally have chosen scenarios involving them to illustrate practice and ethical questions. Some examples are given below together with relevant sources:
  - children, young people and families (Warren, 2007; Ferguson, 2011)
  - mental health service users (Weinstein, 2009)
  - people with learning disabilities (Thompson et al., 2007)
  - black and minority ethnic service users (Graham, 2007b)
- Finally, we might have chosen scenarios that looked more closely at the *limits as well as the possibilities of partnership*. It cannot be assumed that partnership with service users based on person-centred and strengths-based approaches, and developed in services for adults who have capacity, transfers appropriately to other practice situations. Particular care is needed where a person lacks capacity or where there are serious safeguarding concerns or other high risks. Nevertheless, there is an ethical expectation that social workers should always consider the scope for appropriate participation and inclusion (May and Edwards, 2009; Slettebø, 2011).
- The capacity to foster effective partnership while judging where its limits lie is one of the *key ethical challenges of professional social work* and one of its defining skills.

8 | Diversity and difference

Tom Wilks

That diversity has a central place within social work practice is a universally acknowledged truth in professional codes and underlying principles of practice. Both the International Federation of Social Workers and the British Association of Social Workers Codes of Practice (BASW, 2012: 9) stress that 'social workers should recognize and respect the ethnic and cultural diversity of the societies in which they practice, taking account of individual, family, group and community differences' (IFSW/IASSW, 2004: 4.2 Social Justice). Similarly, the US National Association of Social Workers Code of Ethics (NASW, 2008) argues that in pursuing the aims of social justice, social work activities should 'seek to promote sensitivity to and knowledge about oppression and cultural and ethnic diversity'. Dominelli, outlining the principles that she sees as fundamental to social work practice, recognizes the importance of 'acknowledging differences, including those applying to oneself, and celebrating diversity within a human-rights and citizenship based egalitarian framework' (Dominelli 2004: 252).

Achieving these undoubtedly worthy goals for the profession as a whole is not, however, always straightforward in practice. As Dominelli points out elsewhere in the same book, 'not valuing the complexities of diversity is a failing of both social work practitioners and educators' (Dominelli, 2004: 78). This concern with diversity manifests itself in two different ways: first, it is reflected in the broader goals of social work as a professional activity (in the headline statements of ethical codes of practice, for example), at a macro level; second, in the specific roles and tasks undertaken by social workers at a micro level. This distinction between macro and micro issues when thinking about social work values is very much akin to the restricted/extended descriptions of social work values developed by Shardlow. The 'restricted description' focuses on the interaction between social workers and their clients, the 'extended description' on the values that underlie social work's role within society (Shardlow, 2009). The question of how diversity should be addressed by the profession as a whole (and by organizations providing social work services), as a macro-level consideration, and how individual social workers should respond when faced with dilemmas concerning diversity, as a micro-level consideration, are clearly interrelated.

At first sight, the concepts of difference and diversity can appear to stand apart from the study of conventional social work ethics with its roots in moral philosophy, as stated in Chapter 2. They can seem like a parallel part of the world of social work values, where the primary preoccupation is with anti-discriminatory and oppressive practice. However, I think that difference and diversity ought to be central concerns of more conventional ethics and they are arguably crucial in any consideration of both self-determination and respect for persons (at a micro level) and social justice (at a macro level).

The issue of how to work with diversity and difference can generate practice dilemmas at both these levels. At a macro level, important sources of such dilemmas are questions of how far social work should go in its commitment to supporting both diversity and social change. The issue of separate services for specific groups or inclusive services for all can also raise important challenges to social work values. At a micro level, dilemmas can often revolve around what respect for difference means in practice.

I want to begin by looking at some of the debates about diversity and difference that can exist at a macro level. A good starting point for this is a case study.

Case study 8.1

The Park Street Project is a small voluntary agency that runs a drop-in centre for people with mental health problems. The project was set up by a local GP who was concerned about the lack of such support in an area of the city poorly served by public transport, and where access to conventional day care services provided by the NHS Trust and local authority was consequently problematic. The project is supported by fund raising and grants from the NHS, local authority and a local charitable trust.

At a meeting of the project's management committee, a proposal is put forward to use the project's minibus to take a group of project members to a protest against the introduction of capability assessments for those claiming Incapacity Benefit, organized by the Mental Health Resistance Network. The service users on the committee are all in favour of this proposal, as benefits are a major concern of the people who use the centre. However, other members of the committee, including the local vicar, carers' representatives, a GP and representative of the local authority, all express a number of concerns about this, arguing that the centre should not be seen to support political causes and that the funding received from the local authority and the NHS is for providing social care. Jessica, the social worker who is employed by the project to coordinate its activities, argues that the trip is consistent with the project's equal opportunities policy, which aims to combat the discrimination faced by people with mental health problems; she feels that the proposed protest is a crucial way of highlighting a key area of discrimination. The members of the committee opposed to the trip argue that the centre is committed to not discriminating in the services it provides, but that its commitment to this aspect of equal opportunities should not extend beyond the centre itself.

Reflection point

This debate and the dilemmas underlying it are interesting because they illustrate the key questions that can arise when we consider what a commitment to diversity means for social work. Does addressing diversity equate with a commitment to the pursuit of social change, and the promotion of a fairer society, or is it about ensuring equal opportunity within the service that agencies provide? (Johns and Jordan, 2006).

These questions about the nature of social work have been present throughout its history, whether in the contrasts between radical practice and psychodynamic casework (Ferguson and Woodward, 2009), or in the subsequent debates about anti-discriminatory and anti-oppressive practice (Dominelli, 2002b, 2009). The key question here is how far social work ought to be involved in 'transformational social change that alters the balance of power' (Dominelli, 2004: 24) and 'the elimination of structural inequalities' (Dominelli, 2009: 53). Shardlow (2009: 46) argues that 'a highly regulated and performance managed world leaves little room for these debates, which were until relatively recently, the fire in the belly of social work'. However, despite this rather pessimistic prognosis, it is perhaps in relation to difference and diversity that social workers can find the most common ground and where the pursuit of wider goals of social justice is most appropriate.

Discussion point

How far do you think social workers should seek to change society in order to lessen the impacts of discrimination?

In the example of the Park Street Project, the key question is whether engagement with campaigns that aim to secure greater social justice is consistent with the professional goals of social work. A second important question at a macro level is how far services can address the needs of everyone successfully and how far it is appropriate to provide services that only address the needs of specific groups. The following case example is a good illustration of the dilemmas that can arise in this area.

Case study 8.2

A local authority is facing a substantial reduction in its budget and consequently has to explore where funding for services in the voluntary sector could be cut. The authority currently funds a range of provision for older people, including a generic advocacy service, a series of lunch clubs and the Black Elderly Lunch Club and Advocacy Service (BELCAS), a project for African-Caribbean elders, which combines a lunch club with an advice and information service. This combination of services has proved very successful and encouraged older African-Caribbean people to access advocacy. However, austerity is forcing the council into tough decisions. This presents a dilemma around the future of service provision in this area. Two options are being considered. The first is to close BELCAS and use some of the money saved to increase the diversity of food provided within the lunch club service and provide a black outreach worker in the generic advocacy service. The second is to keep BELCAS and institute cuts to lunch clubs and older people's generic advocacy.

Reflection point

What issues does this dilemma raise about the provision of separate services for certain groups?

The argument about whether separate services should be sustained is an interesting one. When reductions are made to advocacy services, those directed towards black and minority ethnic (BME) communities are often most at risk (Rai-Atkins et al., 2002). Thompson (2011) argues that what he terms 'separatism' (the provision of services that address the specific needs of marginalized groups) is justified as a means to the end of eventual equality for all, but not as an end in itself. I am not sure this distinction between means and ends necessarily serves us very well when exploring the sorts of dilemma presented here. In generic services, 'the tendency of dominant groups to reproduce patterns of domination in and through their social interaction' (Thompson, 2011: 178) is always present, and without enormous social change the need for specific services to address particular needs will not disappear. Chahal's (2004) review of research in this area suggests that mainstream services can fail BME communities. There is also an argument that specific services in social care do more than reflect or acknowledge diversity, but they can also provide a tangible celebration of its value.

Discussion point

Consider some of the social care services with which you are familiar. Now think about how these services can work towards celebrating diversity?

Fook (2002) uses the term 'dilemma of difference', originally coined by Minow (1985), when looking at this area. Fook argues that there is a risk that 'in the very act of defining disadvantage, in order to empower we in fact create disadvantage and thus disempower' (Fook, 2002: 52), and that 'by naming difference we also create the possibility of discrimination' (p. 82). Fook argues that more complex and nuanced postmodern understandings of identity in social work are needed, in which she places great emphasis on the idea of narrative; by taking us beyond simple categories of difference we can begin to resolve these dilemmas. The complex nature of identity is a common source of value conflicts in practice at the micro level, as illustrated by the following example.

Case study 8.3

Ayla is a 15-year-old young woman from a Turkish family. Over a number of years Ayla's mother Sara has struggled with problems with drug use and become estranged from her wider family. This estrangement began when, contrary to her parents' wishes (and unlike her two older sisters), Sara went to university when she left school instead of working in the family restaurant business run by her brothers. Ayla is currently doing her GCSEs focusing on science subjects and her eventual aim is to become an environmental scientist. Ayla has been supported by a school-based counsellor, with whom she has a strong relationship. Over the past six months, Ayla has been living with her aunt Pinar (Sarah's sister), after Sara went into rehab because of her drug problems. Unfortunately, Sara left rehab after only a couple of weeks and since then has returned to drug use. At a planning meeting to discuss Ayla's future she reveals that she now intends to leave school and work as a waitress in the family business, rather than pursue her previous career plans. Her social worker and school counsellor both express some concerns about this. However, Pinar points out that Ayla's mother moved away from her culture, changed her name from Zehra to Sara, and despite going to university got involved with drugs and an unsuccessful relationship. Surely, she argues, it is right that we should respect Ayla's decision to become more involved with her family and cultural background.

Reflection point

What competing issues are at play in this scenario? As Ayla's social worker, how might you respond to this situation?

The dilemma for practitioners here is how far it is appropriate to respect a decision that is (arguably) consistent with a set of cultural norms or try to encourage women's emancipation, for example through education. These decisions are complex and not easily resolved. As Parrott (2010: 27) points out, 'valuing difference is a...complex process that requires social workers to be open to understanding different conceptions of the "good life"'. Ayla's identity is multi-faceted. She is a young woman and we need in our social work practice to be aware how she might face discrimination because of this, but she also comes from a particular cultural background and social work practice needs also to respect this aspect of her identity. As social workers, in order to fully understand such dilemmas around difference, it is important to appreciate and understand the nature and impact of our own identities, as we saw in Chapter 4. The next case study begins to look at this aspect.

Case study 8.4

Patience Smith is a black woman in her fifties born and brought up in St Lucia, but who came to the UK in her twenties. She runs a supportive lodging/housing scheme for young people with learning difficulties. Patience has been running the scheme for a number of years and has had great success in supporting people within the scheme, and there has/ have generally been very positive outcomes particularly where fostering independence is concerned. The young people have their own bedrooms, but share a kitchen and bathrooms. They take responsibility for cooking and cleaning on a rota basis and Patience arranges regular house meetings. She also encourages residents to get involved in the community in a whole range of activities.

However, a complaint about the service she provides has recently been received by social services. Patience is a Christian and attends a local Pentecostal church. The parents of one young man, Paul, who has been staying in Patience's supportive housing project have contacted social services to complain that Patience has been encouraging residents to attend her church and after initially not wanting to go, their son has now started going to church meetings a couple of times a week. They feel that Paul has not really made a free choice to do this but has been pressurized by Patience to attend. Their view is that the people who live in the house should be offered practical and emotional support and not religion.

When Patience first heard about the complaint she contacted the Community Team for People with Learning Disabilities, with whom she has a lot of links, and there has been much discussion within the team about it since. Everyone acknowledges the high standards of care Patience provides and how she has identified a wide range of supports for residents and encouraged them to become involved in the community. However, some team members are sympathetic to Patience: they argue that normalization means engaging with these aspects of the wider community and that religion is an important part of everybody's life. Other team members have sympathy for the case made by Paul's parents.

One thing that emerges from the discussion is that individual team members' perceptions of Patience are shaped by their own cultural backgrounds and attitudes to religion. In all these debates about respecting difference, who we are shapes our responses to the situations that we come across and which challenge us. Thus, to work effectively with difference we need to think about this and position ourselves.

Reflection points

- Where do you stand in relation to this case?
- How should we encourage service users to be involved in the community?
- Do your own views on religion impact upon your view?

In our discussions of some of the dilemmas issues of diversity can throw up, we can see how complex 'identity' can be and how in applying social work's professional value base we can struggle to address the challenges that arise because of this. One resource we have available professionally that can help us with these issues is the exercise of empathy, which requires 'a deep understanding of the other person's world and attitudes' (Parrott, 2010: 29). An important concept that develops this idea of empathy further and has been invoked in the context of working with difference is the idea of 'commonality' (White, 1995). Commonality describes the idea of a shared core of experience between social worker and service user, and when we recognize we have things in common we can use this to empathize and understand. This idea of the interconnectedness of social worker and service user has been a powerful feature of feminist social work (Hanmer and Statham, 1999; Dominelli, 2002a), which as always has sought to break down some of the barriers that exist between social worker and service user, and seen the shared gender identity and experience of oppression as one conduit through which this can be achieved.

White (1995) argues that although commonality is a crucial part of how we relate to others and of the feminist social worker/woman service user dyad, the actual experiences of feminist practitioners themselves suggest that this relationship is more complex and nuanced than might first appear. White's conclusions are based on a small-scale qualitative study of feminist social workers' experience of work with women service users. What emerges from the study is the fact that the social workers involved struggled at times to create a connection through gender and commonality with service users, which 'extended beyond the experience of intermittent empathetic feelings' (White, 1995: 154) and that gender was 'not always the primary social division acting oppressively on women service users' lives' (ibid.). The constraints of the statutory context of practice and the power imbalance this introduced into relationships tended to overshadow ideas of 'commonality'. It is worth exploring this issue through another case study.

Case study 8.5

Tim is a newly qualified social worker starting work in a Community Mental Health Team (CMHT) linked to a particular ward in a local psychiatric unit. This is a mixed ward and within it there has traditionally been a women's group, the purpose of which has been to offer mutual aid and support to women on the ward, support new arrivals and explore issues relating to gender and mental health. Within the rather male-dominated Patient's Council in the hospital there has been a discussion of women-only groups on the ward and the council has raised the issue of whether there should be similar provision for men. In response to this idea, the NHS Trust has contacted each CMHT to determine whether there is any possibility of creating a similar resource for men. Tim and his colleague Sean, a staff nurse on the ward, are both interested in exploring the issues that men face within the mental health system (Phillips, 2001), particularly when in-patients, and are keen to try establishing such a group.

A number of men on the ward are keen to attend the group and a clear set of ground rules and agenda for discussion is established in the first few meetings. However, as the group progresses, what strikes Tim and Sean is not the shared common experiences of the men in relation to the mental health system, but the differences between group participants. In an early meeting, Tim and Sean challenge a comment made by one member of the group about 'seeing a bit of totty from the occupational therapy department'; some group members are supportive of this challenge, others see the remark as light-hearted banter. In subsequent meetings, it becomes clear that group members from middle-class professional backgrounds are keen to emphasize how different they are from other group members, that the younger members of the group are resistant to seeing themselves as sharing common ground with older service users who have been in hospital a number of times, and that the black members of the group experience the mental health system as less benign and more coercive than their white counterparts. Sean and Tim, both young white men, are also struck by the differences between their experiences in life and those of the group.

One of the lessons Tim and Sean learnt from this experience is that identity cannot be distilled down to a single identifying quality – that the 'fixed labels and categories with which people identify' (Fook, 2002: 75) are only part of the story. However, despite the differences present in the group, they also saw value in men meeting together, for despite the intersecting social categories that define the identity of each group participant, within this diverse masculinity there is a common thread that links people together. So while there is great value to be derived from commonality, it has to be treated with caution as a framework for working with diversity.

Okitikpi and Aymer point to one way in which we make sense of these multiple facets of our identity. They argue that 'telling stories is the main way we make sense of things' and that therefore 'narrative is a fundamental form of knowing' (Okitikpi and Aymer, 2010: 145) and this is central to understanding identity. This perspective on narrative and story also lies at the heart of Somers' account of narrative identity (Somers, 1994). She argues that our identity lies in the interplay of the different stories we create about our lives. So our identity is not a fixed concept, but a fluid one. The story that comes to the fore in any given set of circumstances may privilege our race or age or culture over other aspects of our identity. Furthermore, these narratives may change; as we move into older age, narratives of parenthood may alter in their focus, for example, from providing care and support to encouraging autonomy and independence. As we saw in Chapter 4, in relation to the social construction of identities, 'narrative identity embeds the actor within relationships and stories that shift over time and space' (Somers, 1994: 621).

Recently, there has been increasing interest in the potential of narrative to provide an alternative to conventional ethical argument based on principles (whether these are Kantian moral imperatives or the principles of utility). Writers interested in medical ethics and to a more limited extent social work ethics (e.g. Fook, 2002) have explored the potential of narrative to offer a different way of understanding moral problems within professional ethics. With its focus on the complex and nuanced ways in which people's personal narratives help shape their identity(ies), it offers an alternative to conventional ethics, one which explicitly addresses issues of diversity and difference. So narrative can be a useful conceptual tool in understanding the complexity of an individual's diverse social identities (Epston and White, 1990). For social workers, this means practising in ways that are sensitive to service users' narratives. The following case example is a useful way of illustrating how this might work in practice.

Case study 8.6

Magda, a district nurse, has referred Montserrat and Miguel, a couple in their eighties, to social services. Both were born and brought up in Spain and moved to the UK in the 1960s when Miguel found work in the engineering industry. Montserrat and Miguel have two children and several grandchildren, none of whom live particularly close by. Over the past four or five years Miguel has suffered from dementia following a stroke. He is very forgetful and needs constant prompting by his wife to help him to do everyday tasks. The couple receive some limited home care support. Miguel also gets quite angry from time to time and shouts at his wife, sometimes in Spanish.

Magda has become concerned by the strain this is putting on Montserrat and has contacted social services for an assessment of her needs as a carer. Magda reports that the couple tend to speak to each other in Spanish at home and that they can be a little bit resistant to accepting help. James, the social worker undertaking the assessment, decides to find an interpreter. He is not clear how well the couple understand English and feels they might prefer to communicate in Spanish. When he arrives at Montserrat and Miguel's flat, Montserrat reacts angrily to the presence of the interpreter. 'What is she doing here, I am English and I speak English. How do you think I would have coped with my husband all these years if I didn't speak English? We haven't just arrived here you know, my children have been to English university, my grandchildren go to English school'. James's motivation for bringing an interpreter is out of respect for difference and diversity, very much in line with the Kantian principles of respect for people. He wants to ensure that Montserrat and Miguel are able to communicate and he is taken aback by Montserrat's reaction. However, reflecting on how she sees her life, he starts to understand how it is shaped by the narrative of her managing a difficult situation well and remaining as autonomous as possible, and the idea that she might need help to communicate runs contrary to this narrative.

The recognition of narrative in this situation helps broaden our understanding and brings a different (and arguably richer) analysis of the ethical issues at play here. Narrative provides a helpful conceptual framework when trying to understand how individuals see themselves and how different strands of their identity come to the fore in changing sets of circumstances. However, it is important when considering working with diversity to think about the interactive professional context within which social work takes place. To understand diversity and identity in social work requires more than the empathetic responses that we can draw on from our commonalities with service users, and using narrative might bring us to a more complex and contextualized understanding of how the people that we work with shape their own identities in particular contexts. When service user and social worker meet, interact and work together, aspects of the social worker's own identity come to impinge on the situation and impact upon the relationship between service user and professional, which lies at the heart of social work practice. Central to understanding the dynamics of this aspect of the social work role is the concept of reflexivity, which has been increasingly recognized as central to anti-oppressive and critical practice. 'Being reflexive involves a recognition of how we our selves as whole people, influence the situations and contexts in which we interact' (Fook, 2002: 130), 'it is about factoring ourselves as players into the situations we practice in' (Fook and Askeland, 2006: 45). In fact, Clifford and Burke describe it as 'an anti-oppressive practice principle' (Clifford and Burke, 2009: 115)

Essentially, reflexivity encompasses two different but related aspects. As we saw in Chapter 5, a reflective practitioner needs first to be aware of both her or his own identity and also the impacts this identity has on interactions with others. For a social worker, 'identity' can have two aspects to it, a personal and a professional aspect. On a personal level, it means 'locating oneself across unequal social boundaries' (Clifford and Burke, 2009: 39). The dynamics of our interactions and relationships with other people are very much shaped by who we are in this sense, and the extent to which our identity is aligned with dominant or subordinated groups within society. Thus, for example, white middle- or upper-class, young, heterosexual, able-bodied men (characteristics many of which apply to me) carry substantial power merely by virtue of their location within dominant social groups.

These aspects of difference cut across all aspects of how we relate to others, even permeating the language we use. A striking example of this is the differential use of unreciprocated terms of endearment in relation to women and men. Terms such as 'dear' and 'love' are normally used to express intimacy when used reciprocally between individuals, 'but used non-reciprocally they suggest one is talking to an inferior or subordinate' (Holmes, 1995: 146). This form of address is far more likely to be applied to women than men (Holmes, 1995).

We have seen how our social location and personal circumstances impact upon our relationships with service users. Trish Hafford-Letchfield reminds us in Chapter 6 that the extent to which we are powerful in a professional context derives in part from these elements of difference. As we have seen from our earlier discussion of commonality, the service user–social worker dyad is commonly marked by differences in power that derive from the contrasting social locations of service user and social worker. However, it is important to remember in social work that over and above this, the power we bring to our work as social workers resides not just in our personal characteristics but also in this professional role. As Hafford-Letchfield notes, this type of power deriving from occupational role is an example of what Smith (2008) terms positional power (as opposed to personal power, which comes from our social position). As I argued earlier in this chapter, power has a structural dimension that is invested in state agencies. Social workers are often representatives of such agencies, their work undertaken within statutory and procedural frameworks, where the individual practitioner has little room for manoeuvre and where scope for empowering practice may be limited (Ferguson and Woodward, 2009). Smith argues that 'the organizational and structural location of social work practitioners places them in the role of legitimate agents of state power' (Smith, 2008: 52).

The reflexive perspective, an approach to ethics and values that is consistent with working with diversity demands, is very different from the more distinct autonomous position of the ethical decision-maker in conventional ethics. Deontological, consequentialist and virtue ethics are all premised on the idea of what is often termed the autonomous moral subject, an individual looking at ethical problems and dilemmas in a disinterested way and separate from them. In contrast to this view from outside, which characterizes standard ethical thinking, a reflexive approach to practice is informed by the view from inside, with dilemmas about values shaped by our interactions with others. Although largely absent from traditional moral philosophy, the distinctive perspective of the reflexive approach to problems of ethics and values is however echoed in feminist thinking. Reflexivity as it is applied to social work practice draws upon the concept's use in feminist research (Fook, 2002; Orme, 2002; Taylor, 2006), where women researchers increasingly began to recognize the importance of an approach to qualitative inquiry that took account of the subjective elements of the research process and took issue with conventional notions of research neutrality, acknowledging 'the active involvement of the researcher in the process of research' (Taylor, 2006: 74).

Furthermore, although traditional ethical thinking has not embraced aspects of reflexivity, feminist ethics have brought a distinctly inter-subjective focus to the whole area of ethical decision-making. The feminist ethic of care takes as its starting point a rejection of the idea of the autonomous moral subject. Gilligan (1982), whose work was instrumental in developing this approach to ethics and subsequent writers (Tronto, 1993; Bowden, 1997) who built on Gilligan's work, all look at ethics from a relational perspective arguing that women faced with moral problems will address them pragmatically focusing on relationships between the people involved rather than always seeking to apply abstract principles (see also Rogers and Weller, 2013). We ought instead to focus on how dilemmas can be understood by paying attention to the relationships between the parties involved with a particular focus on care.

Discussion points

Consider the different elements of your own identity and make a list of your own characteristics. Now think about a challenging discussion with a service user, for example about personal care choices or the intimate aspects of a relationship.

- What impact do you think your identity would have?
- Identify two sets of circumstances, a situation where you and a service user share many characteristics and also one where there are many differences between you.

Chapter summary

It is easy when considering what social work needs to do about diversity and difference to be drawn to two of the key areas we have already discussed: first, ensuring that social workers have the theoretical tools they need to understand this area in a way that reflects the divergent and shifting nature of our identities; and second, using this understanding to inform practice that is anti-discriminatory. However, I think it is important to remember the material impacts that *difference* can have. Difference is not just about the collective categorization of people under one identity, but also about how that identity can be positioned subordinately in relation to those who are more privileged in some way. Thus, for example, men are privileged in relation to gender, heterosexuality is privileged in respect of sexuality, and being white and British is privileged in the sphere of culture and ethnicity.

However, subordinate identities are not only subject to prejudicial treatment, they also experience real structural disadvantage as a result of these aspects of difference. Thus women are disadvantaged in the job market, and members of BME communities are often located in areas of poverty where, for example, housing is in poor condition and the services available are limited. Difference can shape the ways in which we access resources. Interestingly, 'social class' as a category of identity is a hybrid concept in the sense that we are often defining class in both material and cultural terms (hence perhaps John Prescott's famous 1997 assertion that we are 'all middle class now' (BBC News, 2007).

A number of writers have pointed to the fact that one of the most important common experiences that social work service users share is that of poverty (Jones, 2002; Manthorpe and Bradley, 2009; Mantle and Backwith, 2010): 'Poverty is a key defining characteristic of the lives of many social work service users' (Walker and Walker, 2009: 74). If social work's commitment to social justice is to be really meaningful, then it needs to address poverty and material disadvantage, which does not mean 'the subordination of identity issues but their contextualisation within a wider challenge to exclusion and oppression' (Johns and Jordan, 2006: 1272).

Garrett (2002: 187) argues that at times 'there has been a failure to incorporate an understanding of poverty into a discourse which is apt to pivot on notions of diversity and difference', and that social work needs to bring together three aspects of the ethics of difference to deliver on these professional commitments to social justice. The first element is a commitment to understanding and working with difference. However, this needs to be allied with the pursuit of greater social justice, which means a commitment to actively encouraging social change, as we shall see in Chapter 10. A focal point of this commitment ought to be poverty, as it is here where the impacts of discrimination are most starkly demonstrated.

So for Garrett, 'ideas about diversity and difference are inescapably enmeshed with issues associated with poverty and more broadly the politics of redistribution' (p. 188)

A common question asked by students when they first encounter teaching on difference and diversity in social work education is what distinguishes anti-oppressive from anti-discriminatory practice? My short answer to this question (which doesn't entirely capture all the differences but has the virtue of being brief) is to point to the wider scope and ambition of an anti-oppressive stance. Anti-oppressive practice captures the idea of an approach to social work in which the pursuit of social justice is a primary goal. And although we may at times doubt the capacity of social work to deliver on this, it is important that it remains as a central professional aspiration. If social work is to effectively celebrate difference, it needs to ground this celebration in a commitment to social change.

Key points for social work practice

- Working with diversity and difference is central to social work as a profession and to the individual work of social workers with service users.
- There is always a question as to how far the pursuit of social change is a legitimate goal for social workers.
- A person's identity may have many aspects and this is a challenge for social workers. Narrative can be a useful tool in understanding this.
- Our own identities impact upon our work as social workers and we need to work towards a reflective understanding of ourselves in order to work successfully with others.
- Diversity and difference cannot be separated from wider debates about poverty and social justice.

Relationship-based practice

Mina Hyare

Introduction

In this chapter, I will argue that developing 'relationship-based practice' within social work equates to engaging in ethical practice. In essence, relationship-based practice offers a way of engaging with service users that challenges many aspects of contemporary social work practice. I begin by identifying research that discusses the development of relationship-based practice, and note research evidence indicative of social workers possibly engaging in confrontational communication with service users. I will chart the historical journey in terms of attention that has been paid to relational practice, in order to facilitate an understanding of the recent resurgence of such an approach. This leads to a critique of some of the systemic and contextual factors operating at an organizational and macro level that can serve to hinder the development of ethical practice between individual practitioners and service users. This will serve to support my proposition that relationship-based practice is a prerequisite to developing compassionate practice. Carol Gilligan first introduced the concept of the 'ethic of care' (Gilligan, 1982). Essentially, such an approach:

> In contrast to accounts of universal principles, and of the significance of impartiality, individual rights, consequences, and justice in consequentialist and deontological moral theories, the ethic of care emphasises the importance of context, interdependence, relationships and responsibilities to concrete others. (Koggel and Orme, 2010: 109)

We can argue that this position concurs with Munro's (2011) recommendations that relational practice and a systems approach will lead to a more effective child protection system, although the benefits of such an approach extend to all areas of social care and social work.

The development of relationship-based practice

It has consistently been noted that service users perceive the quality of their 'relationship' with their social workers as key to effective social work (for recent research examples, see Leigh and Miller, 2004; de Boer and Coady, 2007; Beresford et al., 2008). Other relational qualities such as an ability to accept, empathize and listen are considered by service users to be central components of good practice. In her review of child protection practice, Munro (2011) noted instances where social workers had never met with the child/young person alone. While this may be difficult to comprehend, Cooper (2005) has noted the difficulty of 'seeing' and 'knowing' in practice, suggesting that anxiety can lead to defensive practice that blinds practitioners to what is happening in front of them. Similarly, Ferguson (2011) notes the fear, anxiety and avoidance that all practitioners are susceptible to, when working with people who can be hostile and frightening. In view of evidence that acknowledges the importance service users attach to relationship, combined with research that indicates that emotions and anxiety are evoked in practice, it is clear that an approach to practice that affords an opportunity to tend to our emotions is a prerequisite to achieving good social work practice and building effective relationships.

Our knowledge regarding the communication and interactions between practitioners and service users is limited, perhaps due to ethical considerations regarding attaining the consent of service users and social workers, as well as the resource implications that such research would necessitate. Research undertaken by Forester et al. (2008: 1) involved exploring the responses of forty social workers to nine 'vignettes' (case scenarios). They found that, 'Overall, social workers tended to use a very confrontational and at times aggressive communication style. This was so consistently observed that it is likely to be a systemic issue.' Thus, despite the rhetoric within the profession regarding relationship, empathy and acceptance, Forrester and colleagues' research suggests that this may not always be achieved within practice. Relationship-based practice can provide practitioners with both the knowledge and the techniques to undertake holistic assessments and develop sophisticated communication skills. It also provides the basis for engaging in use of the self in practice, which can serve to promote compassionate rather than punitive and confrontational practice. A contemporary conception of relationship-based practice is that it is informed by psychodynamic, attachment and systems theory (Ruch, 2010). Such a broadly theoretically encompassing definition of relationship-based practice reflects an evolved definition of relational practice, and redresses historic critiques levelled at more traditional relationship-based and psychoanalytically informed practice.

Ruch (2010) notes that historically, social work has made strong links with psychosocial approaches to practice. The psychosocial casework model developed by Florence Hollis in the 1960s was one of the foundational approaches to social work practice at its inception. Thus, a psychoanalytic tradition within social work prevailed from the 1930s to the 1970s. Critiques levelled at psychoanalytic social work have described such practice as reactionary, individualistic and unpolitical (Cooper, 2010), suggesting that such practice negated the discrimination and marginalization that often permeates the lives of service users. This led to the rise of radical social work, where there was a firm commitment to engaging with the structural inequalities that prevail in the lives of many service users (see also Chapter 8 in this book). The demise of this approach, in succinct terms, can be attributed to the fact that 'Radical social work has always been strong on rhetoric but weak on practical action' (Howe, 1998: 48).

Within this context, inquiries into child abuse cases since Marie Colwell's death in 1973 until Victoria Climbié's death in 2000 and have contributed to a public sector 'audit explosion' (Cooper and Dartington, 2004). Practice has arguably become increasingly procedural and performance-orientated, and in which attention to the emotional aspects of 'doing' social work are overlooked (Ferguson, H, 2005). Such procedure-based practice has frequently led to practitioners missing important information in individual child abuse cases. In the world of performance management, attention to performance (that is, *what* people do) seems to take precedence over *why* people behave the way that they do (Howe, 1998). Cooper (2005) notes that despite new rafts of procedures being introduced after child abuse inquiries, this has not resulted ultimately in a more effective child protection system.

More recently, the death of Peter Connelly in 2007 in the UK led to extensive media coverage and the ensuing public outrage that accumulated resulted in the current and ongoing overhaul of social work practice and education. For the first time since 1973, the profession was able to avoid another government kneejerk response that encompassed introducing a raft of new procedures within a short time-frame. The subsequent long-term overhaul of practice and education in the UK initiated by the Social Work Task Force is now being followed through by The College of Social Work. This has afforded the profession an opportunity to move away from procedure-based surface-level responses, towards practice that engages with emotional processes and context and acknowledges the complexity and uncertainty inherent in the lives of service users, encouraging practitioners to take calculated risks where appropriate.

Ferguson, H (2005) criticizes social work education for compounding the neglect of emotions within practice, due to its emphasis on a neoliberal rights-based agenda that promotes individual choice, autonomy and empowerment, arguably under the guise of anti-oppressive practice. The central characteristic of the neoliberal onslaught is that of the 'free possessive individual' (S. Hall, 2011a). This promotes individual responsibility and choice, and therefore critiques that were aimed at psychoanalytic theory in the 1970s can be justifiably applied to contemporary social work practice, negating any consideration of the impact of structural inequalities upon the lives of service users. Instead, individuals are held accountable for their behaviour, on the simple premise that people *choose* to partake in certain behaviours (Howe, 1996); and so social work practice often involves a punitive response when people choose what is considered unacceptable behaviour. One example of this relates to a shift in the way that we respond to young people who commit crimes. Historically, attention was paid to meeting the welfare needs of such young people. In contemporary practice, there is an emphasis on justice, where young people are punished in proportion to the seriousness of the crimes they commit.

Despite the demise of a psychoanalytic tradition within social work practice in the 1970s, pockets of sustained commitment to a relational approach prevailed. Despite ongoing controversies regarding the nature of social work, many academics and practitioners have maintained a conviction that relationship has some relevance to practice. Howe (1998) distinguishes between three types of relational-based practice. First, he notes that some practitioners regard relationship as a function of the *social work role*. Then, there are those who perceive *relationship skills* as necessary to fulfil their role as a practitioner. Finally, there are those who perceive *relationship as fundamental* in itself, independent of the role of a social worker (Howe, 1998).

Cooper (2011) notes that social workers appear to have lost confidence in working directly with families, and that work often begins and ends with assessment: it is as if 'others' will do the *real* work (e.g. family therapists, therapeutic organizations). In this context, relationship-based practice affords an opportunity for social workers to re-engage and work, for example, with children and families. It offers a model of working that practitioners can use to both enhance their understanding of the lives of service users (e.g. assessment) as well as inform their responses and interactions – that is, what social workers actually say or do (e.g. intervention).

Challenges to implementing relationship-based practice

The current conception of relationship-based practice concurs with Howe's third definition as mentioned earlier, and so relationship can be seen as fundamental in itself. In this context, drawing upon attachment theory, psychoanalytic and systems ideas provide the knowledge base and techniques for facilitating and enabling the development of holistic assessments, as well as enabling highly sophisticated communications skills, in relation to working with diverse service users. It is helpful, however, to acknowledge the troubled historic relationship that has existed between systemic and psychoanalytically informed practitioners (Mandin, 2007). Attention to this could serve to overcome any stereotyping, and so alleviate concerns of systemic and psychoanalytic practitioners who may remain suspicious of each other (Burck and Cooper, 2007).

A number of authors (e.g. Ruch, 2010; Wilson et al., 2011) have noted the ambivalence that many social workers have in relation to relationship-based practice. Hingley-Jones and Mandin (2007) discuss their experiences of teaching systems and psychoanalytic concepts within a module for final-year qualifying social work students. They noted that some students were reluctant to engage with these theoretical frameworks. This is unsurprising given the current procedure-based, rule-following context of practice that has led to a decline in professional autonomy and confidence. This may also be due to the fact that procedure-based practice does afford some degree of containment to practitioners, as it relieves them of having to take responsibility for difficult decisions. Despite this, Hingley-Jones and Mandin (2007) note that student evaluations at the end of their module remained consistently positive, and a gradual engagement with the theories presented appeared to take place during the course of the module for many students. The challenge for social work education is to support students to internalize relationship-based and reflective practice and this picks up on some of the themes we have discussed elsewhere in this book.

Having acknowledged some of the contextual challenges to practitioners engaging with relationship-based practice, I will now introduce the key concepts of relationship-based practice, and demonstrate with a case study how they can complement each other to provide a multi-layered response that facilitates engaging with the complexity of the lives of service users.

Contemporary conceptions of relationship-based practice

Definitions of relationship-based practice remain few and far between. Wilson et al. (2011: 9) note that, 'The central characteristic of relationship-based practice is the emphasis it places on the professional relationship as the medium through which the practitioner can engage with and intervene in the complexity of an individual's internal and external worlds.' Ruch (2005) has reconceptualized Florence Hollis's traditional psychosocial case-work model so that social workers have to think simultaneously about: the uniqueness of service users; the relationship between service users and their social circumstances; the relationship between the social worker and service user; and a notably important new dimension that is highlighted is the social worker relationship with other professionals and their relationship to the socio-political context in which they practise. Such a model therefore necessitates attention not only to the internal and external worlds of the vulnerable people that we work with, but also to the internal and external world of the practitioner; thus, the use of self and reflective practice is inextricably at the heart of relationship-based practice. In this context, all encounters with service users are seen as unique, people are not viewed as rational beings, and so behaviour is recognized as complex and multifaceted (Wilson et al., 2011).

A contemporary conception of relationship-based practice thus requires attention to individual relationships beyond that between the practitioner and the service user; to the context of the vulnerable people we work with; and also importantly to the organizational context that social workers operate within, and the relationship between both individuals (service users and practitioners) and organizations to the macro socio-economic-political context that all parties operate within. Psychoanalytic concepts in combination with attachment theory and systems theory afford an opportunity to consider all of these factors when undertaking assessment and interventions.

The following case study illustrates how attachment, psychoanalytic and systems theory informed an intervention in relation to a young woman, from within an inner London Youth Offending Service.

Case study 9.1

A social worker was supervising a 16-year-old young woman, who was pregnant, addicted to heroin and crack cocaine, and who was suspected of being sexually exploited, although she vehemently denied this. She was subject to a court-ordered supervision order for theft (shoplifting), which meant that she was required to attend the Youth Offending Service on a weekly basis initially.

During these meetings, if the social worker had adhered to procedure-based practice, the National Standards for Youth Justice Services (2008) stipulate that the social worker should use their weekly meetings to discuss the young person's offending behaviour. Children's Services were involved due to concerns as detailed above, and concerns about her unborn child. She was accommodated under Section 20 (Children Act 1989) and placed within supported accommodation, from which she absconded continuously to the point that she was hardly ever there, and she was not keeping appointments with her children and families social worker.

The social worker came to understand that some staff at the residential unit were antagonistic and hostile towards the young woman, as they perceived her as exercising autonomy and choice in terms of her lifestyle and there were concerns that she was involved in the procurement of other young women within the residential accommodation. In order to understand the behaviour of the staff, it is helpful to consider their position from a systemic perspective. Perhaps their compassion and concern for other vulnerable women contributed to their inability to recognize the vulnerability of this young woman. More importantly, perhaps, the fact that at a macro level, neoliberal ideology is firmly embedded within our culture and society, including social policy and social work organizations, practice emphasizing individual choice and autonomy can lead to a punitive rather than a compassionate response.

Reflection point

Think about some of the theoretical underpinnings that the social worker could adopt in this case.

Social work response

In the context of the above case study, the social worker afforded primacy to creating a secure base (*attachment theory*) for this young woman while she was living a chaotic, dangerous and traumatic existence. As such, the social worker, in agreement with her line manager, deviated from procedure-based practice – namely, the National Standards (2008) – and so did not use their weekly meetings to discuss offending, but instead focused on providing a consistent, meeting time and day each week, and was committed to adhering to these weekly appointments, as part of the endeavour to provide a secure base and containing presence. The meetings took place in a local café, a neutral environment (rather than the office), and the social worker was able to access monies to pay for her lunch each time they met, thus offering nurture by contributing towards meeting a basic physiological need. The young woman was sometimes late and her attendance was erratic, although she did attend regularly.

The social worker adopted a *systemic approach* in terms of thinking about why this young woman sometimes turned up late and sometimes did not turn up at all. At a conscious level, and in the context of her chaotic lifestyle, she was always able to proffer a rational explanation for her absences and lateness, and so the social worker wondered about what unconscious thoughts and feelings may have been prevalent for her. The social worker wondered as to her seemingly conflicting position, whereby she simultaneously appeared to desperately seek nurture and support, while another part of her perhaps felt that she was undeserving of compassion and concern. The social worker tried to empathize with her by explicitly acknowledging her lateness and absences, but rather than reprimanding her for this, expressed whether there was a part of her that desperately wanted to meet with the social worker, while at the same time, perhaps, there was a part of her that was very frightened and did not want to meet with her social worker at all. This resonated with how she was feeling and so contributed towards the initial trust and relationship building.

This is a mere snapshot of the work undertaken with this woman, which hopefully serves to illustrate how theory can assist practitioners in understanding and empathizing with vulnerable people, as well as informing what practitioners can say and do in their interactions with service users. Stanford (2010) has referred to the rhetoric of risk used within neoliberal risk society to mobilize fear as an emotive, defensive and strategic medium for advancing the values of safety and security. This is clearly illustrated in the potential for the social worker in this study to reorient her role and practice towards managing and securing what is needed externally as opposed to genuine attempts to respond meaningfully to the young woman's need. Stanford (2010) highlights how this discourse makes social workers fearful for their physical and mental well-being and of being blamed when things are seen to go wrong instead of enacting a moral stance enshrined within the ethics and values of social work. An uncritical stance may incline us towards defensive and morally timid social work practice within a conservative political, social, cultural and economic climate of neoliberal risk society. The case study demonstrates that following a fixed approach to the young women enshrined in national standards claims to offer certainty, facticity, predictability and stability. I will now discuss further some of the theoretical concepts referred to in the above example in more detail and provide an outline of the three core theories applied here.

Key theoretical concepts of relationship-based practice

Psychoanalytic concepts

It is important to be aware that by urging practitioners to draw upon some key psychoanalytic concepts, such as splitting, projective identification and introjections, defence mechanisms, transference, counter-transference and containment, does not equate to practitioners providing psychotherapy to service users, and neither does a relationship-based practice approach advocate this. Rather, using these concepts has the potential to enhance our capacity for reflection and involves paying attention to the individual and emotional aspects of the social work role, as well as the broader context. These concepts can assist social workers in engaging with both the conscious and unconscious worlds of service users, as well as the practitioner's conscious and unconscious worlds (Ruch, 2010). [For a more nuanced account of key psychoanalytic concepts and examples of drawing upon these ideas to inform practice in varied social work settings, see Bower (2005).] At the core of relationship-based practice is the role that anxiety plays in relation to how adults respond to distressing circumstances (Ruch, 2010). Ruch discusses how anxiety can be manifested via aggressive and hostile behaviour, hysteria and mania, and acute and chronic depression and is a natural response to basic fears. If practitioners understand aggression and hostility as a manifestation of anxiety, this can serve to assist them in responding in a caring rather than a punitive manner.

As mentioned earlier, some of the critiques levelled at psychoanalytically informed practice historically include that it was Eurocentric, based on a medical model of treatment, individualistic and demeaning to women, although some feminists have used it to consider male
oppression too (Payne, 2005). However, since the 1950s, psychoanalytic theory has evolved
and so in response to these earlier critiques, Melanie Klein's theory of *object relations* (see
Segal, 1988) and Bion's (1962) concept of reverie and containment clearly acknowledge that
healthy individual emotional development is dependent upon relationship to another. In this
respect, the relational aspect of psychoanalytic theory has evolved (Flaskas, 2007). Furthermore, a contemporary commitment to the 'third position' (Britton, cited in Burck and Cooper,
2007) within psychoanalytic theory that includes attention to race, gender, sexuality and
other forms of difference (Hollway and Jefferson, 2000) is indicative of a move away from a
Eurocentric and traditional medical model of practice. I shall return to discuss Klein's object
relations theory in the organizational contexts section below, but for now I will outline the
key components of attachment theory and note areas of overlap between the two theories.

Attachment theory

John Bowlby's attachment theory (Bowlby, 1988) and psychoanalytic theory both attach
primacy to the importance of early childhood experiences as exerting a powerful influence
throughout our lives, and upon our relationships with others. Both emphasize the importance of an infant's relationship to others, and their desire to seek proximity to a primary
caregiver. There are differences between the two theories in terms of understanding the
root causes of behaviour.

Where the caregiver has the emotional capacity to consistently respond to the child's mind,
something Howe (2005) refers to as 'mind-mindedness', a secure attachment with the caregiver is established, and this enables the infant to develop a positive internal working model
that facilitates social, emotional, physical and cognitive development, and provides a psychological template for how the child approaches the world and makes sense of future experiences (Lefevre, 2010). Attention to the importance of the primary caregiver being emotionally
attuned to the infant is comparable to the psychoanalytic concept of 'reverie' (Bion, 1962),
which refers to a state of mind of the caregiver where difficult emotions can be contained,
managed and reflected upon. Although it is beyond the remit of social workers to reach a con-
clusive assessment regarding an attachment style, social workers can describe and explain
children's behaviour rather than offering definitive categorizations (Lefevre, 2010).

A positive internal working model facilitates the development of intimate personal adult
relationships, where individuals are able to balance autonomy and closeness (Feeney and
Noller, 1996). Understanding that insecure attachments are associated with impaired development can serve to enhance our understanding of behaviour exhibited by children and
adults as well as complex and difficult familial relationships.

As practitioners, we are centrally concerned with assessing relationships and attachment
theory helps us to understand how relationships influence daily functioning and well-being
and why some people engage in relationships that cause deep distress, or that can be violent or abusive; this insight should hopefully serve to enhance our capacity for empathy and
acceptance of service users who exhibit and partake in seemingly self-destructive behaviour.

Systemic theory and techniques

From a systems perspective, individual behaviours are understood in relation to interpersonal relationships in the present. Like psychoanalytic theory, primacy is afforded to
how anxiety is experienced within family relationships, but unlike psychoanalytic theory,

systemic perspectives do not link anxiety with a fear of annihilation (Ruch, 2010). Uncertainty is perceived as a threat to an individual's identity and their relationship network. Systemic practitioners serve to support family members to *tolerate uncertainty* and to *retain curiosity* about what is happening within their family, and this is central to relationship-based practice.

Systemic and psychoanalytically informed practitioners engage with both conscious and unconscious communication. For example, systemic practitioners use mirroring and reflective teams to understand unconscious processes. Mirroring is described as comparable to the concept of transference, and is said to occur when family dynamics are re-enacted in a different but related context and is therefore unconscious (Ruch, 2010). Anderson (1987, cited in Ruch, 2010) describes how systemic practitioners use reflective teams. Some practitioners are involved in working with a family and others observe the process of family–practitioner(s) interactions. During any meeting, the family and practitioner(s) suspend their discussion to afford the observers an opportunity to feed back their observations. The observers pay attention to the affective impact of the meeting, always keeping in mind the possibility that they may be mirroring the dynamics observed.

Ruch (2010) warns that without reflection, practitioner responses may reinforce existing dysfunctional interactions. This approach is based on a social constructionist view of the world where there are no universal truths, and so the views of all parties are valued. Engaging in a reflective collaborative process can be compared, as mentioned earlier, to the concept of utilizing the psychoanalytic 'third position' as a means of engaging in collaborative reflection (Cooper, 2011). This exemplifies again how relationship-based practice is committed to working based on an ethics of care towards service users that includes attention to otherness.

Historically, feminists have challenged the social constructionist aspect of a systemic approach. They have argued that respecting all views, in the context of relationships where there is an imbalance of power, and where domestic violence may be prevalent, equates to colluding with the perpetrator (Flaskas, 2007; Jones, 1993, cited in Mandin, 2007). In response to such critiques, Bilson and Ross (1999) argue that valuing the perspectives of all parties is based on the premise that people are mutually dependent, but that there is no supposition that they are equally to blame, and so observing patterns of interactions in a violent relationship does not equate to condoning such behaviour. Such an approach can assist in challenging the belief that a man can control his partner and therefore support practitioners in choosing the safest level at which to intervene (e.g. to support women, involve extended family, community) with the expectation that change at one level is likely to influence other levels (Mandin, 2007).

Having outlined the key components of the different theories in relation to how they can contribute towards developing relationship-based practice, in keeping with a systemic approach I will now consider the impact that the organizational context can have upon practitioners and their practice.

Organizational contexts and defence mechanisms

Defence mechanisms are normative in the sense that they serve to facilitate our avoidance of painful feelings in response to threatening situations. Defensive behaviour is problematic when it becomes embedded within an individual's behaviour or within an organization's systems.

Segal (1988) describes Melanie Klein's theory of *object relations*, in which she states that the ego has the capacity to experience anxiety from the beginning of life. Thus, a small child's mind comprises intensely opposed elements of love and hate and life and death instincts. Segal proposes that as an early defence, the ego deflects the death instinct, and converts this into aggression. In order to rid itself of these aggressive impulses, the ego splits itself and projects these feelings outwards into an external object, the breast, which then becomes the 'persecutory' breast. Segal explains how good feelings can also be projected into the then 'ideal' breast, in order to keep them 'safe'. She states that gratification (feeding) from the 'ideal' breast not only serves to provide love, but, importantly, it also keeps persecutory feelings at bay. Thus, deprivation is experienced as beyond a lack of gratification, it poses the threat of annihilation. This is the dominant feeling in the 'paranoid-schizoid position' (PS), where paranoia represents the prominent anxiety experienced, and the schizoid reflects the tendency to engage in splitting (Segal, 1988). Thus, the child's world is a split world and the task of development is to overcome this split world and to enable the ego to use more sophisticated methods to manage internal and external conflicts – that is, to achieve integration.

Segal notes that for Klein, integration is achieved through introjection, which involves the projected (loving and persecutory) feelings being returned (introjected) by the infant, in order to gain control over these feelings. She suggests that introjection takes place when the mother has the capacity to process these feelings and return them to the infant, in a way that makes the feelings tolerable, and this is comparable to the concept of an emotionally attuned mother (as discussed earlier in relation to attachment theory). Infants have a tendency to integrate, and continuous integration promotes progression to a new developmental phase, the depressive position (D). Here the infant comes to recognize the whole object – that is, the 'good' and the 'bad' breast are both part of the same person (mother). In the depressive position, the primary source of anxiety is ambivalence, which at its height leads to depressive despair. In this position, painful feelings such as guilt, hate and jealousy can be tolerated, and consequently empathy developed. While this move from the PS to the D position is a necessary stage of development, Klein suggests that as children and adults we continuously oscillate between the PS and D positions (Segal, 1988).

In relation to organizational defences, Isabel Menzies-Lyth's (1988) seminal research found that a teaching hospital had created systems to defend against the staff's anxieties of working with dying patients. The systems fragmented tasks that dehumanized patients, thus creating barriers to staff developing relationships with patients. In contemporary practice, procedure-based practice viewed with the same lens can be seen as a similar organizational defence mechanism that serves to keep service users at bay (Menzies-Lyth, 1988). Indeed, social workers and students often report that they do not have the time to engage in building relationships, as they have too much paperwork to complete. In the context of Menzies-Lyth's research, practitioners' reluctance to engage in spending time with families and building relationships could be interpreted as a reflection of their ambivalence towards emotionally engaging with service users who are capable of doing dreadful things to themselves or to others. Thus, psychoanalytic theory acknowledges that we are all susceptible to fear and denial, and Ferguson (2005) considers the impact that this can have upon practitioners. He refers to the 'Stockholm syndrome' and notes how this can arise due to our self-preservation instincts potentially leading to us empathize with service users and unconsciously collude with or placate potentially violent adult service users. He notes that our fears may dangerously result in the child in the household becoming an after-thought, as we are focused on our relief at having just survived a visit. He notes that it can be difficult to develop a working relationship with a frightening service user, and this can lead to the professional being held as 'captive'.

Cooklin (1999) proposed that organizations have the ability to meet some of our emotional needs via their potential to forge a sense of collective security from the feeling of a sense of belonging to the organization. However, significant changes may have taken place in relation to organizational processes (Cooper and Dartington, 2004), which hinder their capacity for containment. Contemporary organizations within a market state are less bounded than they were and the boundaries that exist are more permeable due to partnership, outsourcing and secondment. These ways of working reflect the trend towards 'networked' organizational functioning' (Cooper and Dartington, 2004).

Importantly, these developments have resulted in organizations being in a constant and rapid state of flux. Cooper and Dartington (2004) state that due to ever-present organizational instability and a preoccupation with risk management, the dependency needs of individuals can no longer be met within organizations, and so new defences against anxiety have evolved and prevail in the workplace. Stokes (1994) suggests that the primary, often unconscious anxieties that practitioners have to contend with are those of inadequacy, helplessness and failure.

Cooper (2010) refers to the macro-social factors that contribute towards organizational processes that are not necessarily conducive to relationship-based practice. He refers to the concept of performativity, which he describes as a culture where primacy is afforded to the behaviour and performance of service users, professionals and organizations, and where performance is judged against performance standards. Ball asserts that 'performativity works best when we come to want for ourselves what is wanted from us' (Ball, 2010: 5). This is indicative that practitioners, including social work academics, have internalized this way of working. Munro's (2011) comments acknowledge this, noting it will take time for practitioners to develop relevant knowledge and skills that will enhance their professional confidence in exercising discretion in practice, as they are used to following the rule book. Whether the current climate and social workers' ambivalence regarding relationship-based practice can be overcome remains to be seen. Cooper (2010) concludes by stating that relationship-based practice practitioners, in the context of a 'changing world order', will have to fight hard if relationship-based practice is to proliferate.

Chapter summary

This chapter argues that developing 'relationship-based practice' within social work equates to engaging in ethical practice. I have identified research that discusses relationship-based practice, including its historical and contemporary development. I have also noted research evidence indicative of social workers engaging in confrontational communication with service users. Using a case example, I was able to identify and discuss relevant theoretical underpinnings that could be applied by social workers, particularly psychoanalytic concepts, attachment theory and systemic theory and techniques. I also critiqued some of the systemic and contextual factors operating at an organizational and macro level that can serve to hinder the development of ethical practice between individual practitioners and service users. As a final point, in consideration of the issues around procedure-based practice, it was noted that the highly publicized death of Peter Connelly in the UK has led to the current ongoing overhaul of social work practice and education. In this context, relationship-based practice is arguably the only way of working that affords an opportunity to redress the surface-level and often punitive practice that prevails (albeit unintentionally), although this is unrealistically presented as promoting human rights and empowering, via the rhetoric of a neoliberal rights-based agenda. Cooper (2010), among others, has noted the fluid and more permeable nature of contemporary organizations and that the current political and economic climate remains in conflict with the development of relationship-based practice. Thus, the challenge remains for social work education to support students to internalize this way of working.

Key points for social work practice

- To develop practice that deals with the complexity, uncertainty and the depth of service users' lives, we should tend to the emotional processes involved in working with service users, colleagues and other agencies as well as the broader context of the social worker and service user's worlds.
- Consider how relationship-based practice affords you the opportunity to develop your approaches to the issues discussed and consider your own ambivalence, if any, towards relationship-based practice and devise strategies to minimize or overcome these.
- Seek support to develop your professional confidence, maturity and ability to utilize discretion. This may involve discussing these issues in your supervision and teams and to critically examine with your colleagues whether the safety that a 'tick-box' practice can offer is really the best way to promote safe practice (as acknowledged by Munro, 2011).
- Make a commitment to and find opportunities in your continuing professional development (CPD) to change the future path of social work practice.

10 Social justice

Alison Higgs

Introduction

This chapter considers how neoliberal economic and social policy has influenced social work, asserting as it has the primacy of the market and operating at an ideological level regarding those who need services (Jordan, 2004; McLaughlin, 2005). Social workers have the 'capacity to care and serve on the one hand and oppress and brutalize on the other' (Singh and Cowden, 2009: 91). It is this capacity that underlines the need for an ethical code in social work that is about more than avoiding professional misdemeanour (Banks, 2006: 12) and which addresses effectively the moral issues at stake in social work interventions. In this chapter, I suggest that these moral issues encompass not only individual conduct or personal belief but also choices about participating in a broader social justice agenda, which should be at the heart of the contemporary social work endeavour. Accounts of social workers' frustration and anxiety about unmanageable caseloads, and statements about the realities of practice expectations as very different from their reasons for training are all too frequent (Baginsky et al., 2009), with social workers reporting a performativity and managerialist culture where effectiveness is measured in terms of cost and where there is little space for reflecting on the complexities of social work (Jones, 2001).

Social justice and social work: philosophy and politics in context

Social work operates in a field of practice informed by both politics and ethics (Millar and Austin, 2006; Sewpaul, 2007). Although sometimes politicians attempt to reduce social work to a set of practical tasks (Singh and Cowden, 2009; McDonald, 2010), ethical dilemmas are part of daily social work practice, requiring complex decision-making and making intellectual activity a key aspect of the role (Singh and Cowden, 2009).

Philosophers have examined what makes a society fair and many continue to influence social work ethics and health and social care policy (Banks, 2006, 2012). As noted earlier, Kant's ideas are evident in the UK professional ethical codes, although their purpose is contested (Banks, 2003). Other philosophers such as Mill and Bentham proposed a utilitarian approach to social justice: defining a fair society as one that maximizes the happiness of the greatest number of people (see Chapter 4). This ethical approach is most regularly applied to the allocation of UK health resources today (Banks, 2006, 2012). Rawls is one of the best known of modern philosophers to develop ideas of social justice drawing on both Kantian and utilitarian themes, examining the implications of putting these into practice and attempting to address the fairer distribution of resources (Dean, 1998). Social justice is referred to, and to a limited extent conceptualized, in the social work profession's international ethical codes (Hugman, 2008), and addressed in key texts for students and practitioners (Banks, 2006, 2012; Adams et al., 2009a).

Encompassing both abstract ideas about fairness and their implications for society, social justice has ethical and political significance – although as Fitzpatrick (2008: 77) states, 'the moral philosophers... have offered surprisingly little discussion of social justice and political economy'. Birkenmaier says more about how the idea of social justice connects with politics and with social work in her reference to 'a vision of a socially just society in which, among other elements, the basic needs of all individuals are met' (Birkenmaier, 2003: 43). This political sphere of influence can be analysed in terms of social workers' own explicit and implicit motivations and accounts of their work, by looking for evidence of social justice commitments in professional ethical codes and by examining the views of politicians and policy-makers (McLaughlin 2005). How to define a fair society, the extent to which social workers should promote this and their role if faced with social injustice has been contested since the earliest days of social work (Butler and Drakeford, 2001; Dickens, 2011). This debate reflects a tension over the extent to which social workers should have a social justice, 'bigger political picture' remit, or whether their proper focus is on individual needs and problems (McDonald et al., 2003; Weinberg, 2010). This tension is not simply one of what the focus should be; it is related to questions social workers are forced to ask themselves about what is actually possible given the constraints imposed by cuts in resources, managerialism and risk aversion (Baginsky et al., 2009).

Social workers do not practise in the abstract, although abstract thought is essential to social work practice (Hugman, 2005a). They cannot simply follow procedures; regardless of pressures to work in increasingly mechanistic and procedure-driven ways (Spandler, 2004), social workers need to make professional judgements, balance competing interests and weigh up different courses of action (Banks, 2006). Referring to a former UK Minister of Social Care's insistence that social work is fundamentally practical and atheoretical, Singh and Cowden critique her assumption that thinking and doing are separate activities. They argue that social work is 'a synthesis of the theoretical and the practical' (Singh and Cowden, 2009: 482) and that it is by insisting on and promoting this synthesis that social workers can address their ethical obligations, including those in respect of social justice. Nevertheless, it is interesting that in the social work ethics literature the discussion of social justice is largely undeveloped and political engagement is rarely addressed beyond the sphere of personal belief and interpersonal interaction (Weinberg, 2010). Perhaps this is because social work ethics is mainly portrayed as being separate from politics, with its meaning located in individual action *vis-à-vis* individual users of social work services (Sewpaul and Jones, 2004). However, arguably this dichotomy is inappropriate for social work, which operates in the domain where philosophy and politics meet (Millar, 2008). In stating that social workers 'are not free to exercise power in ways entirely of their choosing because their power is, to varying degrees, the product of policies and procedures that guide intervention' (2008: 365), Millar suggests that there is an element of choice in respect of professional power. The ethical issues are related to how to use this power and for whom, as discussed by Trish Hafford-Letchfield in Chapter 6 – and therefore in relation to social justice, there remains a space to pursue this even given the constraints of daily practice.

Neoliberalism: the impact on social work and social justice

For at least thirty years, neoliberalism has held sway in the West and increasingly dominates global social and economic policy (Jones, 2001; Ferguson, 2007). The 'liberal' in neoliberalism refers to the free market: an economic ideology that insists that the market is the most effective mechanism for organizing society and hence addressing social need. This ideology and its manifestations have had a profound impact on social work in the UK and internationally throughout this period (Lorenz, 2005; Garrett, 2009). Swenson sums up the relationship of neoliberal economic doctrine to social policy thus: 'Neoliberalism, to the extent that it has a central organizing concept, holds to the notion that market solutions are preferable to government solutions' (Swenson, 2008: 627), hence social need is subject to the profit imperatives of the free market and public spending on support services is drastically reduced (E. Hall, 2011). In respect of social work, Wallace and Pease (2011: 134) argue that 'the impact of neoliberalism ranges across broad structural and organizational frameworks, from policy design and process to consideration of values and constructs of practice'. Hence the neoliberal policy framework influences how services are resourced and delivered, and of necessity (because public spending must be minimized) dependency is demonized and social problems are seen as being located in individuals rather than social divisions (Ferguson and Lavalette, 2006; Carey, 2008b; Danso, 2009).

Many national and international ethical codes and values statements continue to empha- size the importance of social justice (Hatton, 2001), despite the ground that neoliberalism has gained in recent decades (Jordan, 2004; Wallace and Pease, 2011). As Taylor-Gooby (1994) puts it: 'At the level of welfare the theme is reflected in financial constraint, the pri- vatization of services…and the increased inequality between population groups that is evi- dent in many countries, especially the UK.' The increasing marketization of social welfare since at least the 1980s (Jones, 2001; Lymbery, 2010) has resulted in fewer public services and increased privatization (Carey, 2008b). Furthermore, political attempts to redefine human need and pathologize dependence (Lloyd, 2010) have created powerful discourses that impede the development of counter-arguments and influence beliefs about what is pos- sible in social work (Butler and Drakeford, 2001).

Discussion point

How might social workers experience the consequences of marketization of social care?

Social workers experience these consequences in various ways. First, there has been a sustained drive to privatize health and social services, supported by the enforcement of the 'mixed economy' of public and private provision, set in place by the NHS and Community Care Act 1990 (Carey, 2008a; Ferguson, 2008). The Blair New Labour government progressed the neoliberal project in relation to health and social care (Butler and Drakeford, 2001) and today few local authority social workers in the UK are able to carry out anything but the most limited direct work with service users. Many adult and childcare social workers com- plain about desk-bound, procedure-driven work that offers few opportunities to use social work skills (Baginsky et al., 2009). Privatization of services and pressure to use privatized services as part of care packages, fewer opportunities to work long-term with individuals, groups and families, budget cuts and an absence of preventative resources make it increas- ingly difficult for social workers to think about the wider context of practice interventions. A social justice focus can seem irrelevant to busy practitioners who are increasingly pres- surized to focus on measurable, individual outcomes and personal conduct (Lyons, 2006; Baginsky et al., 2009). Where there is also an expectation that interventions are based on approaches and forms of intervention which *unambiguously* 'work' and which are *mani- festly* 'evidence-based' (Garrett, 2009: 203), a consideration of social justice will be seen as an incorrect response to service users' needs, which require an appropriately individualized interpersonal approach.

The economic doctrine of neoliberalism is deeply ideological (Butler and Drakeford, 2001; McLaughlin, 2005) and some writers have suggested that an individualized approach to ethics, values and practice has developed in tandem (Jordan, 2004), emphasizing individual behaviour and tending to 'oversimplify a complex relationship between structural oppression and individual service users' experiences and needs' (Millar, 2008). The assertion that individuals – rather than social divisions – are responsible for personal circumstances is central to neoliberal social policy, which insists that poverty and unemployment result from individual failure (Ferguson and Lavalette, 2004) and that the role of the state in ameliorating disadvantage is at best minimal (Webb, 2003). In other words, as the global neoliberal project has affected the material resources available to social work practitioners, with marketization leading to cuts to public services (Newman et al., 2008), so its ideology has impacted on attitudes about what is possible and what is desirable in terms of social work interventions, ethics and values (Ferguson, 2007; Danso, 2009). Nevertheless, a number of writers have argued that the inherent instability of neoliberalism reduces its hegemonic potential and makes it possible for social workers to participate in 'acts of subterfuge and sabotage' (Carey, 2008a: 357), reasserting a social justice mandate (Ferguson and Lavalette, 2006; Carey, 2008b) that arguably remains a key motivating factor for many entering the profession (Wallace and Pease, 2011).

Postmodernism and neoliberalism

A collective focus that values social justice and acknowledges the class basis of social divisions (Taylor-Gooby, 1994; Garrett, 2009) is in direct contradiction to the postmodern world-view that has influenced social work education for at least twenty years (Smith and White, 1997; Ferguson and Lavalette, 1999). This has resulted in a move away from 'critical' social work (which seeks to address the impact of structural divisions on social problems) towards an emphasis on individual behaviour and identity politics (Allain, 2007; Ferguson, 2007). Where 'critical' social work recognizes and challenges structural disadvantage (Lorenz, 2005; Carey, 2008a), postmodernism insists on the fluidity of 'identity', the importance of different 'discourses' rather than 'grand narratives' and, for social workers, the correct conduct and appropriate individual attitudes and behaviour towards service users (Allain, 2007). Rather than an acknowledgement of the shared (class) interests and campaigning alliances promoted by radical social work (Ferguson, 2007; Carey, 2008a), this individualized approach to ethics and values urges 'service user involvement', rather than political alliances, 'valuing diversity' rather than fighting racism, and 'empowering' practice rather than political engagement against poverty (Hatton, 2001; Coren et al., 2011). As Webb (2010: 201) puts it: 'Social workers who have to respond to crisis, vulnerability and long standing social problems are well aware that their clients are not self determining and autonomous but are enmeshed and situated in a complex socio-cultural world'. It is of note that postmodernist theories in social work have developed at the same time as neoliberalism has gained so much ground (E. Hall, 2011), but it is surely time for social work practitioners and academics to challenge not only the implications of free market policies but their theoretical bases, including the particular view of social division promoted by postmodernism (Taylor-Gooby, 1994; Carey, 2008a; Garrett, 2009).

McLaughlin (2005) discusses the political context of social work's espousal of anti-oppressive practice and links this with the individual rather than collective social work focus that developed as part of the postmodern agenda in social work in the 1990s. Just as the neoliberal orthodoxy holds that the free market offers individuals the choice of buying their way out of poverty and other structural divisions in society (Webb, 2003), so in social work education and much academic discourse there has been a shift from a collective focus on social justice to one of individual behaviour (Sewpaul, 2007) where there are no universal truths (Ferguson and Lavalette, 1999). As Parrott (2009: 621) puts it: 'merely recognizing and celebrating diversity does not confront oppression'.

The lack of critical debate about the personalization of social services is an example of how postmodern ideas about power (Ferguson and Lavalette, 1999) fit with the market-driven demands of neoliberal politics. Government policy and much academic literature applaud personalization as a way in which to 'hand power' to service users and to undermine 'old-fashioned' and 'paternalistic' services (Lymbery, 2010). While some services may have been inflexible, they might have been improved by better training, resourcing and effective management, rather than by wholesale privatization (Ferguson, 2007). With a few exceptions (Spandler, 2004; Leece, 2007; Lymbery, 2010), the personalization agenda in home care services has been portrayed as a demonstration of 'empowerment' and as a contribution towards social justice:

> Personalized care and direct payments or individual budgets in contemporary social work signify a new shift for self-determination. Individual budgets empower service users by providing them with a budget that they can disburse themselves...shifting power away from professionals doing this on their behalf. (Adams et al., 2009a: 23)

Yet this is a partial view of power, privileging the interests of those who wish to employ hourly paid personal assistants (and those local authorities keen to disband home care services) above those of home care workers who previously had access to nationally agreed pay and conditions, supervision, in-house training, support from a local authority infrastructure and even an office to return to, in which to talk to colleagues about the demands of personal care work (Spandler, 2004; Leece, 2007).

While postmodern approaches to social work deny that society is divided by social class, arguably the shared interests of practitioners, service users and academics are all the more obvious as public spending cuts become more severe (Ferguson, 2007). Rather than being powerful in relation to service users, social workers and their academic colleagues, all face cuts in public services, job losses and attacks on working conditions (Ferguson, 2008). These shared interests can be seen in relation to the issue of ageing. Ageing is routinely problematized by politicians on the basis that different healthcare systems 'cannot afford' to meet the 'overwhelming' needs of an ageing population (Fleck, 2011). This raises ethical and political questions, such as: Why is funding for war weapons not problematized or debated publically? Why are services for older people seen as 'costly' by some of the richest nations on earth? Should older people have all or only some of their health needs met, and why? What would be the implications of taxing the richest people in the country an additional percentage of their income? The need for security and adequate care if needed is of interest to social workers as well as current service users and it is on these kinds of issues that global campaigns against neoliberal policies are developing across the globe. As Coren et al. (2011: 602) state in reference to the Marmot Review of health policy in England: 'access to holistic social care services is a health inequalities issue and...sustained, adequate funding...is required to underpin this'. This is just one issue in which users of services and social workers have shared interests in achieving social justice.

The following case study is not particularly unusual in social work. It is included as one illustration of the complexities practitioners face and to suggest some aspects of the impact of the political context and social justice considerations in social work.

Case study 10.1

J is 19. She is pregnant and has previously had four children removed for adoption soon after birth. J used crack and other drugs since she was 12 but recently successfully completed a residential treatment programme and is currently drug-free. J's long-term partner P died in the early stages of this pregnancy. J and P met at school; they were both in foster care at the time. J is now living alone in her flat and wants to be rehoused away from the area and her drug-using friends. J tells her social worker Y that she has a right to be a mother and she needs help to learn how to look after her baby. Y tells her manager in supervision that she is extremely worried about this situation. She finds that she is not sleeping at night and is constantly preoccupied with this case. Her manager tells her that this case is one of many and she will need to learn how to leave work in the office.

There are no longer any Family Support Workers available to help J since the budget was cut. A recent child abuse tragedy in a neighbouring borough has heightened everyone's anxieties and Y's manager tells her that he wants to avoid any kind of risk to this baby. Ministers have also been highlighting the need to speed up the adoption process because there is a 'shortage' of babies for adoptive parents. There have already been enquiries from the local MP and opposition councillors about the department's performance in this area.

Reflection point

What kinds of questions and dilemmas arise in respect of particular views taken about Y's duties to service users, to the profession and to her employer and to herself?

One reason that this scenario is complex relates to the range of ethical issues and dilemmas it raises. These include the competing interests of children, parents and those adults wishing to adopt, the question of whether there is a 'right' to be a parent, as asserted by J, and the consequences for those involved of the different interventions available to social worker Y.

Considering issues of distributive justice (Miley and Dubois, 2007), there is the question of what resources J is entitled to and whether her history as a care leaver gives her a moral entitlement to support. These are only a selection of the ethical issues at stake, and this is not the only aspect of the complexity Y needs to both think about and act on. There are hints at the broader political context: local unease about a recent child abuse tragedy and current debate about adoption is apparently making it difficult for Y's manager to facilitate effective supervision. Anxiety about risk and performance measures appear to dominate consideration of options, while Y's own anxieties are impacting on her well-being and not being properly addressed by her manager. Cuts in public spending mean that Family Support Workers are no longer available: this service would both have made practical support available and contributed to an assessment of J's potential to care for this baby. Similarly, the shortage of housing means that it is going to be difficult for J to make a break from her previous lifestyle.

The complexities of this scenario mean that social worker Y (like most social workers) cannot rely on procedures or legislation to give her one 'right' or 'effective' course of action. She needs to think critically about whom any intervention will be 'effective' and 'right' for and there are ethical choices to be faced. Similarly, a manual of 'how to' approaches for intervention is not going to resolve these issues. Y may feel that she can only intervene at the micro level with a decision about risk to the new baby, yet bigger political issues in relation to cuts in services and poor working conditions for social workers remain. As Millar and Austin (2006: 153) assert, 'social policy is never simply a technical exercise in "what works": it is always about political choices and ideological values'.

As McDonald and colleagues (2003: 199) state, social work 'polices the boundary between professional and political concerns'. This scenario illustrates many aspects of that boundary and shows how neoliberal policies have potential to limit both social work assessment and views about what might be possible for people who are among the most disadvantaged in society. What Carey calls 'a predominantly essentialist and increasingly universal ideological turn' in social work 'involves the political framework of the market penetrating the mind of the care manager, student, carer, client, etc., at both a conscious and subconscious level, to the point where it can become the only type or form of "social work" from which to choose or identify with and understand' (Carey, 2008a: 357). How, then, could social worker Y intervene in a way that addresses social justice issues? Clearly, there are matters that relate to her own working conditions which Y could internalize and blame herself for (being 'unable to leave work at the office'); alternatively, she can join with others to insist that her trade union takes these on as collective political issues of social justice. The same potential to build alliances with others – including service users and other social care workers – exists in respect of cuts to services (Carey, 2008a; Garrett, 2009).

Looking at possible interventions available to her, and bearing in mind that social work involves both thinking and acting (Singh and Cowden, 2009), Y will first need to identify ethical issues involved and resist pressure from her manager to act only on one procedural aspect of the case. Articulating arguments about the complexities of the case, social justice and other ethical considerations and demonstrating that marketization of social care is skewing the assessment process will be required and Y needs much more than a simplistic 'evidence-based' toolkit (Wallace and Pease, 2011) to approach this case, to present to her manager, and to bring to the wider political field. What Y is confronted by is summed up thus by McDonald (2010: 281): 'At the heart of the problem is the structuring of a competitive market of human services that suppresses the social change agenda of agencies', and this influence of neoliberalism on how social work problems are addressed must be understood and confronted in order to reassert the importance of social justice for practice.

It has been demonstrated by a number of writers that political contexts are driving social work as a profession to move away from its stated commitment to social justice towards an individualized conception of 'problem behaviour' and 'social exclusion' (Webb, 2003). Neoliberal social and economic policies continue to have a devastating effect on public service provision. The ideological impact is powerful and, as we have seen, it can be difficult for social workers to keep in sight the social justice remit when support services disappear and when they are urged to focus on interpersonal communication rather than the political implications of any interventions (Mackay and Woodward, 2010). In a climate where public spending cuts become increasingly brutal (Mitchell, 2011), social workers are – as was illustrated in the case scenario above – put under pressure to limit not only how they can act, but how they think about the actual and potential capacities of users of services. As Mackay and Woodward have observed, today's social workers are exhorted to approach service users as individuals who can be 'empowered' to sort out their own situations, and recent applicants to social work programmes 'tended to locate the causes of social problems in the individual rather than the structural' (Mackay and Woodward, 2010: 641).

However, it is important neither to romanticize social work's history nor to underplay power which social workers have to oppress. Weinberg (2010: 41) develops this idea as follows: 'Because they take on the responsibility of determining how normative behaviour is defined, social workers invariably contribute to the construction of how, as a society, people ought to live with certain individuals who are disciplined for living otherwise'. This highlights how the importance of a social justice remit for social work and the extent to which this has needed to be fought for will depend on global and local factors such as state involvement and the specific political context (Weinberg, 2010). As Maschi et al. (2011: 235) put it: 'under a counterfeit shroud of good intentions and friendliness, lurked harsh judgements and devious intentions designed to intrude into the lives of the poor'.

Nevertheless, a commitment to social justice remains a core value for social work as it has been in different forms since the early days of the profession (Dickens, 2011). This is despite the fact that currently, social workers in the UK and elsewhere are being told that their role is simply to manage care plans, to encourage users of services to buy these from the private sector and that structural disadvantage is less important than individual behaviour (Webb, 2003). In these circumstances, it is easier to locate problems faced by service users in designing care packages rather than in social disadvantage. This is the kind of climate whereby even the legitimacy of raising these issues and 'reclaiming' the social justice remit is challenged (Ferguson, 2008).

Referring to the impact of neoliberal doctrine on the social work role, Wallace and Pease (2011: 138) also describe 'the replacement of social and political rights with clinical case management', and it is this that must be reversed if meaningful, campaigning alliances with service users are to replace the often tokenistic 'involvement' whereby social workers and academics appear to believe that their stake in social justice is different from those using services (Ferguson, 2007). Even as neoliberal doctrine and postmodern approaches to social work practice encourage a view that individuals are responsible for their own economic adversity, social workers are increasingly aware that it is not only people who use their services who face unemployment and poverty (Ferguson and Lavalette, 2006). This notion of shared interests cuts across the postmodern insistence that class does not exist and that identity is something that can be chosen at will. Furthermore, there is as yet no evidence that social workers leave university with the intention of sitting behind a desk, 'brokering' care packages (Mackay and Woodward, 2010). Instead, trainees and newly qualified social workers are making choices to work with some of the most disadvantaged people in society and to make some kind of a difference to their life chances (Sewpaul and Jones, 2004). It is this motivation that is being harnessed by campaigns of resistance to the narrow, neoliberal inspired version of social work that is too many practitioners' experience (McDonald et al., 2003; Ferguson, 2008).

It has been suggested that much academic writing in social work over the last three decades gives more or less tacit support to neoliberal ideology by an insistence on postmodernist approaches rather than critical social work (Wallace and Pease, 2011), denying that structural divisions in terms of social class make access to the free market unequal (Carey, 2008a) and suggesting that those who challenge these ideas are unable to keep up with contemporary ways of relating to service users (Lymbery, 2010). It is therefore essential that social work educators and academics think critically about their role in terms of challenging the hegemony of neoliberal ideas, particularly in respect of their translation into social policy (Carey, 2008a). Maschi et al. (2011: 248) assert that 'the jury is still out on the extent to which clinical social workers integrate social justice into practice. What is hauntingly missing from the 20-year discourse are the voices of front line clinical social workers, including from diverse global locations.' Academics and educators have an important role in facilitating these voices to be heard, so that practitioners are supported in their workplaces when they make links between neoliberal policies, cuts in services and social justice implications (Ferguson, 2008). Academics, practitioners, educators and users of services can collaborate on new accounts of theorizing the social justice agenda, enabling arguments to be developed and articulated, and alliances built that recognize the shared interests of people working in and using public services (Ferguson and Lavalette, 1999). Social work educators also have an important role in promoting critical approaches to social work education rather than accepting employer demands for input into a competency-based 'training' curriculum that arguably further the neoliberal agenda (Carey, 2008b).

Promoting social justice requires resisting neoliberalism (McDonald, 2010; Weil, 2011) and this resistance involves thinking as well as acting, in the same way that social work 'practice' requires intellectual activity (Singh and Cowden, 2009). This resistance requires an understanding of the ideological basis for cuts in public spending and negative views of 'dependency', and alliances are developing between students, practitioners, service users and some social work academics (Ferguson, 2008). Rather than accepting that 'austerity' is needed to address a global economic crisis, there is increasing awareness that cuts in public spending are driven by an ideological commitment to neoliberalism. Ferguson and Lavalette (2006: 316) argue that 'much of the current unhappiness of social workers stems precisely from the fact that in neoliberal social work, everything – their professional skills, their time, their relationships with clients – has been turned into a commodity which can be measured and costed'.

The hegemonic influence of neoliberalism is considerable but its power is brittle. The inherent instability of the 'free' market has been amply demonstrated by its inability to regulate itself and by its destructive history of 'boom and bust' (Ferguson, 2007). This instability creates a space for resistance, within which social workers can choose to promote social justice rather than meekly accept attacks on services and working conditions that further social disadvantage (Newman et al., 2008). Reductionist conceptions of social work as well as material and ideological attacks can be resisted (McDonald et al., 2003). Social workers and some academics are making the links with the political context to exploit the instability engendered by neoliberal policies, to reassert the importance of social justice in political alliances with trade unions and service users (Ferguson, 2008).

If, as Maschi et al. (2011) argue, social work ethics need to be contextualized and given that (as has been argued here) philosophical thinking is insufficient on its own, then there is a false polarization in social work politics and ethics (Miley and Dubois, 2007). Social workers have to decide how to act and very often their ethical dilemmas concern social justice (Weinberg, 2010). There is an urgent need, therefore, to set out an account of ethics for social work that encompasses both philosophy and politics. Given that social justice has both political and philosophical meaning and given social work's operation at the meeting point of both disciplines, we might take heed of Weinberg's assertion that,

> when workers struggle with issues that transcend their interpersonal relationships with service users, they commonly view these struggles as idiosyncratic or outside the lens of ethics. The problem with this perspective is that it tends to see politics as the culprit and the solutions as being beyond the purview of individual practitioners. (Weinberg, 2010: 34)

Furthering understanding about the meaning of social justice in the neoliberal context is vital, but it must be combined with political action in order to make changes. The political and philosophical nature of social work requires a definition of social justice that goes beyond an abstract 'thinking about' what a fair society would look like. Social work is about acting and doing as well as thinking, and consequently social justice is something that needs to be struggled for as well as conceptualized. A statement of social work ethics that embraces politics, rather than denies its role in social work, would offer a good starting point, and as Miley and Dubois (2007) suggest, would allow social workers to 'extend their focus beyond individual adaptation to incorporate strategies that create changes within social and political contexts'. The current brutal neoliberal policies being inflicted on populations across the globe are portrayed as the inevitable and sole response to the crisis of world capitalism. This is why there is an urgent need to develop a social work ethics that embraces both intellectual understanding and political action in relation to social justice.

Chapter summary

The ideological and material influences of neoliberalism, and their impact on social work's social justice remit, has been the focus of this chapter. Neoliberalism has been a powerful hegemonic influence in health and social care policy for at least three decades, affecting material resources and promoting a powerful ideology (Carey, 2008b). While as yet in the UK social workers are not facing quite the stark choices referred to by Weinberg (2010), they are likely to feel increasingly compromised in terms of practice that is contrary to social justice, as public spending cuts continue to bite. The 'austerity' measures being implemented by governments across the world in response to the global economic crisis (Weil, 2011) are synonymous with cuts to public spending, increased privatization and a redefinition of concepts of health and social need (Mosebach, 2009), which inevitably impact on social workers themselves and on those with whom they work (Ferguson 2008).

Links have been made here between the development of postmodernist theorizing during the time period where neoliberal social and economic policy has been dominant. Postmodernism's denial of objective structural disadvantage and its promotion of individualizing and identity politics (Allain, 2007; Ferguson, 2008; Maschi et al., 2011) has, it has been suggested, colluded with neoliberal policies and served to undermine the social work role in relation to social justice (Smith and White, 1997; Wallace and Pease, 2011).

Key points for social work practice

- Actively identify, recognize and respond to examples of structural disadvantage in your practice and highlight them to those responsible for allocating and agreeing resources.
- Raise issues about social justice in your supervision, teams and organizations to avoid any blame cultures or labelling of service users with specific problems.
- Use critically reflective practice to embrace the bigger political picture about power and disadvantage in society and to consider different aspects of social work interventions and methods used.
- Keep up to date with current issues and take a historical approach to discussing and analysing issues facing social work practice.
- Discuss the impact of disadvantage with service users and carers and work closely with them to identify solutions that will work for them and link to the support available in the community.

Afterword: Reflecting on ethics and values – continuing the journey

Linda Bell and Trish Hafford-Letchfield

In this edited collection, our aim has been to explore exactly how our contributors view the importance of values and ethics to present-day social work, each of them showing how they think these significant underpinning factors are embedded in various ways within different social work practice(s) and contexts. We recognize that our contributors may themselves have differing ways of 'doing' and 'explaining' social work and that social policy and political agendas are never far away in this professional arena. In Part 1, while we acknowledged that an overall, universalist focus on 'social justice' is important for all social workers, internationally, we also suggested (for example, in Chapter 2) that a wider framework of ethical theories and principles, with a focus on situated and contextualized forms of ethics and values, may be key to understanding how ethics and values are currently being addressed within social work. Starting with issues related to professional education and students' motivations to enter social work as an occupation (Chapter 3) and moving on to how social workers construct their professional identity(ies) (Chapter 4) and work in reflective ways (Chapter 5), we have aimed to explore the strengths and limitations of taking various approaches to social work practice, focusing on concrete examples, seen through the lens of 'ethics and values'.

In Part 2, we identified several key themes that throw up significant ethical dilemmas for social workers in practice and that reveal how social workers' values can be reflected in the actual work they do with various people. Practice examples given in these chapters illustrate just how complex it can be to work effectively and compassionately with notions of 'power', 'partnership', 'diversity and difference', 'social justice' and where the aim is to develop certain forms of 'relationship-based' practice.

Webb (2010) reminds us that postmodern tendencies in social work can militate against a meaningful engagement with issues requiring recognition of social groups who are subject to differential exploitation and prejudice, and the consequences of the vast disparities within a stratified society. He therefore calls for an 'ethical turn' in social work that focuses on developing strategies aimed at creating a just society, echoing the broader aspirations of the IFSW/IAASW. Webb asserts that this sort of analysis is ever more pressing in light of the recent global economic downturn, the origins of which not only lie with fiscal developments but crucially, with the 'structural imbalances associated with the processes of globalization that have over-valued the role of the market and under-valued the institutions of social justice and citizens' participation in economic affairs' (Webb, 2010: 2365).

Returning to the theme of risk discussed earlier, making sense of the politics of social work in its current context is a challenging task, where very strong ideological positions have often been taken up in relation to the emergence of quasi-markets in the public sector (see, for example, Higgs in Chapter 10). As Higgs suggests, issues such as access to and direct privatization of services now occur. Working within these rapidly changing ideological and instrumental environments poses real challenges for social workers in achieving autonomy for those with whom they work. Despite globalization and technological advances, major factors influencing the human condition and circumstance across the world remain grounded in poverty and breaches of human rights (Cocker and Hafford-Letchfield, 2014). While social work may seek to alleviate many causes of poverty through political action and direct support of those impacted upon, the ways in which this is manifested in practice differs dramatically in global terms. Commitment to autonomy through the lens of social justice is one of the key tenets of social work, setting it apart from other professions. This implies, as Dracopoulou suggests in Chapter 2, the continuing importance to social work of some more 'universalist' approaches to applied ethics. Referring back to Beauchamp and Childress's ethical principles, *beneficence* is a term that means 'doing good' and *non-maleficence* means 'not doing harm': it is also recognized that some social work activity may cause harm, for example by disproportionate intervention in some families. Achieving 'social justice' has been identified as one of the most important aims of social work, not just through social workers acting fairly and within the boundaries of legislation, but also through transformative critical action. Social workers may thus engage with circumstances that connect to a structural analysis of aspects of society that are oppressive, unjust and exploitative.

We conclude that ethics are integral to the way social workers utilize *power* invested in practice, particularly power derived from the legislation that governs intervention and informs models of decision-making. Central to acting ethically is the role of people using services; more recently described as a co-productive approach (Needham and Carr, 2009), promoting their involvement and participation is of major importance to reassuring the public that arrangements for meeting their needs are appropriate, genuine and effective. Involvement and participation should also take place at several levels, such as in service planning, delivery, research and evaluation. Within the wider community, developments such as social enterprise and user-led services go hand in hand with challenges to be more ethically or socially responsible in the ways we invest in future services. Following examples from successful business, care services are attempting to engage with principles of sustainability where they demonstrate concern about the environment. This might include further integration of provision through restructuring organizations or collaborating with a range of partners towards maximizing potential for pooling resources. All this implies that contextualized forms of applied ethics will come into play, in addition to more universalist principles of justice and fairness.

The development of new technologies in aspects of care has thrown up a number of challenging questions, not least how far the law should be used to control developments. In relation to new ethical issues, developments in technology have in particular given rise to challenges around reproduction and parenting: questions arise about what frameworks should guide future roles and choices in relation to genetic and substitute parenting and the rights of an individual to be informed of their origins. Several high-profile cases since the turn of this century have given attention to the role of technology in prolonging life, as well as the right to choose life, illustrated in more recent debates about euthanasia, a field rich in moral and ethical debate. Similarly, social workers will inevitably be involved in 'best interest' decisions regarding withholding and withdrawal of treatment in complex situations, and providing assessments and recommendations in relation to contradictions in law and policy that need to be addressed. At a day-to-day level, the introduction of technology to monitor older people in their own homes, sharing of electronic records in multi-agency working, and issues thrown up through charging for care and any compulsory interventions, all raise a range of ethical issues. The challenge is not to avoid them, but to work through issues as best we can with the involvement of all those affected. Recent 'Fitness to

Practice' hearings carried out by the UK Health and Care Professions Council (HCPC) and reported in the press demonstrate not only the overriding importance of competent social work practice, but also that social workers need to demonstrate insight and reflexivity when responding to ethical and professional challenges. Depending on the circumstances of the case, where workers lack capacity to show such insights, the HCPC penalties of suspension or the removal of workers from the register may be more likely.

Human rights legislation will continue to impact on social work by attempting to define parameters between the interests of the individual and the state. An adequate model of justice requires integrating such legislation with a politics of justice and recognition in which social work can actively benefit service users as opposed to just working within the law (Webb, 2003). Internationally, human rights conventions relate to guidelines incorporated into international bodies' declarations that often focus on vulnerable groups needing special protection (Leathard and McLaren, 2007). Since the Human Rights Act 1989, further developments in the UK attempt to balance individual and community interests; we have looked increasingly to the courts to assist decision-making arising from the assertion of rights. For example, further legislation and detailed guidance has sought to address areas of potential conflict. The Mental Capacity Act (Ministry of Justice, 2008) and its amendment the Deprivation of Liberty Safeguards (Department for Constitutional Affairs, 2007) have introduced particular roles and codes of practice when dealing with mental incapacity in the UK. Besides responding to ethical dilemmas through reference to legislation, policy and guidance, there are more tacit or experiential areas for social work practice development. These involve being able to respond to situations involving ethical issues through intuition, drawing on values, evidence about outcomes of certain interventions, theory and knowledge, all of which contribute to action. Thinking ethically and working practically can cause tensions on a day-to-day basis, given the emphasis on targets, performance and viability of resources, and when attempting to balance meeting demands and needs within an increasingly austere environment. Social workers will always encounter conflicts with their professional values and identities in their gate-keeping and resource allocation role, giving rise to further ethical dilemmas. Issues of fairness and administrative justice arise and social workers will need to be able to work with eligibility criteria, thresholds of service provision, all within changing and varied policies, practices and procedures, not least when collaborating and working in partnership. Concern expressed in public enquiries (Corby et al., 2001; Laming, 2003), serious case reviews (Laming, 2009; HM Government, 2010) and government reviews into the state of contemporary social work (DCSF, 2009; Munro, 2011) confirm how much further social work practice is underpinned by business principles premised on a 'neoliberal, managerialist agenda' (Baginsky et al., 2010). As we saw with some examples given in Part 2 of this book in particular, questions continue to be asked about whether, for example, social workers working in statutory settings are able to operate while prioritizing government targets, with a concern about how these may compromise social workers' ability to operate ethically (Preston Shoot, 2010). Webster (2011) has posited that while the core of social work is an altruistic activity entailing a deep commitment, a 'moral impulse', towards the distressed 'other', the 'vicious' times in which we live and subsequent uncomfortable landscape contextualizing practice has led to a number of moral ambiguities and paradoxes in which a simplified, under-theorization of social work ethics and values can thrive. The contributions in this book intend to add something to this overall mix and we hope that you will continue to grapple with these debates in your ongoing practice journey.

References

Abbott, D., Watson, D. and Townsley, R. (2005) The proof of the pudding: what difference does multi-agency working make to families with disabled children with complex health care needs?, *Child and Family Social Work*, 10 (3): 229–38.

Adam, B., Beck, U. and Loon, J. (eds.) (2000) *The Risk Society and Beyond: Critical Issues for Social Theory*. Thousand Oaks, CA: Sage.

Adams, K., Hean, S., Sturgis, P. and McLeod Clark, J. (2006) Investigating the factors influencing professional identity of first-year health and social care students, *Learning in Health and Social Care*, 5 (2): 55–68.

Adams, R., Dominelli, L. and Payne, M. (2009a) *Critical Practice in Social Work* (2nd edn.). Basingstoke: Palgrave Macmillan.

Adams, R., Dominelli, L. and Payne, M. (2009b) *Social Work: Themes, Issues and Critical Debates* (3rd edn.). Basingstoke: Palgrave Macmillan.

Adass (2014) *Social Care Services Unsustainable*; 2nd July, (online) http://www.adass.org.uk/social-care-services-unsustainable-adass/ accessed 18/10/2014.

Allain, L. (2007) An investigation of how a group of social workers respond to the cultural needs of black, minority ethnic looked after children, *Practice*, 19 (2): 127–41.

Arnett, J.J. (2000) Emerging adulthood: a theory of development from the late teens through the twenties, *American Psychologist*, 55 (5): 469–80.

Arras, J.D. (1994) Principles and particularity: the role of cases in bioethics, *Indiana Law Journal*, 69 (4): 983–1014.

Atherton, J. (1991) Resistance to learning: a discussion based on participants in in-service professional training programmes, *Journal of Vocational Education and Training*, 51 (1): 77–90.

Baginsky, M., Moriarty, J., Manthorpe, J., Stevens, M., MacInnes, T. and Nagendran, T. (2010) *Social Workers' Workload Survey: Messages from the Frontline*. London: DCSF.

Ball, S.J. (2010) New voices, new knowledges and the new politics of education research: the gathering of a perfect storm?, *European Educational Research Journal*, 9 (2): 124–37.

Balloch, S. and Taylor, M. (eds.) (2001) *Partnership Working: Policy and Practice*. Bristol: Policy Press.

Banks, S. (2001) *Ethics and Values in Social Work* (2nd edn.). Basingstoke: Palgrave Macmillan.

Banks, S. (2003) From oaths to rulebooks: a critical examination of codes of ethics for the social professions, *European Journal of Social Work*, 6 (2): 133–44.

Banks, S. (2004) *Ethics, Accountability and the Social Professions*. Basingstoke: Palgrave Macmillan.

Banks, S. (2006) *Ethics and Values in Social Work* (3rd edn.). Basingstoke: Palgrave Macmillan.

Banks, S. (2008) Critical commentary: social work ethics, *British Journal of Social Work*, 38 (6): 1238–49.

Banks, S. (2010) *Ethics, Accountability and the Social Professions*. Basingstoke: Palgrave Macmillan.

Banks, S. (2012) *Ethics and Values in Social Work* (4th edn.). Basingstoke: Palgrave Macmillan.

Banks, S. and Gallagher, A. (2009) *Ethics in Professional Life: Virtues for Health and Social Care*. London: Palgrave Macmillan.

Banks, S. and Williams, R. (2005) Accounting for ethical difficulties in social welfare work: issues, problems and dilemmas, *British Journal of Social Work*, 35 (7): 1005–22.

Barnard, A. (2008) Values, ethics and professionalization: a social work history, in A. Barnard, N. Horner and J. Wild (eds.) *Values in the Helping Professions*. London: McGraw-Hill.

Bar-On, A. (2002) Restoring power to social work practice, *British Journal of Social Work*, 32 (8): 997–1014.

Barth, F. (2000) Boundaries and connections, in A.P. Cohen (ed.) *Signifying Identities: Anthropological Perspectives on Boundaries and Contested Values*. London: Routledge.

Bauman, Z. (1993) *Postmodern Ethics*. Oxford: Blackwell.

Baxter, S.K. and Brumfitt, S.M. (2008) Professional differences in interprofessional working, *Journal of Interprofessional Care*, 22 (3): 239–51.

BBC News (2007) *Profile: John Prescott* [http://news.bbc.co.uk/1/hi/uk_politics/6636565.stm].

Beauchamp, T.L. (2005) The nature of applied ethics, in R.G. Frey and C.H. Wellman (eds.) *A Companion to Applied Ethics*. Oxford: Blackwell.

Beauchamp, T.L. and Childress, J.F. (1994) *Principles of Biomedical Ethics* (4th edn.). Oxford: Oxford University Press.

Beauchamp, T.L. and Childress, J.F. (2001) *Principles of Biomedical Ethics* (5th edn.). Oxford: Oxford University Press.

Beauchamp, T. and Childress, J. (2013) *Principles of Biomedical Ethics* (7th revised edn.). Oxford: Oxford University Press.

Beckett, C. and Maynard, A. (2005) *Values and Ethics in Social Work: An Introduction*. London: Sage.

Bell, L. (2007) Training managers constructing their identities in English health and care agencies, *Equal Opportunities International*, 26 (4): 287–304.

Bell, L. and Allain, L. (2011) Exploring professional stereotypes and learning for interprofessional practice: an example from UK qualifying level social work education, *Social Work Education*, 30 (3): 266–80.

Bell, L. and Villadsen, A. (2011) 'A sense of belonging': examining how social work students acquire professional values, identities and practice competence through group support. Paper presented at the *1st European Social Work Research Conference*, St. Catherine's College, Oxford, March.

Beresford, P. (2008) Whose personalisation?, *Soundings*, 40 (Winter): 8–17.

Beresford, P. (2012) From 'vulnerable' to vanguard: challenging the Coalition, in S. Davison and J. Rutherford (eds.) *Welfare Reform: The Dread of Things to Come*. London: Soundings/Lawrence & Wishart.

Beresford, P. and Andrews, E. (2012) *Caring for Our Future: What Service Users Say*. York: Joseph Rowntree Foundation [http://www.jrf.org.uk/sites/files/jrf/caring-for-our-future-peter-beresford.pdf; accessed 20 May 2014].

Beresford, P., Branfield, F., Maslen, B., Sartori, A. and Jenny, Maggie and Manny, and all service users from Shaping Our Lives (2007) Partnership working: service users and social workers learning and working together, in M. Lymbery and K. Postle (eds.) *Social Work: A Companion to Learning*. London: Sage.

Beresford, P., Croft, S. and Adshead, L. (2008) 'We don't see her as a social worker': a service user case study of the importance of the social worker's relationship and humanity, *British Journal of Social Work*, 38 (7): 1388–407.

Beresford, P., Fleming, J., Glynn, M., Bewley, C., Croft, S., Branfield, F. et al. (2011) *Supporting People: Towards a Person-Centred Approach*. Bristol: Policy Press.

Berg, E.B., Barry, J.J. and Chandler, J.P. (2008) New public management and social work in Sweden and England: challenges and opportunities for staff in predominantly female organizations, *International Journal of Sociology and Social Policy*, 28 (3/4): 114–28.

Bernard, C., Fairtlough, A., Fletcher, J. and Ahmet, A. (2010) Social work education as an expedition to the Antarctic. Presentation to the *12th UK Joint Social Work Education Conference*, University of Hertfordshire.

Bilson, A. and Ross, S. (1999) *Social Work Management and Practice* (2nd edn.). London: Jessica Kingsley.

Bion, W.R. (1962) *Learning from Experience*. London: Heinemann.

Bion, W.R. (1967) *Second Thoughts: Selected Papers on Psycho-Analysis*. London: Heinemann.

Birkenmaier, J. (2003) On becoming a social justice practitioner, *Social Thought*, 22 (2): 41–54.

Bisman, C. (2004) Social work values: the moral core of the profession, *British Journal of Social Work*, 34 (1): 109–23.

Bowden, P. (1997) *Caring: Gender-Sensitive Ethics*. London: Routledge.

Bower, M. (ed.) (2005) *Psychoanalytic Theory for Social Work Practice: Thinking Under Fire*. Abingdon: Routledge.

Bowes, A. and Daniel, B. (2010) Introduction: interrogating harm and abuse: a lifespan approach, *Social Policy and Society*, 9 (2): 221–9.

Bowlby, J. (1988) *Clinical Applications of Attachment Theory*. London: Routledge.

Branfield, F., Moriarty, J., Rapaport, P., Beresford, P., Forrest, V., Manthorpe, J. et al. (2007) *The Participation of Adult Service Users, Including Older People, in Developing Social Care*. Practice Guide #17. London: SCIE.

British Association of Social Workers (BASW) (2012) *Code of Ethics for Social Work*. Birmingham: BASW.

British Association of Social Workers (BASW) (2013) *Inquiry into the State of Social Work Report*. Birmingham: BASW on behalf of the All Party Parliamentary Group on Social Work.

Broadhurst, K., White, S., Fish, S., Munro, E., Fletcher, K. and Lincoln, H. (2010) *Ten Pitfalls and How to Avoid Them: What Research Tells Us*. London: NSPCC [http://www.nspcc.org.uk/Inform/publications/downloads/tenpitfalls_wdf48122.pdf; accessed 20 May 2014].

Bunyan, P. (2013) Partnership, the Big Society and community organizing: between romanticizing, problematizing and politicizing community, *Community Development Journal*, 48 (1): 119–33.

Burck, C. and Cooper, A. (2007) Introduction: dialogues and developments in social work practice: applying systemic and psychoanalytic ideas in real world contexts, *Journal of Social Work Practice: Psychotherapeutic Approaches in Health, Welfare and the Community*, 21 (2): 193–6.

Burt, M. (2008) Social work occupations in England 1900–39: changing the focus, *International Social Work*, 51 (6): 749–62.

Butler, I. and Drakeford, M. (2001) 'Which Blair project?' Communitarianism, social authoritarianism and social work, *Journal of Social Work*, 1 (1): 7–19.

Calder, J. (ed.) (1993) *Disaffection and Diversity: Overcoming Barriers for Adult Learners*. London: Falmer Press.

Care Council for Wales (CCW) (2011) *Social Work* [http://www.ccwales.org.uk/qualifications-and-nos-finder/n/social-work/; accessed 19 May 2014].

Care Council for Wales (CCW) (2014) *Practice Guidance for Social Workers* [http://www.ccwales.org.uk/practice-guidance-for-social-workers/; accessed 19 May 2014].

Carers Trust (2013) *What is a Carer?* [http://www.carers.org/what-carer; accessed 20 May 2014].

Carey, M. (2008a) The quasi-market revolution in the head: ideology, discourse, care management, *Journal of Social Work*, 8 (4): 341–62.

Carey, M. (2008b) 'Everything must go?' The privatization of state social work, *British Journal of Social Work*, 38 (5): 918–35.

Carey, M. and Foster, V. (2011) Introducing 'deviant' social work: contextualising the limits of radical social work whilst understanding (fragmented) resistance within the social work labour process, *British Journal of Social Work*, 41 (3): 576–93.

Carpenter, M. and Platt, S. (1997) Professional identity for clinical social workers: impact of changes in health care delivery systems, *Clinical Social Work Journal*, 25(3): 337–50.

Carr, S. (2007) Participation, power, conflict and change: theorizing dynamics of service user participation in the social care system of England and Wales, *Critical Social Policy*, 27 (2): 266–76.

Cartney, P. (1998) *Teaching and Learning in Practice: Process and Outcome*. London: BASW/Open Learning Foundation.

Cartney, P. (2011) Consolidating practice with children and families, in C. Cocker and L. Allain (eds.) *Advanced Social Work with Children and Families*. Exeter: Learning Matters.

Cavadino, M., Crow, I. and Dignan, J. (1999) *Criminal Justice 2000*. Reading: Waterside Press.

Chahal, K. (2004) *Experiencing Ethnicity: Discrimination and Service Provision*. York: Joseph Rowntree Foundation.

Challis, M. (2011) *Professional Capabilities Framework* [http://www.childrenengland.org.uk/upload/WRG%20May%202011%20MC.pdf; accessed 20 May 2014].

Chambon, A.S. (1999) Foucault's approach, in A.S. Chambon, A. Irvine and L. Epstein (eds.) *Reading Foucault for Social Work*. New York: Columbia University Press.

Channell, J. (1990) The student–tutor relationship, in M. Kinnell (ed.) *The Learning Experiences of Overseas Students*. Buckingham: The Society for Research into Higher Education and Open University Press.

Chu, W., Tsui, M. and Yan, M. (2009) Social work as a moral and political practice, *International Social Work*, 52 (3): 287–98.

Clark, C. (2000) *Social Work Ethics: Politics, Principles and Practice*. Basingstoke: Palgrave Macmillan.

Clark, C. (2006) Moral character in social work, *British Journal of Social Work*, 36 (1): 75–89.

Clarke, J. and Newman, J. (1997) *The Managerial State: Power, Politics and Ideology in the Remaking of Social Welfare*. London: Sage.

Clifford, D. and Burke, B. (2008) *Anti-Oppressive Ethics and Values in Social Work*. Basingstoke: Palgrave Macmillan.

Cocker, C. and Hafford-Letchfield, T. (2010) Critical commentary: out and proud? Social work's relationship with lesbian and gay equality, *British Journal of Social Work*, 40 (6): 1996–2008.

Cocker, C. and Hafford-Letchfield, T. (2014) *Rethinking Anti-Discriminatory and Anti-Oppressive Theories for Social Work Practice*. Basingstoke: Palgrave Macmillan.

Commons Health Select Committee (2012) Health Committee – Fourteenth Report, Social Care [http://www.publications.parliament.uk/pa/cm201012/cmselect/cmhealth/1583/158302.htm; accessed 20 May 2014].

Cooklin, A. (1999) Frameworks for the organisation and for the agent of change, in A. Cooklin (ed.) *Changing Organisations*. London: Karnac.

Cooper, A. (2005) Surface and depth in the Victoria Climbié enquiry report, *Child and Family Social Work*, 10 (1): 1–9.

Cooper, A. (2010) What future? Organisational forms, relationship-based social work practice and the changing world order, in G. Ruch, D. Turney and A. Ward (eds.) *Relationship-Based Practice: Getting to the Heart of Practice*. London: Jessica Kingsley.

Cooper, A. (2011) *Opportunities, Risks and Freedoms; Practising and Managing in the Post-Munro World*. Internal Paper #4. London: Tavistock and Portman NHS Foundation Trust and University of East London.

Cooper, A. and Dartington, T. (2004) The vanishing organization: organizational containment in a networked world, in C. Huffington, D. Armstrong, W. Halton, L. Hoyle and J. Poolet (eds.) *Working Below the Surface: The Emotional Life of Contemporary Organizations*. London: Karnac.

Corby, B., Doig, A. and Roberts, V. (2001) *Public Inquiries into Abuse of Children in Residential Care*. London: Jessica Kingsley.

Coren, E., Iredale, W., Rutter, D. and Bywaters, P. (2011) The contribution of social work and social interventions across the life course to the reduction of health inequalities: a new agenda for social work education?, *Social Work Education*, 30 (6): 594–609.

Coulter, S., Campbell, J., Duffya, J. and Reilly, I. (2013) Enabling social work students to deal with the consequences of political conflict: engaging with victim/survivor service users and a 'pedagogy of discomfort', *Social Work Education*, 32 (4): 439–52.

Cropley, A.J. (1992) *More Ways Than One: Fostering Creativity*. Norwood, NJ: Ablex.

Cunningham, S. (2005) Exploring widening participation in one school at a North London university: a case study, *Journal of Health, Social and Environmental Issues*, 6 (1): 5–9.

Dalrymple, J. and Burke, B. (2006) *Anti-Oppressive Practice: Social Care and the Law*. Maidenhead: Open University Press.

Danso, R. (2009) Emancipating and empowering de-valued skilled immigrants: what hope does anti-oppressive social work practice offer?, *British Journal of Social Work*, 39 (3): 539–55.

Davies, C. (1996) The sociology of professions and the profession of gender, *Sociology*, 30 (4): 661–78.

Dawson, A. and Butler, I. (2003) The morally active manager, in J. Henderson and D. Atkinson (eds.) *Managing Care in Context*. London: Routledge.

Dean, H.E. (1998) The primacy of the ethical aim in clinical social work: its relationship to social justice and mental health, *Smith College Studies in Social Work*, 69 (1): 9–24.

Dearing, R. (1997) *Higher Education in the Learning Society: Report of the National Committee of Inquiry into Higher Education* (The Dearing Report). London: HMSO.

de Boer, C. and Coady, N. (2007) Good helping relationships in child welfare: learning from stories of success, *Child and Family Social Work*, 12 (1): 32–42.

Deci, R.I. and Ryan, R.M. (2008) Facilitating optimal motivation and psychological well-being across life's domains, *Canadian Psychology*, 49 (1): 14–23.

Dent, M. and Whitehead, S. (2002) Introduction: configuring the 'new' professional, in M. Dent and S. Whitehead (eds.) *Managing Professional Identities: Knowledge, Performativity and the 'New' Professional*. London: Routledge.

Department for Children, Schools and Families (DCSF) (2009) *Building a Safe, Confident Future: The Final Report of the Social Work Task Force*. London: HMSO.

Department for Constitutional Affairs (DCA) (2007) *Mental Capacity Act 2005 Code of Practice*. London: TSO.

Department for Education and Skills (DfES) (2003) *Widening Participation in Higher Education*. London: HMSO.

Department of Health (DH) (2001a) *Valuing People: A New Strategy for Learning Disability for the 21st Century: Planning with People. Guidance for Implementation Groups*. London: DH [http://webarchive.nationalarchives.gov.uk/20130107105354/http://www.dh.gov.uk/prod_consum_dh/groups/dh_digitalassets/@dh/@en/documents/digitalasset/dh_4059600.pdf; accessed 20 May 2014].

Department of Health (DH) (2001b) *Valuing People: A New Strategy for Learning Disability for the 21st Century. A White Paper*, Cm 5086. London: DH [http://www.archive.official-documents. co.uk/document/cm50/5086/5086.pdf; accessed 20 May 2014].

Department of Health (DH) (2002) *Requirements for Social Work Training*. London: DH.

Department of Health (DH) (2005) *Independence, Well-Being and Choice: Our Vision for the Future of Social Care for Adults in England*. London: DH.

Department of Health (DH) (2010) *Personalisation through Person-Centred Planning*. London: DH [http://webarchive.nationalarchives.gov.uk/20130107105354/http://www.dh.gov.uk/prod_consum_dh/groups/dh_digitalassets/@dh/@en/@ps/documents/digitalasset/dh_115249.pdf; accessed 20 May 2014].

Department of Health (DH) (2012) *Caring for Our Future: Reforming Care and Support*, White Paper, Cm 8378. Norwich: TSO.

Department of Health (DH) (2013) *Integration of Health and Social Care*. London: TSO.

Department of Health (DH) (2014) *Care and Support*. Statutory Guidance [consultation draft] Issued under the Care Act, June.

Dickens, J. (2011) Social work in England at a watershed – as always: from the Seebohm Report to the Social Work Task Force, *British Journal of Social Work*, 41 (1): 22–39.

Dillon, J. (2007) Reflections on widening participation policy: macro influences and micro implications, *Widening Participation and Lifelong Learning*, 9 (2): 16–25.

Dillon, J. (2011) Black minority ethnic students navigating their way from access courses to social work programmes: key considerations for the selection of students, *British Journal of Social Work*, 41 (8): 1477–96.

Doel, M. and Best, L. (2008) *Experiencing Social Work: Learning from Service Users*. London: Sage.

Dominelli, L. (2002a) *Feminist Social Work Theory and Practice*. Basingstoke: Palgrave Macmillan.

Dominelli, L. (2002b) Anti-oppressive practice in context, in R. Adams, L. Dominelli and M. Payne (eds.) *Social Work: Themes, Issues and Critical Debates* (2nd edn.). Basingstoke: Palgrave Macmillan.

Dominelli, L. (2004) *Social Work: Theory and Practice for a Changing Profession*. Oxford: Blackwell/ Polity Press.

Dominelli, L. (2009) Anti-oppressive practice: the challenge of the twenty-first century, in R. Adams, L. Dominelli and M. Payne (eds.) *Social Work: Themes, Issues and Critical Debates* (3rd edn.). Basingstoke: Palgrave Macmillan.

Douglas, A. (2008) *Partnership Working*. London: Routledge.

Dowling, S., Manthorpe, J. and Cowley, S. in association with King, S., Raymond, V., Perez, W. and Weinstein, P. (2006) *Person-Centred Planning in Social Care: A Scoping Review*. York: Joseph Rowntree Foundation [http://www.jrf.org.uk/sites/files/jrf/9781859354803.pdf; accessed 20 May 2014].

Dracopoulou, S. (2005) Applied ethics, health service management and critical thinking, *Res Publica*, 11: 301–10.

Dunk-West, P. (2013) *How to Be a Social Worker*. Basingstoke: Palgrave Macmillan.

Elsey, B (1990) Teaching and learning, in M. Kinnell (ed.) *The Learning Experiences of Overseas Students*. Buckingham: Open University Press.

Epstein, R.M. (1999) Mindful practice, *Journal of the American Medical Association*, 282: 833–9.

Epston, D. and White, M. (1990) *Narrative Means to Therapeutic Ends*. New York: W.W. Norton.

Eraut, M. (1994) *Developing Professional Knowledge and Competence*. London: Routledge.

Feeney, J. and Noller, P. (1996) *Adult Attachment*. London: Sage.

Ferguson, H. (2005) Working with violence, the emotions and the psycho-social dynamics of child protection: reflections on the Victoria Climbié case, *Social Work Education: The International Journal*, 24 (7): 781–95.

Ferguson, H. (2011) *Child Protection Practice*. Basingstoke: Palgrave Macmillan.

Ferguson, I. (2007) Increasing user choice or privatizing risk? The antinomies of personalization, *British Journal of Social Work*, 37 (3): 387–403.

Ferguson, I. (2008) *Reclaiming Social Work: Challenging Neo-Liberalism and Promoting Social Justice*. London: Sage.

Ferguson, I. and Lavalette, M. (1999) Social work, postmodernism, and Marxism, *European Journal of Social Work*, 2 (1): 27–40.

Ferguson, I. and Lavalette, M. (2004) Beyond power discourse: alienation and social work, *British Journal of Social Work*, 34 (3): 297–312.

Ferguson, I. and Lavalette, M. (2006) Globalization and global justice: towards a social work of resistance, *International Social Work*, 49 (3): 309–18.

Ferguson, I. and Woodward, R. (2009) *Radical Social Work in Practice: Making a Difference*. Bristol: Polity Press.

Fitzpatrick, T. (2008) *Applied Ethics and Social Problems*. Bristol: Policy Press.

Flaskas, C. (2007) Systemic and psychoanalytic ideas: using knowledges in social work, *Journal of Social Work Practice: Psychotherapeutic Approaches in Health, Welfare and the Community*, 21 (2): 149–62.

Fleck, L.M. (2011) Just caring: health care rationing, terminal illness, and the medically least well off, *Journal of Law, Medicine and Ethics*, 39 (2): 156–71.

Fook, J. (2002) *Social Work: Critical Theory and Practice*. London: Sage.

Fook, J. and Askeland, G.A. (2006) The 'critical' in critical reflection, in S. White, J. Fook and F. Gardner (eds.) *Critical Reflection in Health and Social Care*. Maidenhead: Open University Press.

Fook, J. and Askeland, G.A. (2007) Challenges of critical reflection: 'nothing ventured, nothing gained', *Social Work Education*, 26 (5): 520–33.

Ford, J. and Harding, N (2004) We went looking for an organization but could find only the metaphysics of its presence, *Sociology*, 38 (4): 815–30.

Forester, D., McCambridge, J., Waissbein, C. and Rollnick, S. (2008) How do child and family social workers talk to parents about child welfare concerns?, *Child Abuse Review*, 17: 23–35.

Foucault, M. (1980) *Power/Knowledge: Selected Interviews and Other Writings by Michel Foucault 1972–1977* (edited by C. Gordon). New York: Pantheon.

Foucault, M. (1983) Afterword: the subject and power, in R. Young (ed.) *Untying the Text: A Post-Structuralist Reader*. London: Routledge & Kegan Paul.

Foucault, M. (1991) Governmentality (translated by Rosi Braidotti and revised by Colin Gordon), in G. Burchell, C. Gordon and P. Miller (eds.) *The Foucault Effect: Studies in Governmentality*. Chicago, IL: University of Chicago Press.

Foucault, M. (1997) The birth of biopolitics, in *Ethics, Subjectivity and Truth* (edited by P. Ravinow). New York: The New Press.

Foucault, M. (2006) *Psychiatric Power: Lectures at the Collège de France 1973–1974*. Basingstoke: Palgrave Macmillan.

Fraser, N. (1996) *Social Justice in the Age of Identity Politics: Redistribution, Recognition, and Participation. The Tanner Lectures on Human Values*, Delivered at Stanford University, 30 April–2 May 1996 [http://www.tannerlectures.utah.edu/lectures/documents/Fraser98.pdf].

Freemen, T. and Peck, E. (2006) Evaluating partnerships: a case study of integrated specialist mental health services, *Health and Social Care in the Community*, 14 (5): 408–17.

Freire, P. (1972) *Pedagogy of the Oppressed*. Harmondsworth: Penguin.

French, J.P. and Raven, B.H. (1986) The bases of social power, in D. Cartwright and A.F. Zander (eds.) *Group Dynamics: Research and Theory* (3rd edn.). New York: Harper & Row.

Frost, E. (2008) Is there a European social work identity?, *European Journal of Social Work*, 11 (4): 341–54.

Garrett, P.M. (2002) Social work and the just society: diversity, difference and the sequestration of poverty, *Journal of Social Work*, 2 (2): 87–210.

Garrett, P.M. (2009) Marx and 'modernization': reading capital as social critique and inspiration for social work resistance to neoliberalization, *Journal of Social Work*, 9 (2): 199–221.

General Social Care Council (GSCC) (2010) *Codes of Practice for Social Care Workers*. London: GSCC.

Gerdes, K. and Segal, E. (2011) Importance of empathy for social work practice: integrating new science, *Social Work*, 56 (2): 141–8.

Gibelman, M. (2000) Commentary: Say it ain't so, Norm! Reflections on who we are, *Social Work*, 45 (5): 463–5.

Gilbert, T. (2009) Ethics in social work: a comparison of the International Statement of Principles in Social Work with the Code of Ethics for British Social Workers, *Journal of Social Work Values and Ethics*, 6 (2) [online].

Gilligan, C. (1982) *In a Different Voice: Psychological Theory and Women's Development*. Cambridge, MA: Harvard University Press.

Gillon, R. (1986) *Philosophical Medical Ethics*. Oxford: Wiley-Blackwell.

Gillon, R. (1994) Medical ethics: four principles plus attention to scope, *British Medical Journal*, 309 (6948): 184–8.

Glasby, J. and Littlechild, R. (2009) *Direct Payments and Personal Budgets: Putting Personalisation into Practice* (2nd revised edn.). Bristol: Policy Press.

Glendinning, C. (2009) The consumer in social care, in R. Simmons, M. Powell and I. Greener (eds.) *The Consumer in Public Services*. Bristol: The Policy Press.

Glendinning, C., Clarke, S., Hare, P., Kotchetkova, I., Maddison, J. and Newbronner, L. (2006) *Outcome-Focused Services for Older People*, Knowledge Review #13. Bristol: Policy Press with the Social Care Institute for Excellence.

Goldstein, I. and Ford, K. (2001) *Training in Organizations: Needs Assessment, Development and Evaluation*. Belmont, CA: Wadsworth.

Gosling, J. and Martin, J. (2012) *Making Partnerships with Service Users and Advocacy Groups Work*. London: Jessica Kingsley.

Gould, S.J. (1996) *The Mismeasure of Man* (revised edn.). New York: W.W. Norton.

Graham, J.R. and Shier, M.L. (2010) The social work profession and subjective well-being: the impact of a profession on overall subjective well-being, *British Journal of Social Work*, 40 (5): 1553–72.

Graham, M. (2007a) The ethics of care, black women and the social professions: implications of a new analysis, *Ethics and Social Welfare*, 1 (2): 1194–1207.

Graham, M. (2007b) *Black Issues in Social Work and Social Care*. Bristol: Policy Press.

Gray, M. (2010) Moral sources and emergent ethical theories in social work, *British Journal of Social Work*, 40 (6): 1794–1811.

Gregory, M. (2010) Reflection and resistance: probation practice and the ethic of care, *British Journal of Social Work*, 40 (7): 2274–90.

Grenier, A. and Guberman, N. (2009) Creating and sustaining disadvantage: the relevance of a social exclusion framework, *Health and Social Care in the Community*, 79 (2): 116–24.

Habermas, J. (1984) *The Theory of Communicative Action, Vol. 1: Reason and Rationalization of Society* (translated by T. McCarthy). Cambridge: Polity Press.

Hafford-Letchfield, T. (2007) Factors affecting student retention on a social work degree in a university in the South-East of England, *Learning in Health and Social Care*, 6 (3): 170–84.

Hafford-Letchfield, T. (2010a) The age of opportunity? Revisiting assumptions about the lifelong learning needs of older people using social care services, *British Journal of Social Work*, 40 (2): 496–512.

Hafford-Letchfield, T. (2010b) A glimpse of the truth: evaluating 'debate' and 'role play' as pedagogical tools for learning about sexuality issues on a law and ethics module, *Social Work Education*, 29 (3): 244–58.

Hafford-Letchfield, T. (2011) Grey matter really matters: a study of the learning opportunities and learning experiences of older people using social care services, *International Journal of Education and Ageing*, 2 (1): 8–23.

Hafford-Letchfield, T., Leonard, K., Begum, N. and Chick, N.F. (2009) *Leadership and Management in Social Work and Social Care*. London: Sage.

Hafford-Letchfield, T., Lambley, S., Spolander, G. and Cocker, C. (2014) *Inclusive Leadership in Social Work and Social Care*. Bristol: Policy Press.

Hall, E. (2011) Shopping for support: personalisation and the new spaces and relations of commodified care for people with learning disabilities, *Social and Cultural Geography*, 12 (6): 589–603.

Hall, S. (2011a) The neoliberal revolution, *Cultural Studies*, 25 (6): 705–28.

Hall, S. (2011b) The march of the neoliberals, *The Guardian*, 12 September [http://www.guardian.co.uk/politics/2011/sep/12/march-of-the-neoliberals; accessed 20 May 2014].

Hanmer, J. and Statham, D (1999) *Women and Social Work: Towards a Woman-Centred Practice*. Basingstoke: Macmillan.

Haringey Local Safeguarding Children Board (LSCB) (2009) *Serious Case Review: Baby Peter, Executive Summary*. London: Haringey LSCB.

Harris, A. and Allen, T. (2011) Young people's views of multi-agency working, *British Educational Research Journal*, 37 (3): 405–19.

Harris, J. (2003) *The Social Work Business*. London: Routledge.

Hatton, K. (2001) Translating values: making sense of different value bases – reflections from Denmark and the UK, *International Journal of Social Research Methodology*, 4 (4): 265–78.

Health and Care Professions Council (HCPC) (2012a) *Standards of Proficiency: Social Workers in England*. London: HCPC.

Health and Care Professions Council (HCPC) (2012b) *Standards of Conduct, Performance and Ethics*, London: HCPC.

Healy, K. (2005) *Social Work Theories in Context: Creating Frameworks for Practice*. Basingstoke: Palgrave Macmillan.

Hean, S., Macleod Clark, J., Adams, K. and Humphries, D. (2006) Will opposites attract? Similarities and differences in students' perceptions of the stereotype profiles of other health and social care professional groups, *Journal of Interprofessional Care*, 20 (2): 162–81.

Heath, B. (2010) The partnership approach to drug misuse, in A. Pycroft and D. Gough (eds.) *Multi-Agency Working in Criminal Justice: Control and Care in Contemporary Correctional Practice*. Bristol: The Policy Press.

Heffernan, K. (2006) Social work, new public management and the language of 'service user', *British Journal of Social Work*, 36 (1): 139–47.

Held, V. (2006) *The Ethics of Care: Personal, Political and Global*. Oxford: Oxford University Press.

Her Majesty's Government (2008) *Transforming Social Care*. Local Authority Circular LAC (DH) (2008) (1). London: TSO.

Her Majesty's Government (2010) *The Government's Response to Lord Laming: One Year On*. London: TSO.

Her Majesty's Government (2013) *Working Together to Safeguard Children* [https://www.gov.uk/government/uploads/system/uploads/attachment_data/file/281368/Working_together_to_safeguard_children.pdf; accessed 20 May 2014].

Her Majesty's Government (2014) *Open Public Services: 2014 Progress Report* [https://www.gov.uk/government/publications/open-public-services-2014-progress-report; accessed 20 May 2014].

Hicks, S. (2014) Rethinking the family, in C. Cocker and T. Hafford-Letchfield (eds.) *Rethinking Anti-Discriminatory and Anti-Oppressive Social Work: Theories for Practice*. Basingstoke: Palgrave Macmillan.

Higher Education Funding Council for England (HEFCE) (2006) *Widening Participation: A Review. Report to the Minister of State for Higher Education and Lifelong Learning*. Bristol: HEFCE.

Higher Education Funding Council for England (HEFCE) (2009) *Strategic Plan 2006–11, Updated June 2009*. Bristol: HEFCE.

Hingley-Jones, H. and Mandin, P. (2007) Getting to the root of problems: the role of systemic ideas in helping social work students to develop relationship-bsed practice, *Journal of Social Work Practice*, 21 (2): 177–91.

Højlund, H. (2009) Hybrid inclusion – the new consumerism of Danish welfare services, *Journal of European Social Policy*, 19 (5): 421–31.

Hollway, W. and Jefferson, T. (2000) *Doing Qualitative Research Differently: Free Association, Narrative and the Interview Method*. London: Sage.

Holmes, J. (1995) *Women, Men and Politeness*. Harlow: Longman.

Howe, D. (1996) Surface and depth in social work practice, in N. Parton (ed.) *Social Theory, Social Change and Social Work*. London: Routledge.

Howe, D. (1998) Relationship-based thinking and practice in social work, *Journal of Social Work Practice: Psychotherapeutic Approaches in Health, Welfare and the Community*, 12 (1): 45–56.

Howe, D. (2005) *Child Abuse and Neglect: Attachment, Development and Intervention*. Basingstoke: Palgrave Macmillan.

Hugman, R. (2005a) *New Approaches to Ethics for the Caring Professions: Taking Account of Change for Caring Professions*. Basingstoke: Palgrave Macmillan.

Hugman, R. (2005b) Looking back: the view from here, *British Journal of Social Work*, 35 (5): 609–20.

Hugman, R. (2008) Ethics in a world of difference, *Ethics and Social Welfare*, 2 (2): 118–32.

Hugman, R. (2009) But is it social work? Some reflections on mistaken identities, *British Journal of Social Work*, 39 (6): 1138–53.

Hurd, N. (2011) *Introduction to Big Society Discussion Paper* [http://www.conservativepolicy-forum.com/sites/www.conservativepolicyforum.com/files/2011_01_17_big_society_paper.pdf; accessed 20 May 2014].

Hursthouse, R. (1999) *On Virtue Ethics*. Oxford: Oxford University Press.

Hussein, S., Moriarty, J. and Manthorpe, J. (2009) *Variations in Progression of Social Work Students in England: Using Student Data to Help Promote Achievement: Undergraduate Full-Time Students' Progression on the Social Work Degree*. London: GSCC/Social Care Workforce Development Unit.

International Federation of Social Workers (IFSW) (2000) *IFSW Code of Ethics*. Montreal: IFSW.

International Federation of Social Workers (IFSW) (2013) *Global Definition of Social Work* [http://ifsw.org/get-involved/global-definition-of-social-work/; accessed 20 May 2014].

International Federation of Social Workers/International Association of Schools of Social Work (IFSW/IASSW) (2004) *Ethics in Social Work: Statement of Principles*. Approved at the General Meetings of the IFSW/IASSW in Adelaide, SA, October 2004.

Ixer, G. (1999) There's no such thing as reflection, *British Journal of Social Work*, 29 (4): 513–27.

Jenkins, R. (2004) *Social Identity* (2nd edn.). London: Routledge.

Jensen, K. and Aamodt, P. (2002) Moral motivation and the battle for students: the case of studies in nursing and social work in Norway, *Higher Education*, 44 (3/4): 361–78.

Jeyasingham, D. (2008) Knowledge/ignorance and the construction of sexuality in social work education, *Social Work Education*, 2 (27): 138–51.

Johns, N. and Jordan, J. (2006) Social work, merit and ethnic diversity, *British Journal of Social Work*, 36 (8): 1271–88.

Johnson, P., Wistow, G., Schulz, R. and Hardy, B. (2003) Interagency and interprofessional collaboration in community care: the interdependence of structures and values, *Journal of Interprofessional Care*, 17 (1): 69–83.

Jones, C. (2001) Voices from the front line: state social workers and New Labour, in H. Beynon and T. Nichols (eds.) *Patterns of Work in the Post-Fordist Era: Fordism and Post-Fordism*, Vol. 2. Cheltenham: Elgar.

Jones, C. (2002) Social work and society, in R. Adams, L. Dominelli and M. Payne (eds.) *Social Work: Themes, Issues and Critical Debates* (2nd edn.). Basingstoke: Palgrave Macmillan.

Jordan, B. (2004) Emancipatory social work? Opportunity or oxymoron, *British Journal of Social Work*, 34 (1): 5–19.

Kearney, M.H. (2001) Enduring love: a grounded formal theory of women's experience of domestic violence, *Research in Nursing and Health*, 24 (4): 270–82.

Kemp, S. and Brandwein, R. (2010) Feminisms and social work in the United States: an intertwined history, *Affilia*, 25 (4): 341–64.

Kjellberg, G. and French, R. (2011) A new pedagogical approach for integrating social work students and services users, *Social Work Education*, 30 (8): 948–63.

Knezevic, M. (1999) Social work students and work values, *International Social Work*, 42 (4): 419–30.

Knott, C. and Scragg, T. (2007) *Reflective Practice in Social Work*. Exeter: Learning Matters.

Koggel, C. and Orme, J. (2010) Care ethics: new theories and applications, *Ethics and Social Welfare*, 4 (2): 109–14.

Laming, Lord (2003) The Victoria Climbié Inquiry: Report of an Inquiry by Lord Laming, Cm 5730. Norwich: TSO.

Laming, Lord (2009) *The Protection of Children in England: A Progress Report*. London: TSO.

Leathard, A. and McLaren, S. (2007) Introduction, in A. Leathard and S. McLaren (eds.) *Ethics: Contemporary Challenges in Health and Social Care*. Bristol: Policy Press.

Leathwood, C. and O'Connell, P. (2003) 'It's a struggle': the construction of 'new student' in higher education, *Journal of Education Policy*, 18 (6): 597–615.

Lee, S. (2009) The rising profile of informal care: modernisation and the future of care services, in D. Galpin and N. Bates (eds.) *Social Work Practice with Adults*. Exeter: Learning Matters.

Leece, D. and Leece, J. (2006) Direct payments: creating a two-tiered system in social care?, *British Journal of Social Work*, 36 (8): 1379–93.

Leece, J. (2007) Direct payments and user-controlled support: the challenges for social care commissioning, *Practice*, 19 (3): 185–98.

Leece, J. and Leece, D. (2011) Personalisation: perceptions of the role of social work in a world of brokers and budgets, *British Journal of Social Work*, 41 (2): 204–23.

Lees, S. (2000) *Health, Rape and Domestic Violence* [www.bunker8.pwp.blueyonder.co.uk/Sue/health.htm; accessed 15 August 2012].

Lefevre, M. (2010) *Communicating with Children and Young People: Making a Difference*. Bristol: Policy Press.

Leigh, S. and Miller, C. (2004) Is the third way the best way? Social work intervention with children and families, *Journal of Social Work*, 4 (3): 245–67.

Lloyd, L. (2010) The individual in social care: the ethics of care and the 'personalisation agenda' in services for older people in England, *Ethics and Social Welfare*, 4 (2): 188–200.

Local Government Group (2011) *New Partnerships, New Opportunities: A Resource to Assist Setting Up and Running Health and Wellbeing Boards – Executive Summary* [http://www.local.gov.uk/c/document_library/get_file?uuid=f924fb06-5f3e-4b73-9a1c-77a6cc61f3fc&groupId=10180; accessed 20 May 2014].

Lorenz, W. (2005) Social work and a new social order – challenging neo-liberalism's erosion of solidarity, *Social Work and Society International Online Journal*, 3(1) [accessed 3 March 2010].

Loughlin, M. (2002) *Ethics, Management and Mythology: Rational Decision-Making for Health Professionals*. Oxford: Radcliffe Medical Press.

Lukes, S. (2005). *Power: A Radical View* (2nd edn.). New York: Palgrave Macmillan.

Lundberg, B. (2013) *Serious Case Review: In Respect of the Death of Keanu Williams Inquiry*. Birmingham: Birmingham Safeguarding Board.

Lymbery, M. (2006) United we stand? Partnership working in health and social care and the role of social work in services for older people, *British Journal of Social Work*, 36 (7): 1119–34.

Lymbery, M. (2010) A new vision for adult social care? Continuities and change in the care of older people, *Critical Social Policy*, 30 (1): 5–26.

Lymbery, M. and Postle, K. (2010) Social work in the context of adult social care in England and the resultant implications for social work education, *British Journal of Social Work*, 40 (8): 2502–22.

Lyons, K. (2006), Globalization and social work: international and local implications, *British Journal of Social Work*, 36 (3): 365–80.

MacIntyre, A.C. (1985) *After Virtue: A Study in Moral Theory* (2nd edn.). London: Duckworth.

Mackay, K. and Woodward, R. (2010) Exploring the place of values in the new social work degree in Scotland, *Social Work Education*, 29 (6): 633–45.

Mandin, P. (2007) The contribution of systems and object relations theories to an understanding of the therapeutic relationship in social work practice, *Journal of Social Work Practice: Psychotherapeutic Approaches in Health, Welfare and the Community*, 21 (2): 149–62.

Manthorpe, J. and Bradley, G. (2009) Managing finances, in R. Adams, L. Dominelli and M. Payne (eds.) *Practising Social Work in a Complex World*. Basingstoke: Palgrave Macmillan.

Mantle, G. and Backwith, D. (2010) Poverty and social work, *British Journal of Social Work*, 40 (8): 2380–97.

Mappes, T.A. and Degrazia, D. (2005) *Biomedical Ethics* (6th edn.). New York: McGraw-Hill Education.

Maschi, T., Baer, J. and Turner, S.G. (2011) The psychological goods on clinical social work: a content analysis of the clinical social work and social justice literature, *Journal of Social Work Practice*, 25 (2): 233–53.

May, H. and Edwards, P. (2009) *Enriched Care Planning for People with Dementia: A Good Practice Guide for Delivering Person-Centred Care*. London: Jessica Kingsley.

McDonald, C., Harris, J. and Wintersteen, R. (2003) Contingent on context? Social work and the state in Australia, Britain and the USA, *British Journal of Social Work*, 33 (2): 191–208.

McDonald, J. (2010) Neo-liberalism and the pathologising of public issues: the displacement of feminist service models in domestic violence support, *Australian Social Work*, 583 (3): 275–84.

McLaughlin, K. (2005) From ridicule to institutionalization: anti-oppression, the state and social work, *Critical Social Policy*, 25: 283–305.

McLeod Clark, J. (2006) Investigating the factors influencing professional identity of first-year health and social care students, *Learning in Health and Social Care*, 5 (2): 55–68.

Memmot, J. and Brennan, E. (1998) Learner–learning environment fit: an adult learning model for social work education, *Journal of Teaching in Social Work Education*, 16 (1/2): 75–98.

Menzies Lyth, I. (1988) The functioning of social systems as a defence against anxiety, in *Containing Anxiety in Institutions: Selected Essays*. London: FAB.

Mezirow, J. (1981) A critical theory of adult learning and education, *Adult Education*, 32 (1): 3–23.

Mezirow, J. (1991) *Transformative Dimensions of Adult Learning*. San Francisco, CA: Jossey-Bass.

Mezirow, J. (2009) An overview on transformative learning, in K. Illeris (ed.) *Contemporary Theories of Learning: Learning Theorists... in Their Own Words*. London: Routledge.

Miehls, D. and Moffatt, K. (2000) Constructing social work identity based on the reflexive self, *British Journal of Social Work*, 3 (3): 339–48.

Miley, K. and Dubois, B. (2007) Ethical preferences for the clinical practice of empowerment social work, *Social Work in Health Care*, 44 (1/2): 29–44.

Millar, J. and Austin, M.J. (2006) The role of social workers in welfare to work programs: international perspectives on policy and practice, *Journal of Policy Practice*, 5 (2): 149–58.

Millar, M. (2008) Anti-oppressiveness: critical comments on a discourse and its context, *British Journal of Social Work*, 38 (2): 362–75.

Minister for Government Policy (2011) *Open Public Services White Paper*, Cm 8145 [http://files.openpublicservices.cabinetoffice.gov.uk/OpenPublicServices-WhitePaper.pdf; accessed 20 May 2014].

Ministry of Justice (2008) *The Mental Capacity Act* [https://www.justice.gov.uk/protecting-the-vulnerable/mental-capacity-act].

Minow, M. (1985) Learning to live with the dilemma of difference, *Law and Contemporary Problems*, 18 (2): 157–211.

Mitchell, W. (2011) Beyond austerity: deficit mania is built on a series of destructive neoliberal myths, *Nation*, 292 (14): 11–17.

Moreno, J.D. (1999) Ethics consultation as moral engagement, in H. Kuhse and P. Singer (eds.) *Bioethics: An Anthology*. Oxford: Blackwell.

Morley, L. (2003) *Quality and Power in Higher Education*. Milton Keynes: Open University Press.

Morris, K. (ed.) (2008) *Social Work and Multi-Agency Working*. Bristol: Policy Press.

Mosebach, K. (2009) Commercializing German hospital care? Effects of new public management and managed care under neoliberal conditions, *German Policy Studies/Politikfeldanalyse*, 5 (1): 65–98.

Mudge, S.L. (2008) What is neo-liberalism?, *Socio-Economic Review*, 6 (4): 703–31.

Munro, E. (2011) *The Munro Review of Child Protection: Final Report – A Child Centred System*, Cm 8062. London: Department for Education.

Narey, M. (2014) *Making the Education of Social Workers Consistently Effective: Report of Sir Martin Narey's Independent Review of the Education of Children's Social Workers*. London: Department for Education.

National Association of Social Workers (NASW) (2001, 2008) *Code of Ethics for Social Work Practice*. Washington, DC: NASW.

Needham, C. (2011) *Personalising Public Services: Understanding the Personalisation Narrative*. Bristol: Policy Press.

Needham, C. and Carr, S. (2009) *Co-Production: An Emerging Evidence Base for Adult Social Care Transformation*, Research Briefing #31. London: Social Care Institute for Excellence.

Newman, J., Glendinning, C. and Hughes, M. (2008) Beyond modernisation? Social care and the transformation of welfare governance, *Journal of Social Policy*, 37 (4): 531–57.

Newton, R. (2011) *Open Public Services White Paper, July 2011: Urban Forum Policy Briefing* [http://www.urbanforum.org.uk/files/briefings/2011_07_open_public_services_briefing.pdf; accessed 20 May 2014].

Noddings, N. (2002) *Starting at Home: Caring and Social Policy*. Berkeley, CA: University of California Press.

Noddings, N. (2003) *Caring: A Feminist Approach to Ethics and Moral Education* (2nd edn.). Berkeley, CA: University of California Press.

Nussbaum, M. (2001) *Upheavals of Thought: The Intelligence of Emotions*. New York: Cambridge University Press.

Okitikpi, T. and Aymer, C. (2010) *Key Concepts in Anti-Discriminatory Social Work*. London: Sage.

Oliver, M. (2009) *Understanding Disability: From Theory to Practice* (2nd edn.). Basingstoke: Palgrave Macmillan.

Orme, J. (2002) Social work: gender, care and justice, *British Journal of Social Work*, 32 (6): 799–814

Orme, J. (2003) 'It's feminist because I say so!' Feminism, social work and critical practice in the UK, *Qualitative Social Work*, 2 (2): 131–53.

Panaser, A. (2003) Sikhing social work, in V. Cree (ed.) *Becoming a Social Worker*. London: Routledge.

Papadaki, E. and Papadaki, E. (2008) Ethically difficult situations related to organizational conditions: social workers' experiences in Crete, Greece, *Journal of Social Work*, 8 (2): 163–81.

Parrott, L. (2009) Constructive marginality: conflicts and dilemmas in cultural competence and anti-oppressive practice, *Social Work Education*, 28 (6): 617–30.

Parrott, L. (2010) *Values and Ethics in Social Work Practice*. Exeter: Learning Matters.

Parton, N. (2000) Some thoughts on the relationship between theory and practice in and for social work, *British Journal of Social Work*, 30 (4): 449–504.

Parton, N. (2003) Rethinking professional practice: the contributions of social constructionism and the feminist 'ethics of care', *British Journal of Social Work*, 33 (1): 1–16.

Payne, M. (2005) *Modern Social Work Theory* (3rd edn.). Basingstoke: Palgrave Macmillan.

Pease, B. (2011) Men in social work: challenging or reproducing an unequal gender regime?, *Affilia*, 26 (4): 406–18.

Perkins, N., Penhale, B., Reid, D., Pinkney, L., Hussein, S. and Manthorpe, J. (2007) Partnership means protection? Perceptions of the effectiveness of multiagency working and the regulatory framework within adult protection in England and Wales, *Journal of Adult Protection*, 9 (3): 9–23.

Perry, R. and Cree, V. (2003) The changing gender profile of applicants to qualifying social work training in the UK, *Social Work Education*, 22 (4): 375–83.

Pettigrew, T.F. (1998) Intergroup contact theory, *Annual Review of Psychology*, 49 (1): 65–85.

Phillips, N. (2001) Men and mental health services: a view from social work practice, in A. Christie (ed.) *Men and Social Work: Theories and Practices*. Basingstoke: Palgrave Macmillan.

Phillipson, C. (2000) Critical and educational gerontology: relationships and future developments, in F. Glendenning (ed.) *Teaching and Learning in Later Life*. Farnham: Ashgate.

Pinkey, S. (2011) Participation and emotions: troubling encounters between children and social welfare professionals, *Children and Society*, 25 (1): 37–46.

Polanyi, M. (1967) *The Tacit Dimension*. London: Routledge.

Powell, J. (2005) 'Value talk' in social work research: reflection, rhetoric and reality, *European Journal of Social Work*, 8 (1): 21–37.

Preston-Shoot, M. (2010) Help social workers serve the law, not their employers, *Community Care*, 24 June, p. 21.

Pullen-Sansfacon, A. (2010) Virtue ethics for social work: a new pedagogy for practical reasoning, *Social Work Education*, 29 (4): 402–15.

Qureshi, H. and Henwood, M. (2000) *Older People's Definitions of Quality Services*. York: Joseph Rowntree Foundation.

Rai-Atkins, A., Jama, A.A., Wright, N., Scott, V., Perring, C., Craig, G. et al. (2002) *Best Practice in Mental Health: Advocacy for African, Caribbean and South Asian Communities*. Bristol: Policy Press.

Rodriguez-Keyes, E., Schneider, D.A. and King Keenan, E.K. (2013) Being known in undergraduate social work education: the role of instructors in fostering student engagement and motivation, *Social Work Education*, 32 (6): 785–99.

Rogers, C. and Weller, S. (eds.) (2013) *Critical Approaches to Care: Understanding Caring Relations, Identities and Cultures*. Abingdon: Routledge.

Rowe, W. (2011) Client-centred theory: the enduring principles of a person-centred approach, in F.J. Turner (ed.) *Social Work Treatment: Interlocking Theoretical Approaches* (5th edn.). Oxford: Oxford University Press.

Ruch, G. (2002) From triangle to spiral: reflective practice in social work education, practice and research, *Social Work Education*, 21 (2): 199–216.

Ruch, G. (2005) Relationship-based practice and reflective practice: holistic approaches to contemporary child care social work, *Child and Family Social Work*, 10: 111–23.

Ruch, G. (2007) Reflective practice in contemporary child-care social work: the role of containment, *British Journal of Social Work*, 37 (4): 659–80.

Ruch, G. (2010) Theoretical frameworks informing relationship-based practice, in G. Ruch, D. Turney and A. Ward (eds.) *Relationship-Based Practice: Getting to the Heart of Practice*. London: Jessica Kingsley.

Ruch, G. (2011) Where have all the feelings gone? Developing reflective and relationship-based management in child care social work, *British Journal of Social Work* (DOI: 10.1093/bjsw/bcr134).

Ruch, G., Turney, D. and Ward, A. (eds.) (2010) *Relationship-Based Practice: Getting to the Heart of Practice*. London: Jessica Kingsley.

Rushton, I. and Suter, M. (2012) *Reflective Practice for Teaching in Lifelong Learning*. Maidenhead: Open University Press.

Sadd, J. (2011) *'We are more than our story': Service User and Carer Participation in Social Work Education*, SCIE Report #42. London: SCIE.

Sakamoto, I. and Pitner, R.O. (2005) Use of critical consciousness in anti-oppressive social work practice: disentangling power dynamics at personal and structural levels, *British Journal of Social Work*, 33 (4): 435–52.

Schon, D. (1983) *The Reflective Practitioner*. New York: Basic Books.

Schon, D. (1987) *Educating the Reflective Practitioner*. San Francisco, CA: Jossey-Bass.

Scourfield, P. (2007) Social care and the modern citizen: client, consumer, service user, manager and entrepreneur, *British Journal of Social Work*, 37 (1): 107–22.

Scragg, T. and Mantell, A. (eds.) (2011) *Safeguarding Adults in Social Work* (2nd edn.). Exeter: Learning Matters.

Segal, H. (1988) *Introduction to the Work of Melanie Klein*. London: Karnac.

Sewpaul, V. (2007) Challenging East–West value dichotomies and essentialising discourse on culture and social work, *International Journal of Social Welfare*, 16 (4): 398–407.

Sewpaul, V. and Jones, D. (2004) Global standards for social work education and training, *Social Work Education*, 23 (5): 493–513.

Shardlow, S.M. (2009) Values, ethics and social work, in R. Adams, L. Dominelli and M. Payne (eds.) *Social Work: Themes, Issues and Critical Debates* (3rd edn.). Basingstoke: Palgrave Macmillan.

Singh, G. and Cowden, S. (2009) The social worker as intellectual, *European Journal of Social Work*, 12 (4): 479–93.

Slettebø, T. (2011) Partnership with parents of children in care: a study of collective user participation in child protection services, *British Journal of Social Work* (DOI: 10.1093/bjsw/bcr188).

Slocock, C. (2012) *The Big Society Audit 2012* [http://www.civilexchange.org.uk/the-big-society-audit; accessed 20 May 2014].

Smith, C. and White, S. (1997) Parton, Howe and postmodernity: a critical comment on mistaken identity, *British Journal of Social Work*, 27 (2): 275–95.

Smith, R. (2008) *Social Work and Power*. Basingstoke: Palgrave Macmillan.

Smyth, J. (1989) Developing and sustaining critical reflection in teacher education, *Journal of Teacher Education*, 40 (2): 2–9.

Social Care Institute for Excellence (SCIE) (2011) *Keeping Personal Budgets Personal: Learning from the Experiences of Older People, People with Mental Health Problems and Their Carers*, SCIE Report #40 [http://www.scie.org.uk/publications/reports/report40/index.asp; accessed 20 May 2014].

Social Care Institute for Excellence (SCIE) (2013) *Fair Access to Care Services (FACS): Prioritising Eligibility for Care and Support*, SCIE Guide #33 [http://www.scie.org.uk/publications/guides/guide33/files/guide33.pdf; accessed 20 May 2014].

Social Care Institute for Excellence/Pan London Adult Safeguarding Editorial Board (SCIE/PLASED) (2011) *Protecting Adults at Risk: London Multi-Agency Policy and Procedures to Safeguard Adults from Abuse*, SCIE Report #39 [http://www.scie.org.uk/publications/reports/report39.pdf; accessed 20 May 2014].

Social Work Reform Board (2010) *Building a Safe and Confident Future: One Year On*. London: Department of Education.

Somers, M. (1994) The narrative constitution of identity: a relational network approach, *Theory and Society*, 23 (5): 605–49.

Spandler, H. (2004) Friend or foe? Towards a critical assessment of direct payments, *Critical Social Policy*, 24 (2): 187–209.

Stanford, S. (2010) 'Speaking back' to fear: responding to the moral dilemmas of risk in social work practice, *British Journal of Social Work*, 40 (4): 1065–80.

Stevens, M., Glendinning, C., Jacobs, S., Moran, N., Challis, D., Manthorpe, J. et al. (2011) Assessing the role of increasing choice in English social care services, *Journal of Social Policy*, 40 (2): 257–74.

Stevenson, O. (2005) Genericism and specialization: the story since 1970, *British Journal of Social Work*, 35 (5): 569–86.

Stokes, J. (1994) The unconscious at work in groups and teams: contributions from the work of Wilfred Bion, in A. Obholzer and V. Zagier-Roberts (eds.) *The Unconscious at Work: Individual and Organizational Stress in the Human Services*. Hove: Brunner Routledge.

Super, D.E. and Šverko, B. (eds.) (1995) *Life Roles, Values, and Careers: International Findings of the Work Importance Study*. San Francisco, CA: Jossey-Bass.

Swenson, S. (2008) Neoliberalism and human services: threat and innovation, *Journal of Intellectual Disability Research*, 52 (7): 626–33.

Taylor, C. (2006) Practising reflexivity: narrative, reflection and the moral order, in S. White, J. Fook and F. Gardner (eds.) *Critical Reflection in Health and Social Care*. Maidenhead: Open University Press.

Taylor, I., Sharland, E., Sebba, J., Le Riche, P., Keep, E. and Orr, D. (2006) *The Learning, Teaching and Assessment of Partnership Work in Social Work Education*. Knowledge Review #10. London: SCIE.

Taylor, Z. (1999) Values, theories and methods in social work education: a culturally transferable core?, *International Social Work*, 42 (3): 309–18.

Taylor-Gooby, P. (1994) Postmodernism and social policy: a great leap backwards?, *Journal of Social Policy*, 23 (3): 385–404.

The College of Social Work (TCSW) (2011) *Professional Capabilities Framework* [www.tcsw.org.uk/pcf.aspx].

The College of Social Work (TCSW) (2012a) *The College of Social Work launches campaign to protect the role of social workers within adult social care services*, Press Release, 3 February.

The College of Social Work (TCSW) (2012b) *PCF: Qualifying to Advanced*, February. London: TCSW.

The College of Social Work (TCSW) (2013) *A Code of Ethics for Membership of the College of Social Work* [http://www.tcsw.org.uk/uploadedFiles/TheCollege/Members_area/CodeofEthicsAug2013.pdf; accessed 19 May 2014].

Thompson, J., Kilbane, J. and Sanderson, H. (2007) *Person Centred Practice for Professionals*. Maidenhead: Open University Press.

Thompson, N. (2011) *Promoting Equality: Working with Diversity and Difference* (3rd edn.). Basingstoke: Palgrave Macmillan.

TOPSS England (2004) *Values and Ethics Statement of Expectations from Individuals, Families, Carers, Groups and Communities Who Use Services and Those Who Care for Them* [www.hpc-uk.org/assets/documents/1000338CItem11-enc9a3-NatOccStands-SW.pdf; accessed 20 May 2014].

Townsend, P. (2006) Policies for the aged in the 21st century: more 'structured dependency' or the realisation of human rights, *Ageing and Society*, 26 (2): 161–80.

Tronto, J (1993) *Moral Boundaries: A Political Argument for an Ethic of Care*. London: Routledge.

Walby, S. and Allen, J. (2004) *Domestic Violence, Sexual Assault and Stalking: Findings from the British Crime Survey*. London: Home Office Research, Development and Statistics Directorate.

Walker, C. and Walker, A. (2009) Social policy, poverty and social work, in R. Adams, L. Dominelli and M. Payne (eds.) *Social Work: Themes, Issues and Critical Debates* (3rd edn.). Basingstoke: Palgrave Macmillan.

Wallace, J.E. (1995) Organizational and professional commitment in professional and non-professional organizations, *Administrative Science Quarterly*, 40: 228–55.

Wallace, J. and Pease, B. (2011) Neoliberalism and Australian social work: accommodation or resistance?, *Journal of Social Work*, 11 (2): 132–42.

Wallman, S. (1986) Ethnicity and the boundary process in context, in J. Rex and D. Mason (eds.) *Theories of Race and Ethnic Relations*. Cambridge: Cambridge University Press.

Walton, D. (2005) *Fundamentals of Critical Argumentation*, Cambridge: Cambridge University Press.

Warren, J. (2007) *Service User and Carer Participation in Social Work*. Exeter: Learning Matters.

Webb, S.A. (2003) Local orders and global chaos in social work, *European Journal of Social Work*, 6 (2): 191–203.

Webb, S.A. (2006) *Social Work in a Risk Society: Social and Political Perspectives*. Basingstoke: Palgrave Macmillan.

Webb, S.A. (2010) (Re)assembling the Left: the politics of redistribution and recognition in social work, *British Journal of Social Work*, 40 (8): 2364–79.

Webster, P. (2011) *A critical analytic literature review of virtue ethics for social work: beyond codified conduct towards virtuous social work*. Unpublished thesis for the Doctor of Social Work, University of Sussex [http://sro.sussex.ac.uk/7085/1/Webster,_Paul.pdf].

Weil, T.P. (2011) Privatization of hospitals: meeting divergent interests, *Journal of Health Care Finance*, 38 (2): 1–11.

Weinberg, M. (2010) The social construction of social work ethics: politicizing and broadening the lens, *Journal of Progressive Human Services*, 21 (1): 32–44.

Weinstein, J. (2009) *Mental Health, Service User Involvement and Recovery*. London: Jessica Kingsley.

Westen, P. (1985) 'Freedom' and 'coercion': virtue words and vice words, *Duke Law Journal*, 3/4: 541.

White, V. (1995) Commonality and diversity in feminist social work, *British Journal of Social Work*, 25 (2): 143–56.

Whittington, C. (2003a) Collaboration and partnership in context, in J. Weinstein, C. Whittington and T. Leiba (eds.) *Collaboration in Social Work Practice*. London: Jessica Kingsley.

Whittington, C. (2003b) A model of collaboration, in J. Weinstein, C. Whittington and T. Leiba (eds.) *Collaboration in Social Work Practice*. London: Jessica Kingsley.

Whittington, C. (2007) The rise and rise of interprofessional education?, in M. Lymbery and K. Postle (eds.) *Social Work: A Companion to Learning*. London: Sage.

Whittington, C. and Bell, L. (2001) Learning for interprofessional and inter-agency practice in the new social work curriculum: evidence from an earlier research study, *Journal of Interprofessional Care*, 15 (2): 153–69.

Whittington, C. and Whittington, M. (2007) Ethics and social care: political, organizational and inter-agency dimensions, in A. Leathard and S. McLaren (eds.) *Ethics: Contemporary Challenges in Health and Social Care*. Bristol: Policy Press.

Whittington, C., Whittington, M., Quinney, A. and Thomas, J. (2009a) *Key Policy and Legislation with Implications for Iterprofessional and Inter-Agency Collaboration (IPIAC): A Timeline of Examples 1968–2008*. London: SCIE [http://www.scie.org.uk/assets/elearning/ipiac/ipiac08/resource/flash/index.html; accessed 20 May 2014].

Whittington, C., Thomas, J. and Quinney, A. (2009b) *Interprofessional and Inter-Agency Collaboration (IPIAC)*. London: SCIE [http://www.scie.org.uk/publications/elearning/ipiac/index.asp; accessed 20 May 2014].

Whittington, C., Quinney, A. and Thomas, J. (2009c) *A Model of Practice and Collaboration.* London: SCIE [http://www.scie.org.uk/assets/elearning/ipiac/ipiac05/resource/flash/index.html; accessed 20 May 2014].

Whittington, C., Thomas, J. and Quinney, A. (2009d) *An Introduction to Interprofessional and Inter-Agency Collaboration.* London: SCIE [http://www.scie.org.uk/assets/elearning/ipiac/ipiac01/resource/flash/index.html; accessed 20 May 2014].

Whittington, C., Quinney, A. and Thomas, J. (2009e) *The Practitioner, the Agency and Inter-Agency Collaboration.* London: SCIE [http://www.scie.org.uk/assets/elearning/ipiac/ipiac07/resource/flash/index.html; accessed 20 May 2014].

Wilks, T. (2005) Social work and narrative ethics, *British Journal of Social Work,* 35 (8): 1249–64.

Williams, B. (1985) *Ethics and the Limits of Philosophy.* Cambridge, MA: Harvard University Press.

Williams, I. (2009) Offender health and social care: a review of the evidence on inter-agency collaboration, *Health and Social Care in the Community,* 17 (6): 573–80.

Williams, R. (2012) *Faith in the Public Square.* London: Bloomsbury Continuum.

Wilson, K., Ruch, G., Lymbery, M. and Cooper, A. (2011) *Social Work: An Introduction to Contemporary Practice.* (2nd edn.). Harlow: Pearson.

Winkler, E. (1993) From Kantianism to contextualism, in E.R. Winkler and J.R. Coombs (eds.) *Applied Ethics.* Oxford: Blackwell.

Woodward, R. and Mackay, K. (2012) Mind the gap! Students' understanding and application of social work values, *Social Work Education,* 31 (8): 1090–104.

Wright, P., Turner, C., Clay, D. and Mills, H. (2006) *The Participation of Children and Young People in Developing Social Care,* Practice Guide #6. London: SCIE [http://www.scie.org.uk/publications/guides/guide11/files/guide11.pdf].

Index

Abbott, 80
'Access to Social Work' courses, 26
accountability, 7, 39, 73, 78, 81, 82, 83
Adam, 6
Adams, K, 42
Adams, R, 112, 116
Adoption, 65, 117
adult social care see also case examples, 46, 67, 80,
    86, 88, 92, 116, 123
advocacy, 40, 66, 70, 92
aging, 68–69, 86, 88, 116, 123
alienation see also Marx, 70, 71
Allain, 42, 115, 121
altruism, 46
anti-discriminatory and anti-oppressive practice,
    6, 100
anti-heterosexism, 30
anxiety, managing student/social worker, 31, 38, 51,
    59, 73, 101, 102, 106, 110, 112, 117
applied ethics see also healthcare ethics, xv, 3, 4, 8,
    9, 12–22, 47, 48, 57, 123
Aristotelian virtues, 20, 21
Arnett, 27
Arras, 16, 18
assessment, carer, 89, 96
assessment, holistic, 102, 103
assessment, service user, 46, 50, 64, 65, 66, 68, 71,
    72, 85, 86, 87, 88, 91, 103, 104, 107, 117, 118,
    123
assessment, student, 24, 30, 33, 34
Atherton, 32
attachment theory, 71, 102, 103, 104, 105, 107, 109,
    110
audit, 82, 102
austerity see economic policy
authority see also power, 25, 30, 36, 63, 64, 65, 73
autonomy, see also principles, ethical, 12, 26, 40, 41,
    43, 104, 105, 107

Baginsky, 112, 113, 114, 124
Ball, 110
Balloch, 77
Banks, 3, 4, 5, 6, 12, 16, 20, 21, 29, 32, 34, 44, 45, 57,
    58, 82, 112, 113
Barnard, 4, 5
Bar-On, 63, 66
Barth, 39
BASW, 5, 63, 80, 81, 83, 90

Bauman, 4
Baxter, 42
Beauchamp, xv, 4, 13, 16, 18, 20, 22, 57, 123
Beck, U, 6
Beckett, 3, 4
'becoming' a social worker, 9, 23, 24–25, 35
Bell, 29, 34, 39, 42, 43
beneficence, see principles, ethical
Bentham, Jeremy see Utilitarianism
Bereavement, 85, 86, 87, 88
Beresford, 77, 78, 79, 81, 84, 101
Berg, 43
Bernard, 28
Big Society, 78, 79
Bilson, 108
biomedical ethics see healthcare ethics
biomedicine, 12, 13
Bion, 107
Birkenmaier, 113
Birmingham Safeguarding Children Board
    see Lundberg
Bisman, 42
Blair Government, 78, 114
boundaries, 7, 33, 34, 39, 40, 97, 110, 123
Bowden, 98
Bower, 106
Bowes, 71, 73
Bowlby, 107
Branfield, 33
British Association of Social Workers see BASW
Broadhurst, 80
brokerage, 66, 85, 86
Bunyan, 79
bureaucracy, 6, 40, 43, 51
Burck, 103, 107
Burt, 41
Butler, 113, 114, 115

Calder, 28
Canada see also international perspectives, 40
Care Council for Wales (CCW), 81, 83
care, delivery, 5, 6, 7, 73
care, heteronormative models, 30
carer perspectives, 5, 7, 27, 32, 33, 64, 67, 68, 69, 73,
    77, 79, 80, 81, 83, 84, 88, 89, 91, 96, 121
Care Plan, 85, 86, 119
Carers Trust, 89
Carey, 70, 114, 115, 118, 119, 120, 121

Caring for our Future (White Paper), 78, 79
caring professions, 20, 21, 22
Carpenter, 41
Carr, 66, 68, 123
Cartney, 49, 50, 52
case examples, working with:
    domestic violence, 53–54 (case 5.1), 72 (case 6.2)
    families, 53–54 (case 5.1) 72 (case 6.2) 117
        (case 10.1)
    mental health, 72 (case 6.2), 91 (case 8.1), 95
        (case 8.5)
    older people, 17 (case 2.1), 67–68 (case 6.1),
        84–88 (case 7.1), 96–97 (case 8.6)
    people with learning difficulties, 94 (case 8.4)
    specific user groups, 92 (case 8.2)
    substance abuse, 93 (case 8.3), 105 (case 9.1)
    young people, 93 (case 8.3), 94 (case 8.4),
        105 (case 9.1)
Cavadino, 51
Chahal, 92
Challis, 81
Chambon, 70, 74
Channell, 34
child protection, 52, 57, 59, 73, 101, 102
    see also case examples, Munro, safeguarding
Children Act 1989 - section 20, 105
choice, 18, 29, 57, 66, 67, 68, 73, 78, 79, 81, 84, 86, 87,
    94, 99, 103, 105, 113, 115, 118, 123
Chu, 39, 45
citizenship, 30, 53, 69, 72, 90
Clark, C, 3, 4, 5, 7, 12, 17, 20, 37, 38, 44, 81
Clarke, J, 43
Clifford, 84, 97
Cocker, 5, 30, 31, 35, 63, 123
codes of practice, 5, 6, 10, 23, 39, 81, 90, 124
coercive power *see* power, typologies
collaboration *see also* partnership, 76, 77–78, 79, 80,
    83, 84, 86, 88, 89
collectivities and identity, 37, 39
commissioning care, 69, 71, 78
Commons Health Select Committee, 80
communication, 69, 85, 101, 102, 108, 110, 118
    skills, 10, 21, 33, 34, 102, 103
communities, 4, 7, 21, 22, 24, 33, 36, 58, 73, 74, 79,
    92, 99
Community Health services, 85
compassion, 20, 21, 22, 58, 101, 102, 105, 106, 122
compliance, 65
confidence, 10, 25, 31, 34, 36, 84, 103, 104, 110, 111
confidentiality, 7, 17, 19, 29, 83, 84, 85
confrontation, 101, 102, 110
consent, 7, 17, 65, 83, 102
Consequentialism *see also* Utilitarianism, xv, 4, 8,
    13–14, 22, 37
Conservative-Liberal Democrat Coalition, 66, 78

consumerism and social care, 6, 7, 46, 66, 69, 78,
    82, 88
containment *see* psychoanalytic concepts
contextualized ethics, xv, 4, 8, 18–21, 22, 58, 120,
    122, 123
contextualized practice, 47, 58, 71, 97
continuing professional development (CPD), 7, 8, 9,
    23, 25, 35, 111
'continuous improvement' discourse *see also*
    managerialism, 39
continuum of social work, 3, 11, 23, 48
Cooklin, 109
Cooper, 101, 102, 103, 108, 110
co-productive approach, 33, 68, 123
Corby, 124
Coren, 115, 116
Coulter, 25, 32, 33
counter transference *see* psychoanalytic concepts
creativity, 7, 35
critical enquiry, 32
critical incidents, 34
critical social work, 4, 35, 115, 119
critical theory *see also* Foucault, 34, 64, 75
Croatia, 45
Cropley, 35
cultural contexts, 9, 10, 39, 42, 44, 45, 46, 71, 96–97
    (case 8.6), 108–109
Cunningham, 25

Dalrymple, 9, 23
Danso, 114, 115
Davies, 43
Dawson, 7
Dean, 112
Dearing, 28
de Boer, 101
Deci, 26
decision-making, 6, 11, 16, 18, 22, 44, 45, 51, 52, 59,
    63, 65, 73, 80, 83, 98, 112, 123, 124
deductivism, 14, 16
defence mechanisms *see* psychoanalytic concepts
defensive social work practice, 6, 63, 101
Denmark, 45
Dent, 37, 40, 41, 43
Deontology, xv, 4, 8, 13–16, 22, 37, 98, 101
Department for Children, Schools and Families
    (DCSF), 24, 25, 71, 124
Department for Constitutional Affairs (DCA), 88
Department for Education & Skills (DfES), 28
Department of Health (DH), 25, 65, 78, 79, 83
Deprivation of Liberty Safeguards (2009), 65, 124
Dickens, 113, 119
difference, 31, 32, 45, 84, 90–100
Dillon, 25, 26, 27, 28, 31, 32
direct payments, 66, 78, 116

disabilities, 26, 28, 88, 94
disclosure, 74
discrimination, 5, 29, 31, 73, 83, 84, 91, 92, 93, 99, 102
diversity, working with, 3, 10, 25, 28, 30, 31, 32, 64,
        90–100, 115, 116
Doel, 84
domestic violence, 53, 57, 72, 108
domination, *see* power
Dominelli, 42, 90, 91, 95
Douglas, 77
Dowling, 78
Dracopoulou, 18, 20
Dunk-West, 23, 24, 28, 35, 71

economic policy, 4, 5, 6, 10, 11, 18, 19, 27, 34, 36, 51,
        64, 71, 92, 106, 110, 112, 113, 114, 115, 118,
        119, 120, 121, 122
education, professional, 3, 4, 5, 6, 7–8, 9, 20, 22,
        23–36, 37, 38, 39, 42, 43, 45, 48, 74, 100, 102,
        103, 104, 110, 115, 116, 120, 122
education, widening participation, 25, 28–29, 36
'ego', 38, 108, 109
eligibility, 67, 68, 71, 124
Elsey, 34
emotions, 5, 7, 10, 20, 32, 34, 36, 43, 49, 52, 53, 54, 55,
        56, 58, 59, 68, 73, 74, 85, 94, 102, 103, 106 107,
        109, 111
empathy, 20, 24, 25, 38, 94, 95, 102, 107, 109
empowerment, 9, 10, 63, 64, 67, 69, 70, 71, 74, 78, 79,
        80, 82, 88, 103, 116
Epstein, 69
Epston, 96
Eraut, 52
ethical codes, 10, 39, 44, 80, 81–82, 83, 88, 89, 112,
        113, 114
ethics, normative *see* normative ethics
'ethics of care', xv, 4, 5, 8, 9, 20–21, 22, 37, 58, 108
ethics theories and principles, xv, 12–22
ethnicity, 44, 94, 99
'ethos', 4
Eurocentrism, 39, 45
Europe *see also* international perspectives, 39, 40,
        44, 45, 82
evaluation, 36, 55, 123
expert power *see* power, typologies
expertise *see also* knowledge, 7, 19, 33, 40, 42, 43,
        45, 52, 54, 58, 63, 65, 68. 73, 83

family dynamics, 108
Family Support Workers, 117
fear, safety and security discourses *see also* risk,
        6, 106
feminism, xv, 4, 5, 8, 20, 43, 44, 57, 70, 72, 95, 98,
        107, 108
Ferguson, H, 89, 101, 102, 103, 109

Ferguson, I, 42, 51, 70, 71, 91, 98, 113, 114, 115, 116,
        119, 120, 121
fitness for practice hearings, 5, 123
Fitzpatrick, 113
Flaskas, 107, 108
Fleck, 116
Fook, 74, 93, 96, 97, 98
Ford, 42
Forester, 102
foster care, 51, 65, 117
Foucault, 10, 35, 64, 69, 70, 75
Fraser, 71
Freeman, 80
Freire, 74
French, 65
Freud, 45
Frost, 37, 39, 44, 45
funding, 19, 53, 79, 91, 92, 116

Garrett, 99, 100, 114, 115, 118
gatekeepers *see also* professional conduct, 29, 38, 67
gender, 28, 34, 43, 44, 95 (case 8.5), 99, 107
General Practitioner (GP), 85–88, 91
General Social Care Council (GSCC), 5, 81
Gerdes, 38
Gibelman, 44
Gilbert, 5, 6
Gilligan, 98, 101
Glasby, 78
Glendinning, 66, 69
globalization, 5, 6, 11, 40, 45, 113, 115, 116, 119, 120,
        121, 122, 123
Goldstein, 35
Gosling, 77, 84
Gould, 35
governance, 6, 23, 78, 82, 88
Graham, 5, 40, 44, 89
Gray, 4, 5, 8, 22, 37
Greece *see also* international perspectives, 39, 41
Gregory, 51, 52
Grenier, 67, 68
group work, 32, 34, 95

Habermas, 74
Hafford-Letchfield, 5, 6, 7, 24, 27, 28, 30, 31, 35, 63,
        66, 68, 74
Hall, E, 114, 115
Hall, S, 79, 103
Hanmer, 95
Haringey, 79, 81
Harris, A, 79, 80
Harris, J, 63
Hatton, 45, 114, 115
Health and Care Professions Council (HCPC), 5, 25,
        81, 83, 124

healthcare ethics *see also* applied ethics, 12, 13, 17, 18
healthcare management, 19, 116
healthcare rationing, 18
Healy, 82, 84
Hean, 7, 42
Heath, 80
Heffernan, 66
Held, 21
HM Government, 66, 79, 124
Hicks, 65
Higher Education Funding Council for England (HEFCE), 28
Hingley-Jones, 104
Höjlund, 45, 46
Hollis *see also* psychosocial casework, 102, 104
Hollway, 107
Holmes, 98
Homophobia, 29, 31
Howe, 102, 103, 107
Hugman, 3, 4, 20, 39, 45, 112, 113
human rights, 5, 6, 65, 72, 73, 81, 90, 110, 123, 124
Human Rights Act (1998), 32, 124
Hurd, 78, 79
Hursthouse, 20
Hussein, 28, 43

identities, 3, 4, 9, 24, 27, 31, 35, 37–46, 48, 49, 67, 68, 69, 71–73, 93, 94, 95, 96, 97, 99, 100, 108, 115, 119, 121, 122, 124
inclusive practice, 3, 8, 9, 23
individualized budgets *see* personal budgets
individuals, 15, 18, 20, 32, 37, 39, 66, 97, 98, 103, 104, 107, 114, 115, 118, 119
inequalities, 28, 44, 69, 84, 91, 102, 103, 116
institutional policies, 19
intergroup contact theory, 32
IFSW, 5, 39, 81, 82, 90, 122
IASSW, 5, 82, 90
inter-agency, 77, 78, 79, 80, 83, 89
International Association of Schools of Social Work *see* IFSW/IASSW
International Federation of Social Workers *see* IFSW/IASSW
international perspectives, 5, 6, 11, 39, 40, 41, 44, 45, 81, 82, 90, 113, 115, 116, 119, 120, 121, 122, 123
introjections *see* psychoanalytic concepts
intuition, 18, 124
Ixer, 48

Jenkins, 37, 39
Jensen, 42
Jeyasingham, 30, 31
Johns, 91, 99

Johnson, 80
Jones, 99, 108, 112, 113, 114
Jordan, 112, 114, 115
justice *see* principles, ethical

Kantian ethics *also* Deontology, xv, 14 –16, 30, 96, 97, 112
Kearney, 54
Kemp, 43
Kjellberg, 32
Klein, M, 107, 108, 109
Knezevic, 44, 45, 46
Knott, 48
knowledge, 6, 7, 9, 10, 15, 16, 17, 24, 25, 30, 31, 33, 38, 42, 43, 47, 48, 50, 51, 52, 56, 58, 59, 65, 66, 70, 75, 84, 85, 87, 90, 102, 103, 124
   practice based, 6, 9, 25, 33, 47, 48, 52, 53, 54, 58, 70
   research evidence, 9, 15, 24, 50, 51, 52, 54, 66, 103
   see also expertise
Koggel, 101

Laming, 63, 124
language, xv, 4, 5, 32, 66–69, 70, 96–97 (case 8.6)
law, case-law, 5, 41, 123, 124
leadership, 23, 65
learning, 23–56, 38
learning contracts, 34
learning cultures, 29, 31
learning experiences, 32, 35
learning styles, 31, 32
Leathard, 4, 6, 124
Leathwood, 31
Lee, 89
Leece, 66, 67, 116
Lees, 54
Lefevre, 107
Leigh, 101
legislation, 4, 23, 51, 53, 55, 65, 78, 117, 123, 124
legitimate power *see* power, typologies
life experiences, 26, 28, 36, 52, 53
lifelong learning, 8, 9, 23, 25, 35, 36
listening skills, 34, 85
Lloyd, 114
Local Government Group, 79
Lorenz, 114, 115
Loughlin, 17, 18, 19, 20
Lukes, 64
Lymbery, 66, 69, 80, 114, 116, 119
Lyons, 114

MacIntyre, 21
Mackay, 118, 119
management, 7, 18, 19, 42, 43, 51, 63, 85, 86, 91, 116, 119

managerialism, 40, 43, 51, 63, 71, 82, 113
Mandin, 103, 108
Manthorpe, 99
Mantle, 99
Mappes, 20
Marx, 45, 70, 71
Maschi, 119, 120, 121
mature students, 31
May, 89
McDonald, 112, 113, 118, 119, 120
McLaughlin, 112, 113, 115
Memmot, 38
Mental Capacity Act (2005), 65, 124
Menzies Lyth, 109
mentoring, 34
metaethics, xv, 12, 57
methodology, 13, 16, 18, 22
Mezirow, 35, 74
micro level, 4, 10, 23, 70, 90, 91, 93, 117
Miehls, 38, 40, 42
Miley, 117, 120
Mill, J. S. see Utilitarianism
Millar, J, 112, 118
Millar, M, 113, 115
Minister for Government Policy, 78
Ministry of Justice, 124
minority groups, 32, 73, 92
Minow, 93
mission statements, 7
Mitchell, 118
moral character, 4, 22
morally active practitioner, 4, 10, 38, 44
moral philosophy, 4, 8, 12, 13, 17, 90, 98
Moreno, 18
Morley, 43
Morris, 89
Mosebach, 121
Mudge, 6
motivation to enter social work, 26–27 (case 3.1)
multi-agency, xi, 8, 77, 80, 123
Munro, 7, 52, 54, 57, 63, 71, 101, 110, 111, 124

Narey, 7
narrative approaches, 10, 33, 64, 71, 73–74, 76, 78, 85, 93, 96, 97, 100
National Association of Social Workers (NASW), 25, 90
NHS and Community Care Act 1990, 114
NHS, 85, 91, 95
National Standards for Youth Justice Services (2008), 114
Needham, 68, 78, 123
neoliberalism, 6, 11, 66, 70, 103, 105, 106, 110, 112, 113–121
Newman, 43, 78, 115, 120

Newton, 78
Noddings, 20, 21
non-maleficence see principles, ethical
'non-professional' tasks, 42
normative ethics, xv, 12, 13
Northern Ireland, 81
Norway see also international perspectives, 42
Nussbaum, 20, 22

occupational therapist, 85–88
Okitikpi, 96
Oliver, 80, 88
Open Public Services (White Paper), 78, 79
oppression, 5, 29, 31, 32, 35, 70, 71, 73, 90, 95, 99, 107, 115, 116
organizational cultures, 5, 108–110
organizational hierarchies, 63, 66
organizations, 6, 7, 9, 10, 33, 35, 37, 39, 40–41, 42, 43, 46, 65, 67, 73, 77, 78, 80, 81, 82, 83, 84, 85, 86, 88, 90, 98, 101, 103, 104, 105, 114, 121, 123
Orme, 4, 5, 20, 98

Panaser, 44
Papadaki, 39, 41, 44, 45
parenting, 54, 123
Parrot, 93, 94, 116
participation, 7, 33, 34, 66, 67, 73, 74, 79, 82, 83, 87, 88, 122, 123
partnership, 10, 33, 34, 50, 66, 69, 76–89, 110, 124
partnership-related values, 83–84, 88, 89
Parton, 4, 20, 57
Payne, 107
Pease, 44
'pedagogy of discomfort', 32
peer support, 28, 34
performance measurement, 7, 51, 91, 102, 110, 117, 124
Perkins, 80
Perry, 44
person-centred planning see also personalization, 78, 83
person-centred support see also personalization, 78, 80, 81–82
personal commitment to social work values, 5, 10, 23, 25, 27, 28, 31, 36, 71, 77, 85, 90, 111, 119, 124
personal budgets, 78
personal conduct, 7, 114
personalization, 66, 67, 78, 79, 80, 86, 116
Pettigrew, 32
philanthropy, 26
Phillips, 95
Phillipson, 71
philosophical theories, 12–22

Pinkey, 66, 71, 73
policy drivers, 78
political action, 11, 34, 66, 120, 121
politics, 4, 6, 30, 34, 45, 51, 66, 67, 69, 71, 74, 75, 76,
  82, 91, 102, 104, 106, 110, 113, 114, 115, 116,
  117, 121, 122, 123
political rights, 119, 120
postmodernism, 115
poverty, 72, 99, 100, 115, 116, 119, 123
Powell, 4
power, 7, 9, 10, 33, 34, 35, 40, 41, 43, 54, 55, 56, 57,
  63–75, 77, 79, 80, 83, 84, 91, 95, 97, 98, 108,
  113, 116, 118, 121, 123
power, typologies, 64–66
practice educator, 29, 30, 33, 38
practice learning, 34, 35
practice wisdom *see* knowledge
Preston-Shoot, 41
principles, ethical
  autonomy, xv, 4, 16, 17, 18, 19, 57, 58, 67, 85, 87,
    96, 103, 123
  beneficence, xv, 4, 15, 16, 17, 18, 57, 58, 123
  non-maleficence, xv, 4, 15, 16, 17, 57, 123
  justice., xv, 4, 7, 16, 17, 20, 30, 35, 37, 101
principles, international statements of, 5
Principlism, xv, 4, 16–18
professional capabilities, 48, 81, 83
Professional Capabilities Framework (PCF),
  81, 83
professional conduct, 3, 44
professional identity *see* identities
professional integrity, 5, 44, 57
professional norms, 3, 35, 42
professional regulation, 6, 29, 38, 81
professional roles, 5, 8, 10, 19, 21, 24, 31, 43, 63, 67,
  90, 123, 124
professional socialization, 24, 27, 42
professions, female-dominated, 43, 44
projective identification *see* psychoanalytic
  concepts
psychoanalytic concepts, 104, 106, 110
psychodynamic approaches, 10, 53, 56, 91, 102
public enquiries, 5, 124
Pullen-Sansfacon, 58

Qureshi, 69

race theory, 4
racism, 72, 115
radical social work, 70–71, 102, 115
Rai-Atkins, 92
referent power *see* power, typologies
reflective practice, 9, 36, 47–59, 104, 121
reflective practice, model, 54–59
reflexivity, 11, 19, 29, 36, 38, 40, 71, 97, 98, 124

relationship based practice, 5, 10, 30, 34, 49, 52, 64,
  101–111, 122
relationships, 7, 10, 16, 22, 27, 32, 34, 35, 37, 38, 39,
  54, 56, 63, 64, 66, 67, 68, 71, 72, 74, 76, 77, 81,
  83, 84, 95, 96, 97, 98, 101, 102, 104, 107, 108,
  109, 120
relativism, 21, 22
religion, 27, 94
research evidence *see* knowledge – research
  evidence
resilience, 24, 25, 28, 71
resistance, 52, 69, 73, 91, 119, 120
resources, 7, 17, 19, 41, 66, 67, 69, 71, 84, 99, 112,
  113, 114, 115, 117, 121, 123
respect, xv, 5, 10, 14, 15, 16, 17, 20, 30, 32, 39, 43, 54,
  57, 65, 69, 76, 79, 81, 82, 83, 85, 86, 88, 90, 91,
  93, 94, 97, 108
responsibility, 15, 6, 21, 28, 29, 30, 32, 34, 37, 41, 56,
  58, 59, 69, 79, 81, 82, 103, 104, 118
reward power *see* power, typologies
risk, 6, 7, 49, 51, 54, 57, 63, 67, 69, 80, 82, 84, 85, 87,
  88, 89, 103, 106, 110, 113, 117, 122
Rodriquez-Keyes, 27
Rogers, 4, 20, 83, 98
role models, 34, 38
Rowe, 83
Ruch, 51, 54, 76, 102, 104, 106, 108
Rushton, 48

Sadd, 79
safeguarding, 64, 66, 71, 73, 77, 79, 80, 89
Sakamoto, 63
Schon, 50, 51
Scotland, 81
Scourfield, 69
Scragg, 79
Segal, 107, 108, 109
'self' awareness, 5, 19, 28, 30, 31, 34, 36, 38, 42, 47,
  49, 55, 56, 59, 71, 74, 90, 97, 102, 104
separatism, 92
serious case reviews, 5, 7, 63, 64, 124, 132
service costs, 78
service user perspectives, 10, 32, 33–34, 36, 40, 45,
  66, 68, 69, 70, 74, 77, 82, 83, 87, 88, 89, 91, 96,
  119, 120
service users' narratives, 33, 66, 70, 96
Sewpaul, 112, 113, 116, 119
Shardlow, 4, 90, 91
Singh, 112, 113, 118, 120
Slocock, 79
Smith, C, 115, 121
Smith, R, 63, 65, 98
Smyth, 54–59
social capital, 66, 69
social care and health, 80

Social Care Institute for Excellence (SCIE), 77, 85, 86
social change, 10, 19, 69, 72, 74, 90, 91, 92, 99, 100, 118
social class, 31, 34, 40, 44, 95, 97, 99, 115, 116, 119
social exclusion, 67, 68, 73, 75, 118
social inclusion, 30, 65, 81, 89
social justice see also principles, ethical, 3, 5, 8, 9, 11, 23, 27, 41, 45, 64, 81, 90, 91, 92, 99, 100, 112–121
social model of care, 88
social movements, 6, 74, 78, 79, 88
social pedagogy, 74
social work and the media, 63, 102
social work as a profession, 4, 22, 24, 41, 102, 104, 115, 117, 118, 119, 123
social work education see education, professional
Social Work Reform Board, 28, 48, 81
social work identity/ies see identities
social work, recruitment and retention, 9, 24
social work skills, 7, 10, 21, 25, 33, 34, 38, 70, 84, 85, 103
social work students, 23–36, 42, 43, 46
social work students, ethical dilemmas, 29 (case 3.2)
social work students, recruitment and selection, 9, 25, 36
social work values, 4, 5, 6, 7, 8, 16, 26, 27, 28, 32, 33, 34, 35, 36, 38, 39, 40, 41, 42, 44, 46, 50, 57, 59, 64, 81–82, 83, 88, 90, 114, 115, 122
see also spheres of values, streams of values
social worker 'journey', 24, 25, 27, 28, 29–32, 36, 124
Somers, 96
Spandler, 113, 116
spheres of values, 4
splitting see psychoanalytic concepts
stakeholder involvement, 7, 63
Stanford, 6, 106
the State, 64, 69, 79, 115, 124
statutory responsibilities, 55, 56, 57, 58, 59, 64, 65, 79, 95, 98, 124
stereotypes, 42
Stevens, 66
Stevenson, 42
Stokes, 110
streams of values, 82, 88
strengths-based approach, 84, 89
stress, workplace, 7, 73
student-tutor relationship, 29, 30, 33, 38, 43
substance misuse, 29, 93, 117
suitability' for social work, 5, 25, 28, 29, 38
Super, 45
supervision, 7, 54, 56, 65, 86, 87, 88, 105, 111, 116, 117, 121
supportive learning, 29, 31

Swenson, 114
systemic theory see systems theory
systems theory, 10, 46, 101, 102, 103, 104, 105, 107, 108, 110

Taylor, C, 98
Taylor, I, 76
Taylor, Z, 45
Taylor-Gooby, 114, 115
team-building, 34
team working, 65, 70, 77, 88, 94, 95, 108, 111
technological changes, 6, 46, 123
terminology see language
The College of Social Work (TCSW), 31, 80, 81, 83, 86, 102
theory see knowledge
Thompson, J, 89
Thompson, N, 92
Tokenism, 33, 119
TOPSS England, 80, 81
Townsend, 67
training, local authorities, 39, 116
trajectories see social worker 'journey'
transference see psychoanalytic concepts
transferable learning, 5, 43
transformational learning, 35
traumatic learning, 32
Tronto, 21, 98
tutor, 29, 30, 33, 38, 43

UK Care Councils see also HCPC, 5, 81, 83
UK Social Work Task Force, 71, 81, 102
uncertainty, coping with, 35, 49, 103, 108, 111
Utilitarianism, xv, 13, 14, 15, 16, 22

values see social work values
'virtue ethics', xv, 4, 5, 9, 20, 21–22, 37, 44, 58, 98
voluntary sector, 56, 92

Walby, 54
Wales, 81, 83
Walker, 99
Wallace, 40, 41, 114, 115, 118, 119, 121
Wallman, 39
Walton, 76
Warren, 77, 78, 89
'ways of knowing', see also knowledge, 47, 48
Webb, 4, 6, 64, 115, 116, 118, 119, 122, 124
Webster, 124
Weil, 120, 121
Weinberg, 5, 19, 113, 118, 119, 120, 121
Weinstein, 89
welfare regimes, 45, 46
Westen, 76
Western liberal ethics, xv, 4, 5, 13, 37

White, 95
Whittington, 7, 42, 44, 76, 77, 78, 79, 80, 81, 82, 84, 89
Wilks, 44
Williams, B, 16
Williams, I, 80
Williams, R, 79
Wilson, 49, 104

Winkler, 16, 18
Woodward, 34
workforce development /management, 7, 9, 24, 79
Wright, 33

youth justice, 104, 105
Youth Offending Service (YOS), 104, 105

**AN INTRODUCTION TO APPLYING SOCIAL
WORK THEORIES AND METHODS**

Second Edition

Barbra Teater

9780335247639 (Paperback)
April 2014

eBook also available

This bestselling book is the leading introduction to the most commonly used theories and methods in social work practice. Now in its second edition, the book explores the concepts of a 'theory' and a 'method', the difference between the two and the ways in which they are connected. Assuming little to no prior knowledge, each chapter explores a single theory or method in depth and uses a variety of interactive tools to encourage the reader to explore their own theories and beliefs.

Key features:

- New chapter on **Community Work** provides a step-by-step approach to community work
- New chapter on **Groupwork** provides an overview of the rationale for groupwork
- New **case studies** exploring areas of growing priority in practice such as dementia

www.openup.co.uk

THE SOCIAL WORK PORTFOLIO
A STUDENT'S GUIDE TO EVIDENCING YOUR PRACTICE

Lee-Ann Fenge, Kate Howe, Mel Hughes and Gill Thomas

June 2014 114pp
978-0-335-24531-4 – Paperback

eBook also available

The portfolio is an essential part of the summative assessment within qualifying social work programmes. All students are required to complete a practice portfolio to provide evidence of their learning in practice. This essential book demonstrates how students can use the portfolio to demonstrate their learning in terms of developing core knowledge, values and skills.

Topics covered include:

- What a portfolio is, and how to make best use of it in your learning journey
- How to evidence your capability using the Professional Capabilities Framework for Social Workers
- How to reflect on your own learning needs and learning style
- How to work with your practice educator in terms of practice learning and portfolio development
- How to evidence the use of theory in your portfolio
- How to evidence meaningful service user and carer involvement within your placement and portfolio
- How to use your portfolio as a basis for future CPD learning, including the need to develop Personal Development Plans and the role of AYSE

Written by a team of experts from Bournemouth University, each chapter uses a range of reflective activities, practice educator comments, and student testimony to illustrate the discussion.

www.openup.co.uk

CONTEMPORARY SOCIAL WORK PRACTICE
A Handbook for Students

Barbra Teater

9780335246038 (Paperback)
February 2014

eBook also available

This exciting new book provides an overview of fifteen different contemporary social work practice settings, spanning across the statutory, voluntary, private and third sectors. It serves as the perfect introduction to the various roles social workers can have and the numerous places they can work, equipping students with the knowledge, skills and values required to work in areas ranging from mental health to fostering and adoption, and from alcohol and drug treatment services to youth offending.

Key features:

- An overview of the setting, including the role of the social worker, how service users gain access to the service and key issues, definitions or terms specific to the setting
- Legislation and policy guidance related to the specific setting
- The key theories and methods related to the setting

www.openup.co.uk

OPEN UNIVERSITY PRESS
McGraw - Hill Education